IMAGES
of America

GREENVILLE

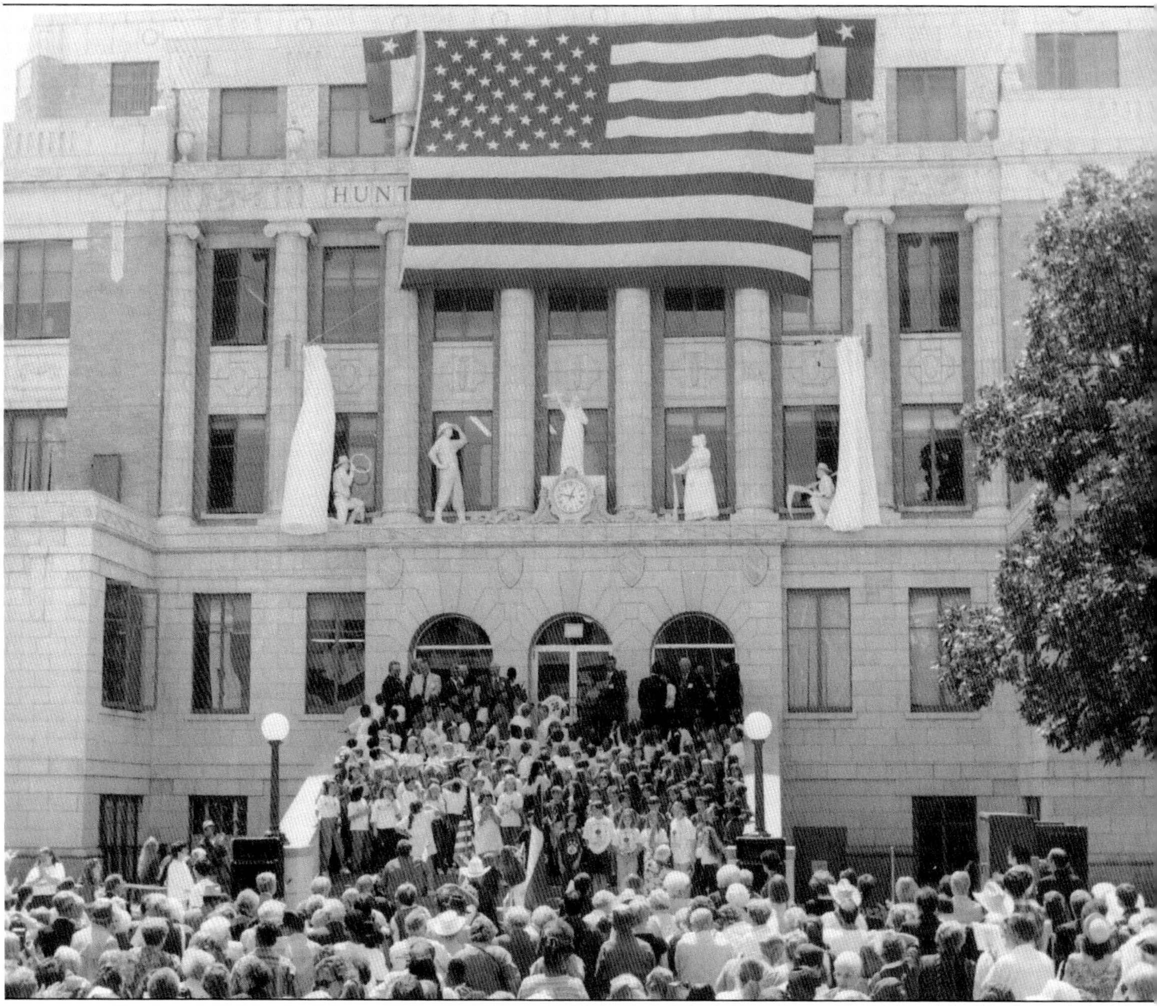

In April 1996, the Hunt County Historical Commission celebrated the 150th anniversary of the creation of Hunt County and Greenville as the county seat. The event spotlighted the 1929 courthouse with a re-creation of the original dedication. On both occasions, the finale included a tableau representing Pioneer Cowboy, Texas Ranger, Justice, Pioneer Woman, and Pioneer Farmer. (Courtesy of the author.)

ON THE COVER: The formal opening of the 1929 Hunt County Courthouse in the center of the public square in Greenville was held on April 11, 1929. The event also marked the 83rd anniversary of the creation of the county and town. (Courtesy of the Hunt County Historical Commission.)

IMAGES
of America

GREENVILLE

Carol Taylor and the
Hunt County Historical Commission

ARCADIA
PUBLISHING

ISBN 978-0-7385-7910-8

Published by Arcadia Publishing
Charleston, South Carolina

Printed in the United States of America

Library of Congress Control Number: 2010921324

For all general information contact Arcadia Publishing at:
Telephone 843-853-2070
Fax 843-853-0044
E-mail sales@arcadiapublishing.com
For customer service and orders:
Toll-Free 1-888-313-2665

Visit us on the Internet at www.arcadiapublishing.com

Dedicated to the men and women of all races whose vision and hard work changed Greenville from a small frontier village to a progressive city.

Contents

ACKNOWLEDGMENTS

This book is a collection of images belonging to countless persons whose photographs, yearbooks, and scrapbooks found their way into major collections in Greenville and Hunt County. Others were in personal collections whose owners readily agreed to share with readers. To all we owe a debt of gratitude.

The major collections include the Special Collections at the Gee Library on the campus of Texas A&M University-Commerce, the Hunt County Historical Commission, and the W. Walworth Harrison Public Library. The City of Greenville; the Greenville Board of Development; and GEUS, the municipally owned power company, allowed me to use their collections. Jack Horton graciously offered his photograph collection of a magnificent parade held in Greenville in 1901.

I owe a debt of gratitude to Dr. James Conrad and countless others who were always willing to discuss the history of Greenville. The patient guidance and understanding of Luke Cunningham and Hannah Carney of Arcadia Publishing made the technical aspect of this project much easier.

Finally, I would like to thank my husband, Michael, and our son, Matthew. Without their support and encouragement, this book would still be an idea.

INTRODUCTION

Greenville, Texas, grew from an isolated frontier village in the 1840s to a major market center in the first half of the 20th century. The transition can be attributed to the fertile black land prairies surrounding the town and the determination of its citizens to create a progressive community following the Civil War. That transition will be the main focus of this book, amply illustrated with many photographic pieces used by the Booster Club in selling Greenville to new residents, new industry, and new ideas.

The First Legislature of the State of Texas created 31 new counties, which included Hunt County. Two sites were offered for the county seat, to be named Greenville in honor of Thomas Jefferson Green, patriot of the Republic of Texas. The citizens chose the site offered by McQuinney Howell Wright on the black land prairie some 16 miles from the headwaters of the Sabine River. Town lots sold at auction on January 15, 1847. The little town grew slowly at first. Isolated from the rest of the world, with no newspaper, no railroads, and often surrounded by a sea of mud, Greenville at first struggled with a limited supply of water and timber for fuel and building.

The end of the Civil War brought new settlers seeking new homes to rebuild their lives. Greenville, like other Texas towns, grew steadily. The merchants enlarged their stores, contributed funds to bring railroads to town, and began to transform the village into a town. The first railroad arrived on October 2, 1880, which changed Greenville forever. Cotton could be shipped to Galveston and on to European markets much quicker and cheaper. Banks were built, an opera house provided entertainment, and churches flourished.

By the beginning of World War I, Greenville was home to numerous retail businesses, two soft drink manufacturers, three newspapers, and four colleges. Bankers dealt directly with their New York counterparts. Grain and cotton oil mills as well as several cotton gins and a cotton compress employed local men. The newspapers and city officials constantly encouraged new industry. Brooms, mattresses, and bee hives were some of the items produced in town.

Railroads had a dramatic influence on the growth of Greenville. In the fall of 1880, the Missouri, Kansas, and Texas Railroad, better known as the Katy, arrived in Greenville with a grand celebration. Cotton production was doubled by the fall of 1881. Later rail lines included the East Line and Red River, the Texas Midland, and the Cotton Belt. The trains also brought visitors to the city including the Frisco Land and Immigration Association in 1904, a Grand Class Initiation of the Woodmen of the World in 1909, and state reunions of Confederate veterans held in 1913 and again in 1914.

While the railroads allowed Greenville citizens to travel to other parts of the country and outsiders to visit and relocate to the area, transportation within town was a nightmare during periods of heavy rainfall. The black land prairies are composed of a clay soil that not only expanded when wet but assumed the consistency of tar. When rain inundated the region, ox teams became mired in the roads. At one point in the 1870s, the local newspaper had to suspend printing for lack of newsprint. Stores ran out of goods. Some comedian put a sign on the main street that declared "No Fishing."

The enterprising businessmen tried paving the street from the Katy depot to the courthouse square with wooden bricks, cut from bois d'arc trees. Bois d'arc was used to line cisterns and served as fence posts because of its density and resistance to rotting. However, the bois d'arc bricks tended to shrink when dry and expand when wet. The blocks floated out of the road bed after a rain and made the road extremely bumpy during dry weather. Regular paving bricks were later used.

Tracks for the Greenville Electric Street Railway were laid in 1910 and service began in 1911. Fares were 5¢, if the passenger had the money. If not, he or she rode free. The railway leased the city park about 3 miles from the public square and added a band shell; dance pavilion; bowling alley; skating rink; a theater, which seated 600 and had a large stage; a zoo; playground equipment; and electric lights at night, all to encourage ridership. However, the endeavor was not financially successful. The Greenville Electric Street Railway sold the cars in 1918.

The streetcars and park were just two of many civil improvements in Greenville. On March 4, 1891, the city council began operation of the municipally owned electric plant. A small steam engine powered two dynamos for 40 streetlights and 1,000 lights for homes. The plant ran only at night until 1909. Two years earlier in 1889, the Greenville Water Works dammed up the Sabine River north of town in an effort to address the critical need for water. In 1903, the Women's Review Club received $15,000 from Andrew Carnegie for a public library that opened to the public in 1904. All of the improvements were welcomed with great celebrations.

As the population of Greenville expanded, housing was built to the north, south, and west with the Sabine River forming the town limits on the east. Several housing developments included large homes with indoor plumbing, running water, and electric lighting prior to the beginning of the 20th century. Large churches were built in the downtown area. Four colleges located in Greenville between 1899 and 1935. Students were able to attend the Greenville Business College and the following three church supported institutions: Texas Holiness University, Burleson College, and Wesley College. Unfortunately, declining enrollments and economic crisis forced all four to close by 1935.

Greenville was an agricultural marketing center until the beginning of World War II when the Army Air Corps opened a pilot training school at the newly commissioned Majors Field south of town. At the end of the war, the field was turned over to the city. It became the start of an industrial movement that continues to the present. No longer dependent on the fertile black land prairie, Greenville has sustained that progressive attitude over 150 years of growth and development.

One

Early Days

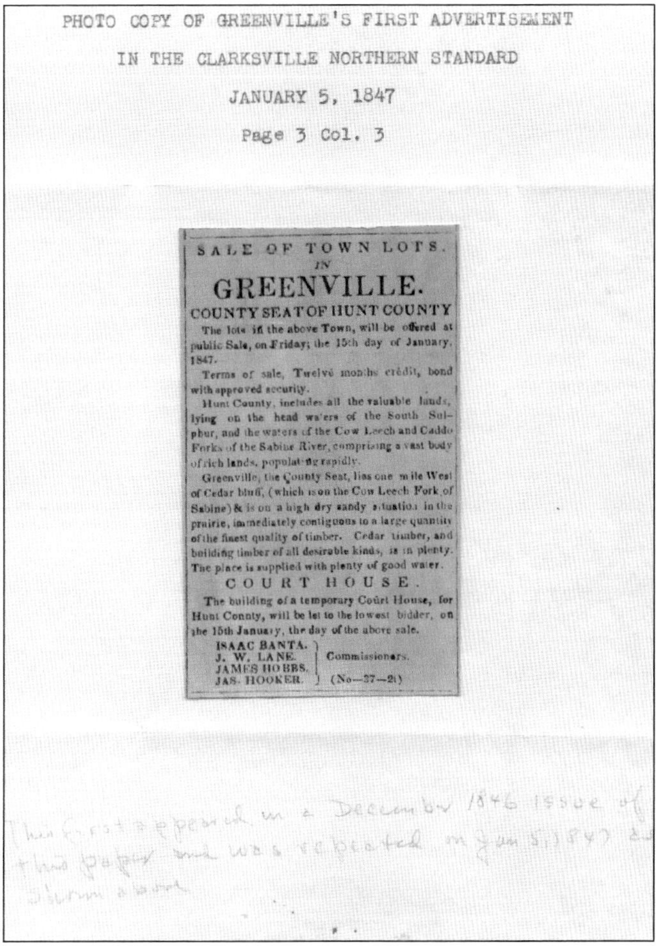

PHOTO COPY OF GREENVILLE'S FIRST ADVERTISEMENT

IN THE CLARKSVILLE NORTHERN STANDARD

JANUARY 5, 1847

Page 3 Col. 3

SALE OF TOWN LOTS.

IN

GREENVILLE.

COUNTY SEAT OF HUNT COUNTY

The lots in the above Town, will be offered at public Sale, on Friday; the 15th day of January, 1847.

Terms of sale, Twelve months credit, bond with approved security.

Hunt County, includes all the valuable lands, lying on the head waters of the South Sulphur, and the waters of the Cow Leech and Caddo Forks of the Sabine River, comprising a vast body of rich lands, populating rapidly.

Greenville, the County Seat, lies one mile West of Cedar bluff, (which is on the Cow Leech Fork of Sabine) & is on a high dry sandy situation in the prairie, immediately contiguous to a large quantity of the finest quality of timber. Cedar timber, and building timber of all desirable kinds, is in plenty. The place is supplied with plenty of good water.

COURT HOUSE.

The building of a temporary Court House, for Hunt County, will be let to the lowest bidder, on the 15th January, the day of the above sale.

ISAAC BANTA,
J. W. LANE,
JAMES HOBBS,
JAS. HOOKER. } Commissioners.

(No—37—2t)

Two men offered sites for Greenville to be decided by vote of the white male population. After two votes, the present site of Greenville was chosen by a narrow margin. In December 1846, this promotional piece appeared in the *Clarksville Northern Standard* advertising the first auction of town lots in the new county seat of Hunt County. (Courtesy of Special Collections, Gee Library, Texas A&M University-Commerce.)

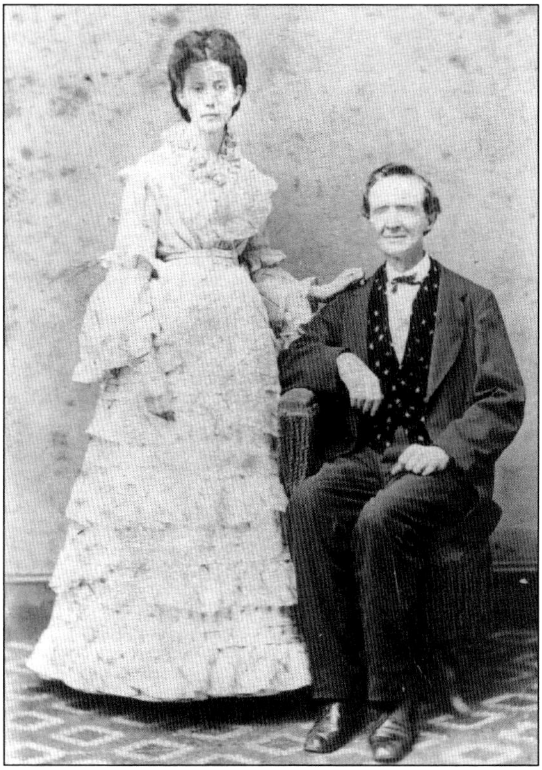

McQuinney Howell Wright (1813–1890) donated 160 acres for the new town of Greenville. To show his support for the new town, he purchased several of the town lots and opened one of the early mercantile stores. Shown here is Wright with his second wife, Nancy Emily Davis Turner, whom he married in 1870. (Courtesy of Hunt County Historical Commission.)

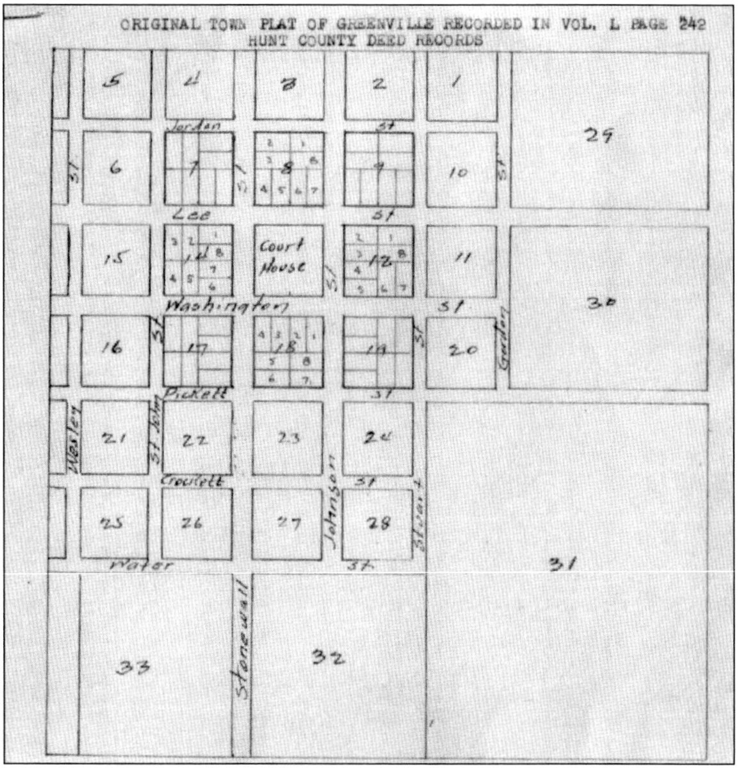

The town of Greenville was surveyed and lots were laid out in December 1846, which was some eight months after the county was created and the name of the town selected. Only those lots facing the public square were sold at the first auction. The center of the square was reserved for a future brick courthouse. (Courtesy of W. Walworth Harrison Public Library.)

Hunt County was named in honor of Memucan Hunt, a close friend of then Texas governor James Pinckney Henderson and Thomas Jefferson Green, who arrived in Texas from Mississippi shortly after the Battle of San Jacinto. Hunt served as secretary of the Texas Navy and minister to the United States during the Republic of Texas. (Courtesy of W. Walworth Harrison Public Library.)

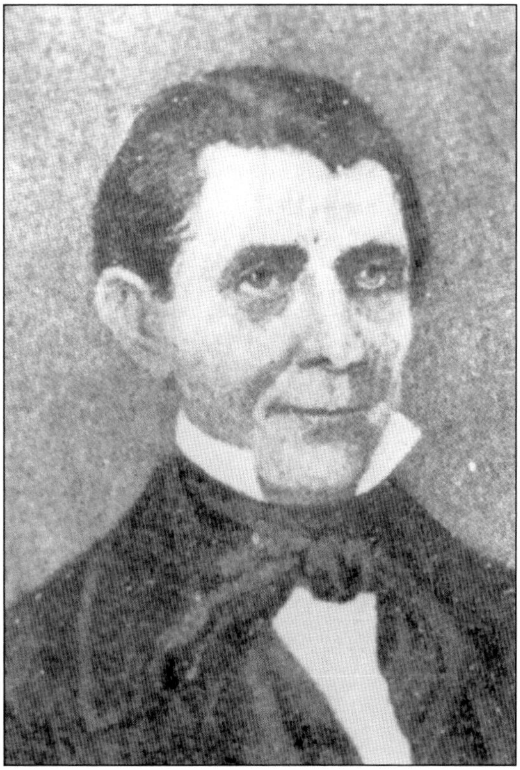

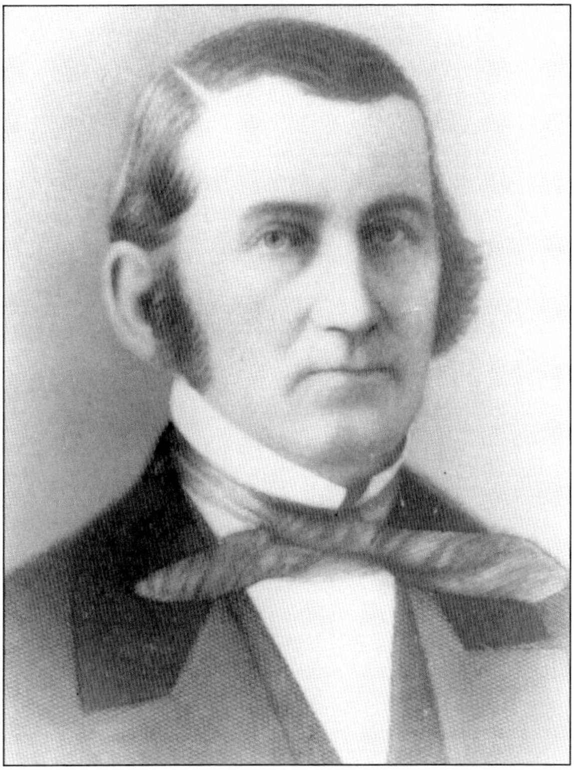

Greenville was named in honor of Thomas Jefferson Green. He was an officer in the Texas Army who was sent to Mississippi to recruit men and supplies. There he was aided by Memucan Hunt and James Pinckney Henderson. Green later took part in the Mier Expedition where he was captured and imprisoned at Perote Castle. Green escaped and finally returned to Texas. (Courtesy of W. Walworth Harrison Public Library.)

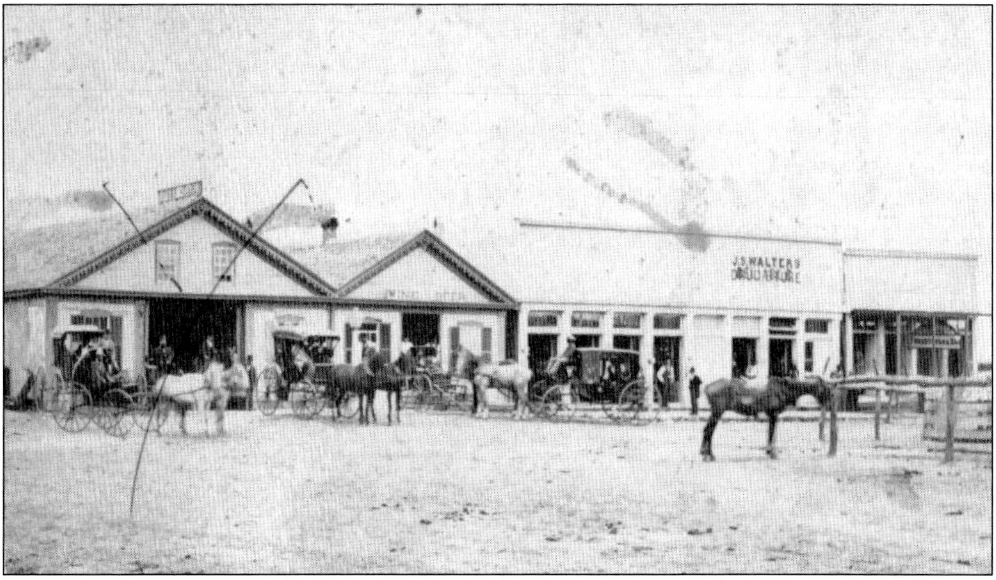

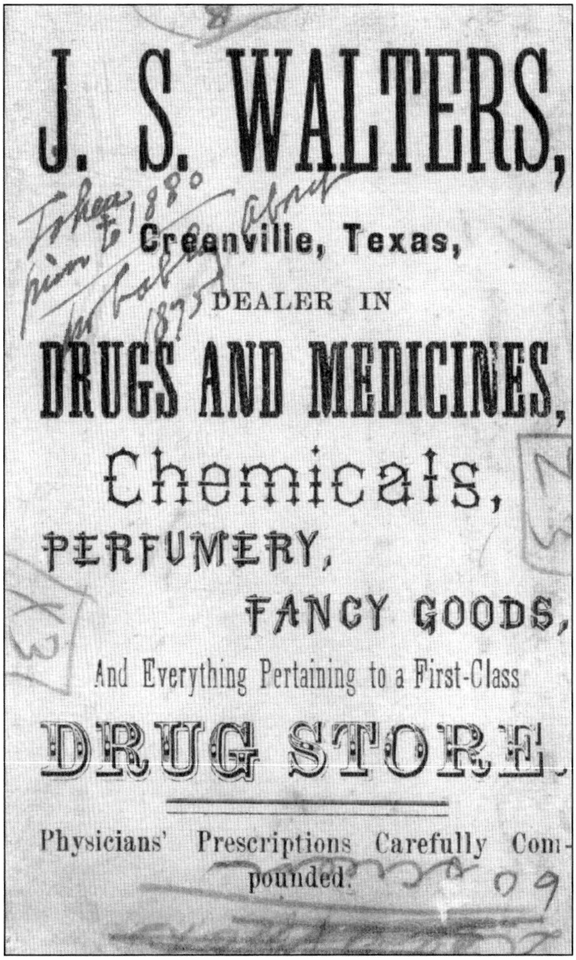

No antebellum photographs of Greenville are extant. The photograph above shows the west side of the public square during the late 1860s. This was taken by one of the first photographers who followed the U.S. 6th Army when troops occupied the region during Reconstruction. The horse on the right is tied to the rail that surrounded the 1857 courthouse, the first built in the center of the public square. The carriages and coaches are quite elaborate for the time and place, indicating that this was not a casual snapshot. Located in the center of the block was J. S. Walters's drugstore, one of the more specialized stores that opened after the Civil War. (Both courtesy of the author.)

Two

Progressives at Work

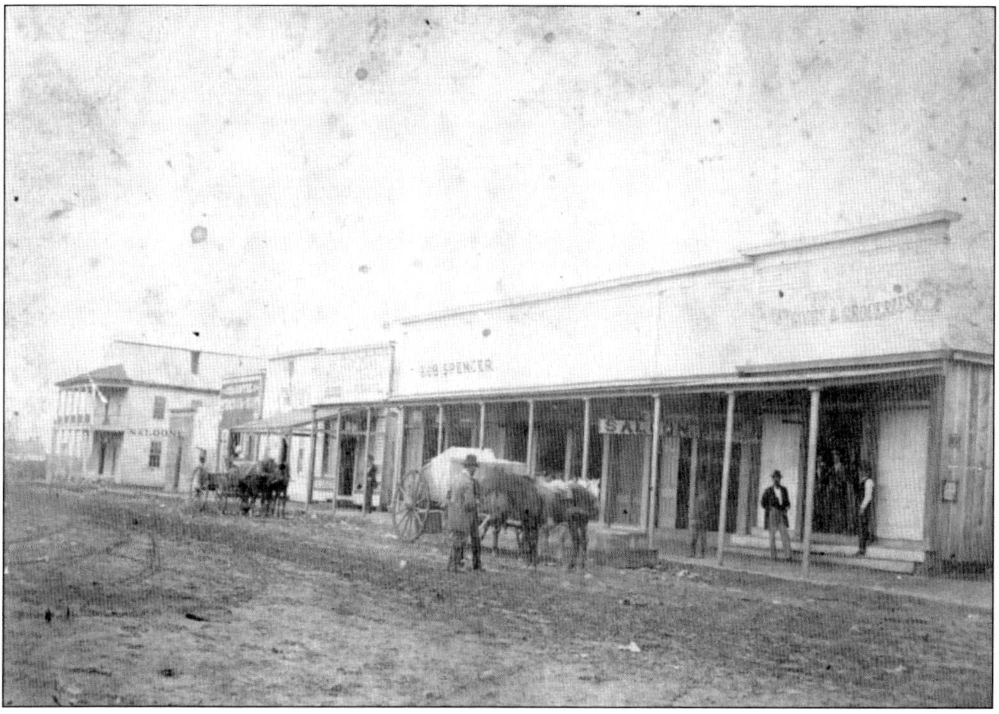

The west side of the public square is shown here sometime in the 1870s. The two-story building on the far left was the Star Hotel, one of the earliest in town. Two saloons were located on this side of the square. The wagon on the right holds a bale of cotton. Both wagons have high rear wheels to maneuver the black land mud. (Courtesy of Gee Library, Texas A&M University-Commerce.)

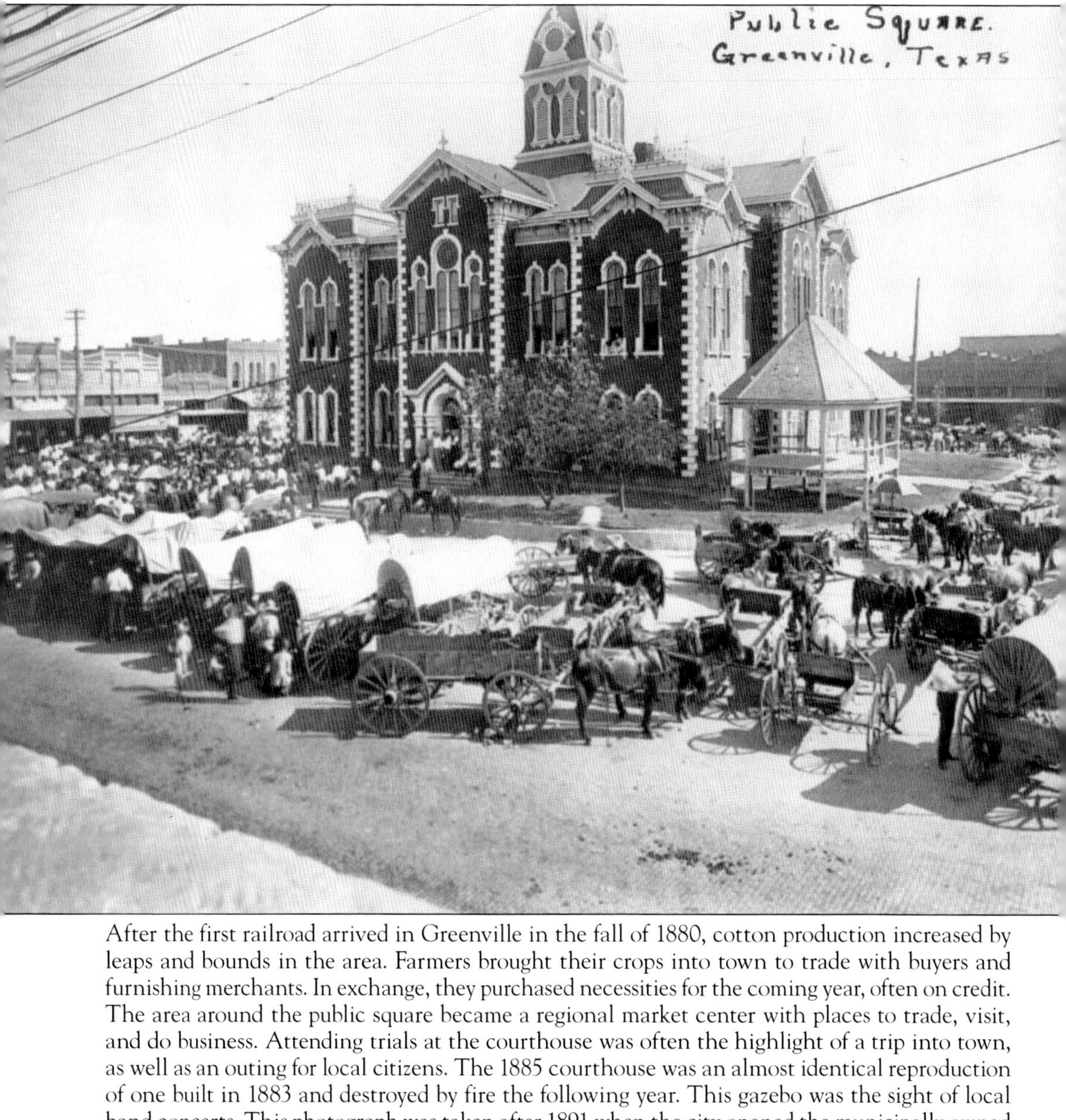

After the first railroad arrived in Greenville in the fall of 1880, cotton production increased by leaps and bounds in the area. Farmers brought their crops into town to trade with buyers and furnishing merchants. In exchange, they purchased necessities for the coming year, often on credit. The area around the public square became a regional market center with places to trade, visit, and do business. Attending trials at the courthouse was often the highlight of a trip into town, as well as an outing for local citizens. The 1885 courthouse was an almost identical reproduction of one built in 1883 and destroyed by fire the following year. This gazebo was the sight of local band concerts. This photograph was taken after 1891 when the city opened the municipally owned power plant. Merchants and other leading citizens were determined that Greenville become a modern progressive city. (Courtesy of the author.)

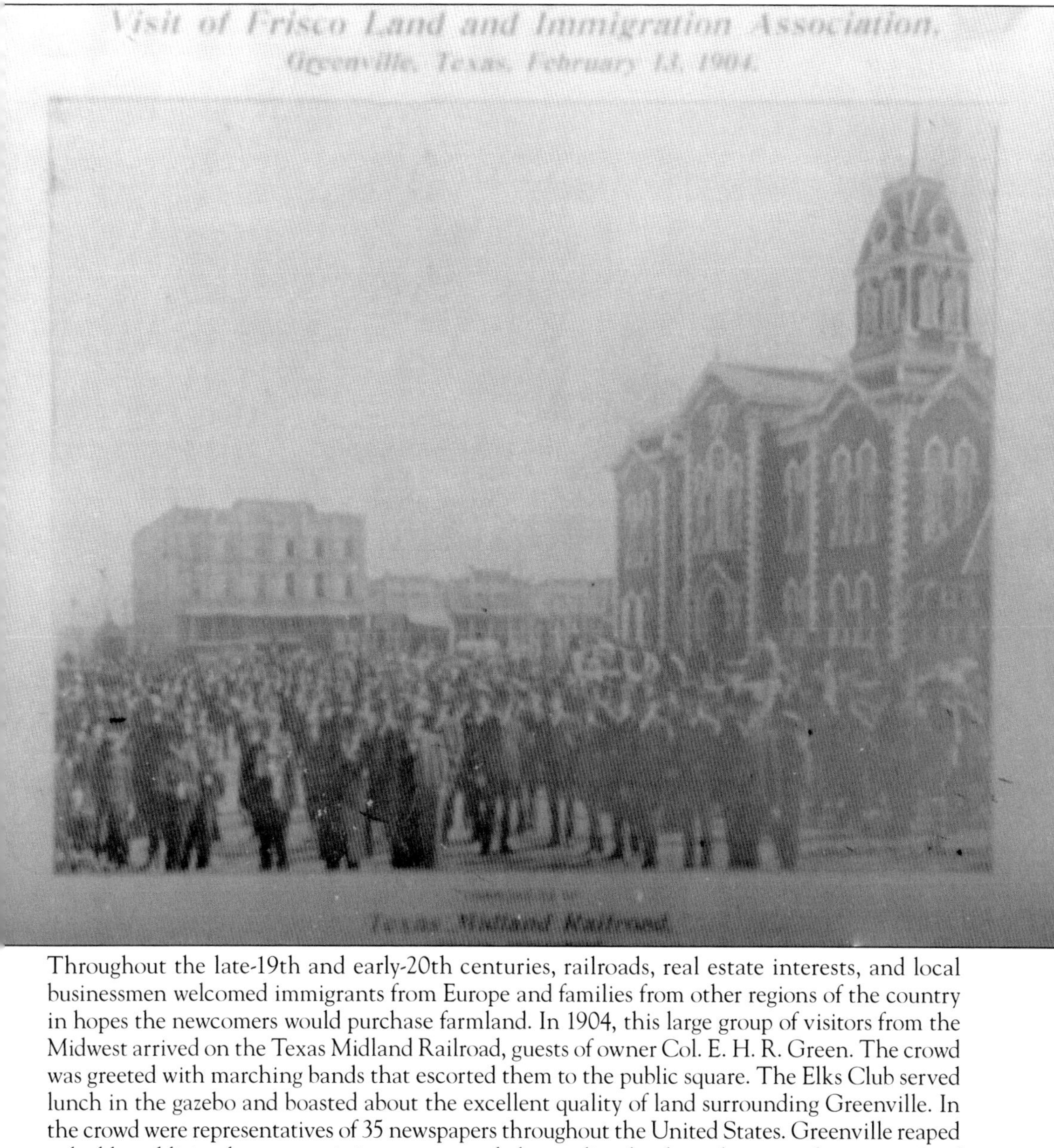

Throughout the late-19th and early-20th centuries, railroads, real estate interests, and local businessmen welcomed immigrants from Europe and families from other regions of the country in hopes the newcomers would purchase farmland. In 1904, this large group of visitors from the Midwest arrived on the Texas Midland Railroad, guests of owner Col. E. H. R. Green. The crowd was greeted with marching bands that escorted them to the public square. The Elks Club served lunch in the gazebo and boasted about the excellent quality of land surrounding Greenville. In the crowd were representatives of 35 newspapers throughout the United States. Greenville reaped valuable publicity, but no statistics were recorded regarding land purchases made as a result of the promotion. Yet this event set the stage for numerous similar occasions to come. All the time, prices of farm lands continued to soar. (Courtesy of the W. Walworth Harrison Public Library.)

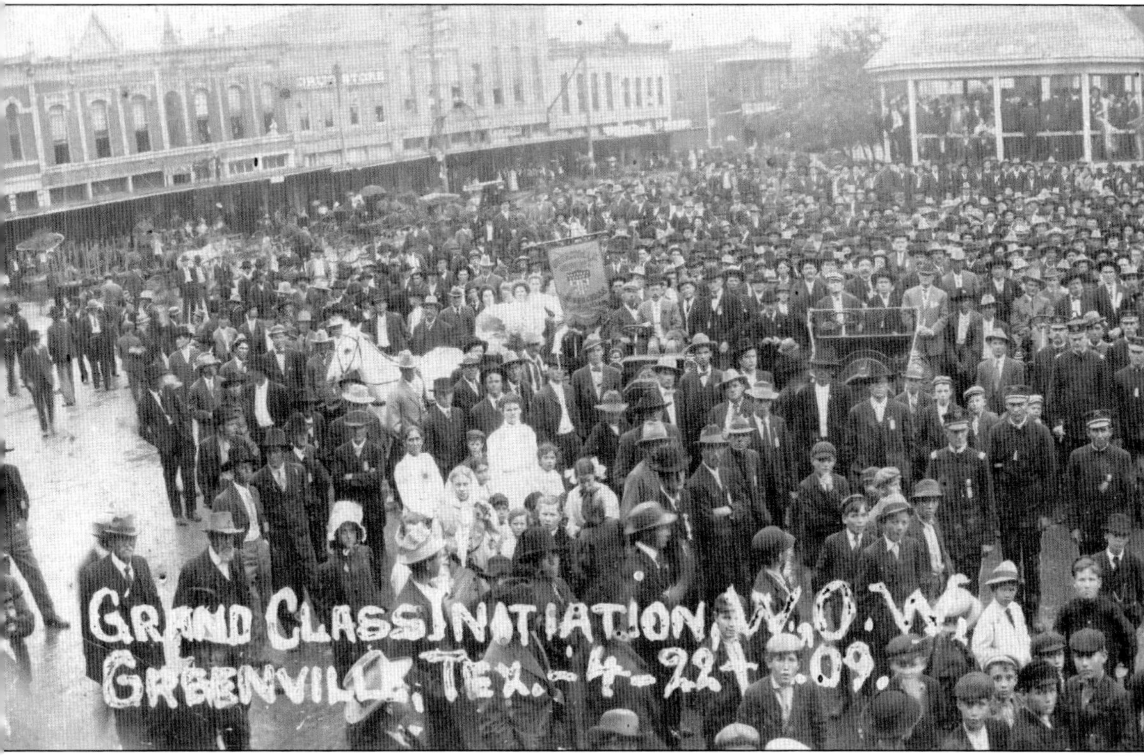

The Grand Class Invitation meeting of the Woodmen of the World met in Greenville on April 22, 1909. Families throughout the state arrived by special train for the festivities. Marching bands and floats paraded through the business district to the public square where the courthouse stood. Woodmen of the World was a popular fraternal benevolence society in Greenville and throughout the nation, especially in rural areas and small towns. The lodge, located one block south of

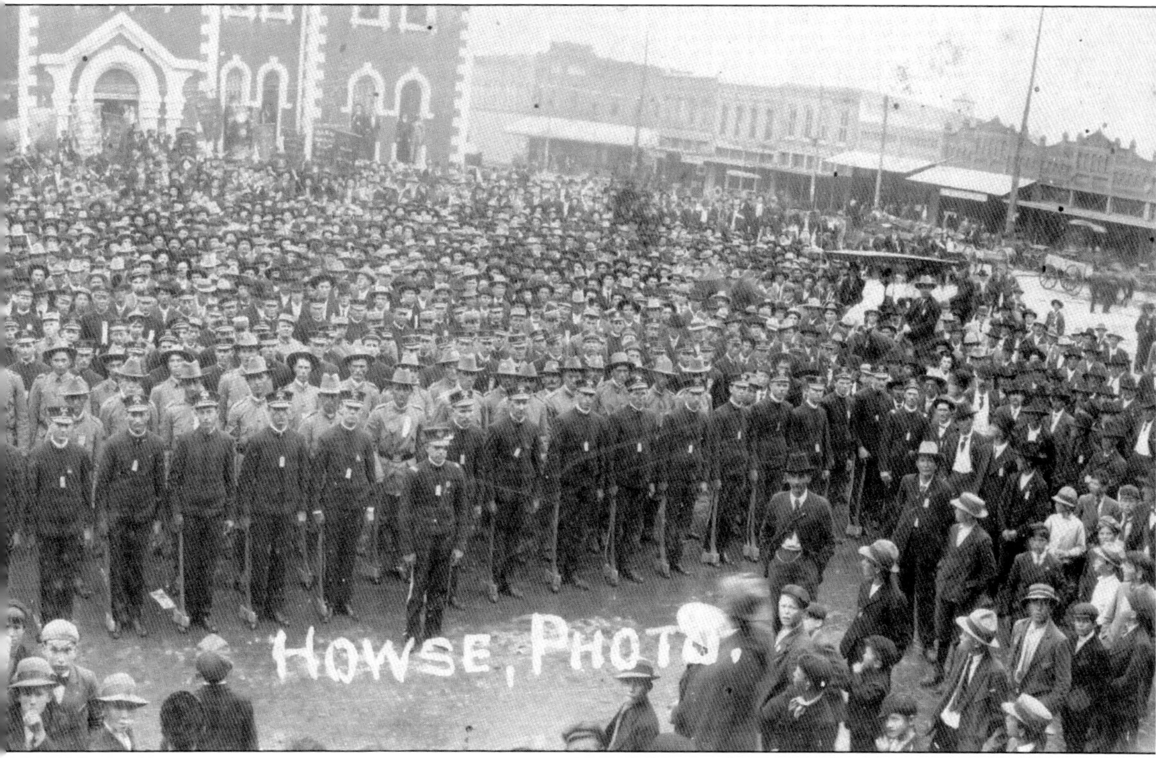

the square, provided activities for men, women, and young boys. The society stressed volunteerism and care of those of the lodge in time of need. One lasting memory of the Woodmen of the World was the iconic tombstones in the shape of a tree. Both East Mount Cemetery, the oldest in Greenville, and Forest Park Cemetery are profusely endowed with these sculptural headstones. (Courtesy of the W. Walworth Harrison Public Library.)

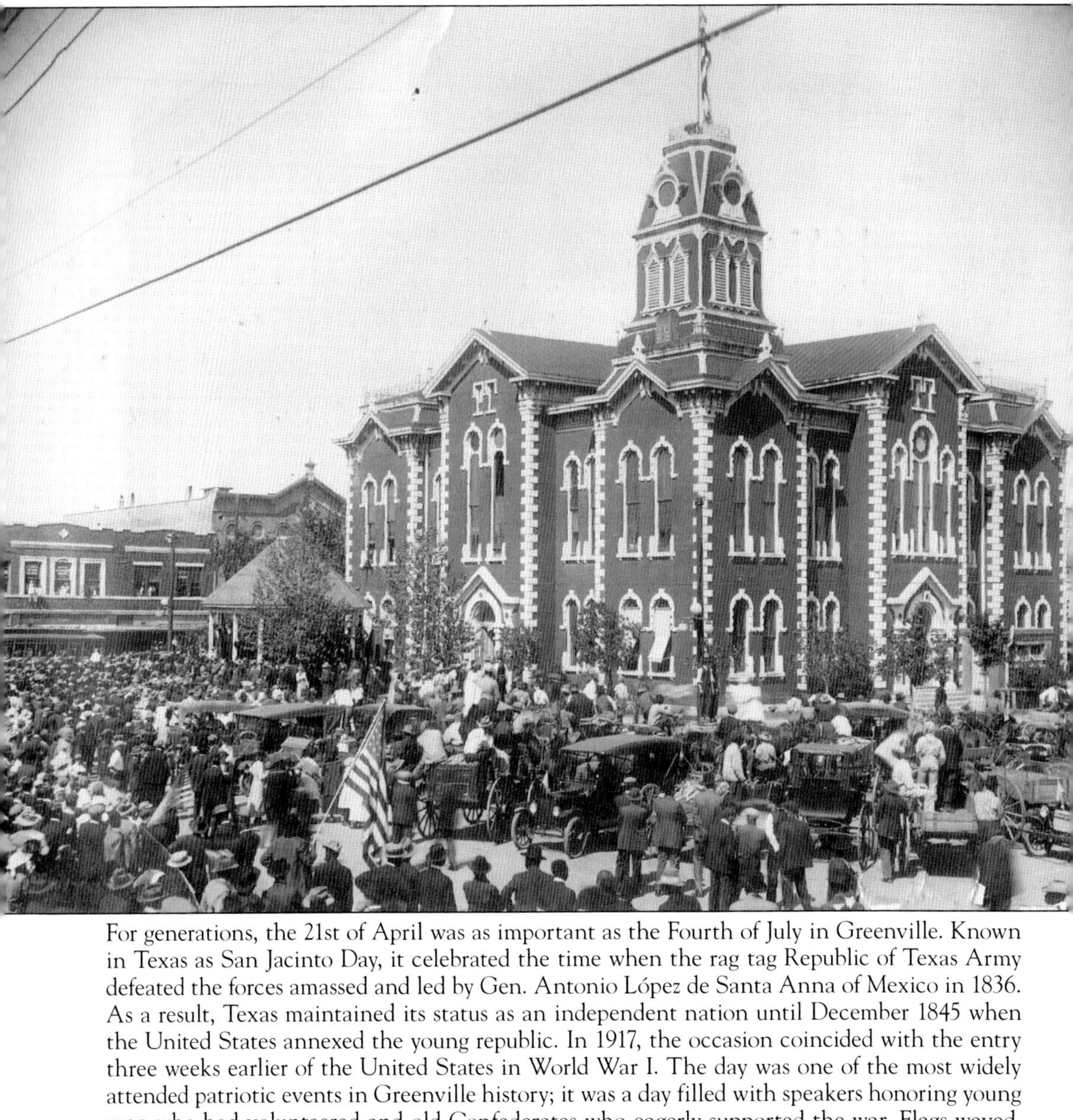

For generations, the 21st of April was as important as the Fourth of July in Greenville. Known in Texas as San Jacinto Day, it celebrated the time when the rag tag Republic of Texas Army defeated the forces amassed and led by Gen. Antonio López de Santa Anna of Mexico in 1836. As a result, Texas maintained its status as an independent nation until December 1845 when the United States annexed the young republic. In 1917, the occasion coincided with the entry three weeks earlier of the United States in World War I. The day was one of the most widely attended patriotic events in Greenville history; it was a day filled with speakers honoring young men who had volunteered and old Confederates who eagerly supported the war. Flags waved, bands played, and the crowd cheered. Greenville citizens eagerly joined in the drive to "feed the troops." (Courtesy of the author.)

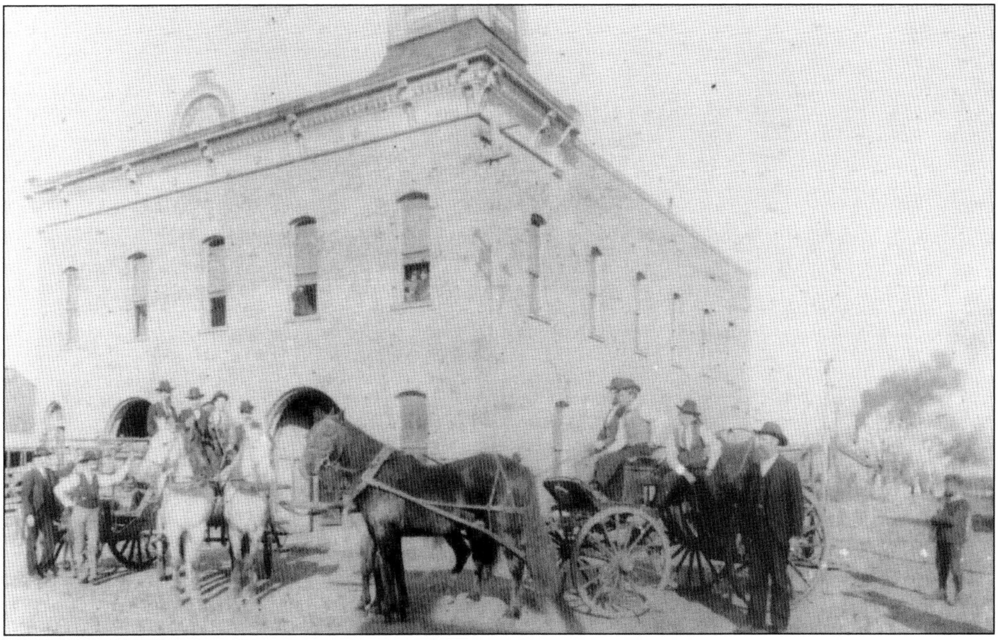

Fred Ende (1832–1897) was active in enticing railroads to Greenville and soon built a grand hotel on the site of his mercantile business. After a deadly fire killed 13 at the Ende Hotel on the southeast corner of the square on April 7, 1883, the Greenville City Council organized a fire department a month later. The horse drawn engines were housed in a large two-story building on the same block as the old hotel. Later fires did less damage, thanks to the fire department. (Courtesy of the Hunt County Historical Commission.)

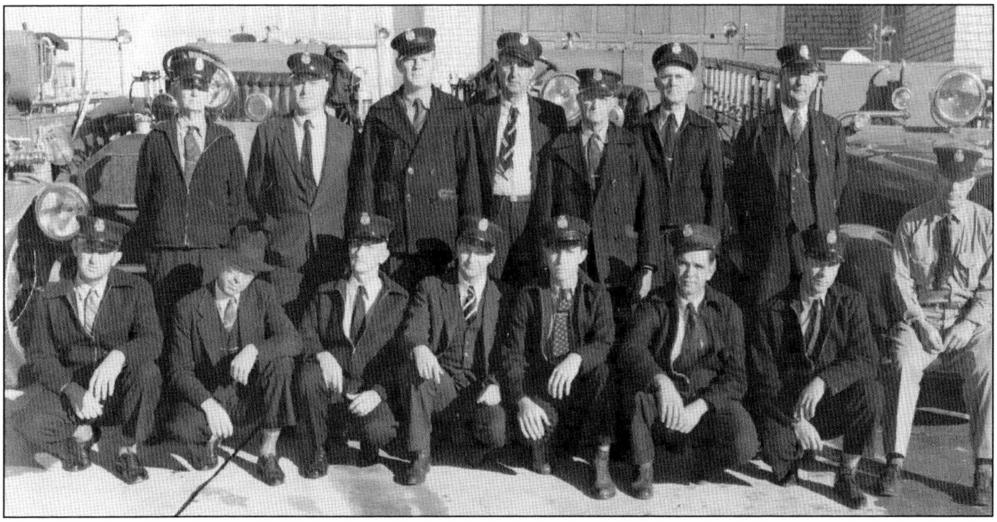

One of the dreams of Greenville citizens in the early 20th century was to build a large public auditorium. This plan did not materialize, even though a new courthouse, banks, and hotels were constructed during the 1920s. In the late 1930s, the City of Greenville received word that WPA (Works Progress Administration) assistance would build a new city hall with a grand auditorium and an attached central fire station. The station included upstairs space for firemen to live while on duty. After World War II, the city had a total of four modern fire trucks and a full-time professional fire department. (Courtesy of the W. Walworth Harrison Public Library.)

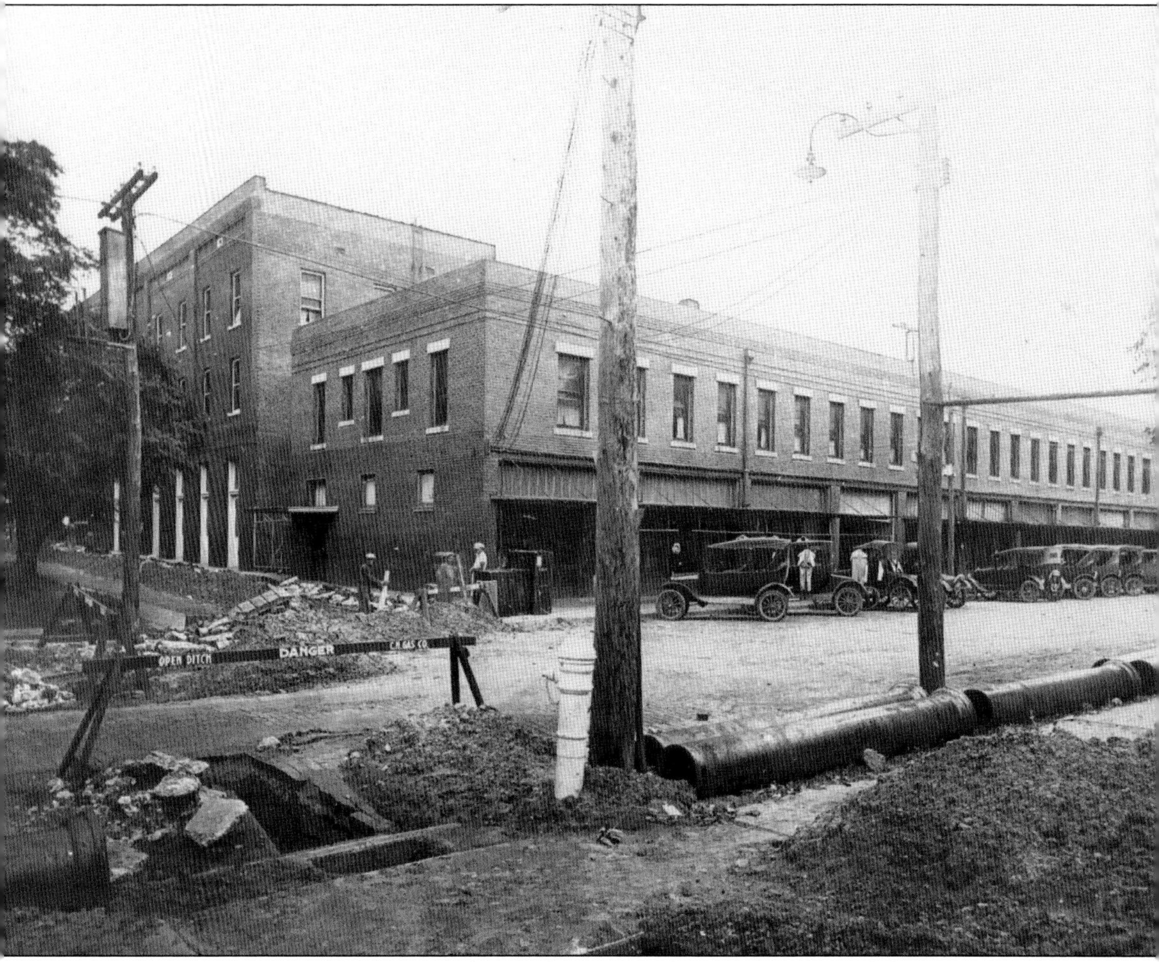

Artificial gas was developed in the late 19th century when scientists feared the natural gas supply would soon become exhausted. In 1905, J. B. Murphy was issued an artificial gas plant franchise in Greenville to manufacture the safe and economic by-product of coal. Artificial gas was used for lighting and cooking, although it produced less heat units than either coal or natural gas. City leaders feared it would compete with the municipally owned power plant as a cheaper but less convenient alternative to electric lighting. They pursued the natural gas option until 1926 when a natural gas supply became available in Greenville. Lines, such as these in the 2800 block of Washington Street, ran throughout town. The Booster Club solicited 2,000 customers who paid $20 each to cover meter deposits and connection fees for homes and businesses. Homes now had the convenience of hot water and heating without the danger of fires caused by open flame lights. (Courtesy of the author.)

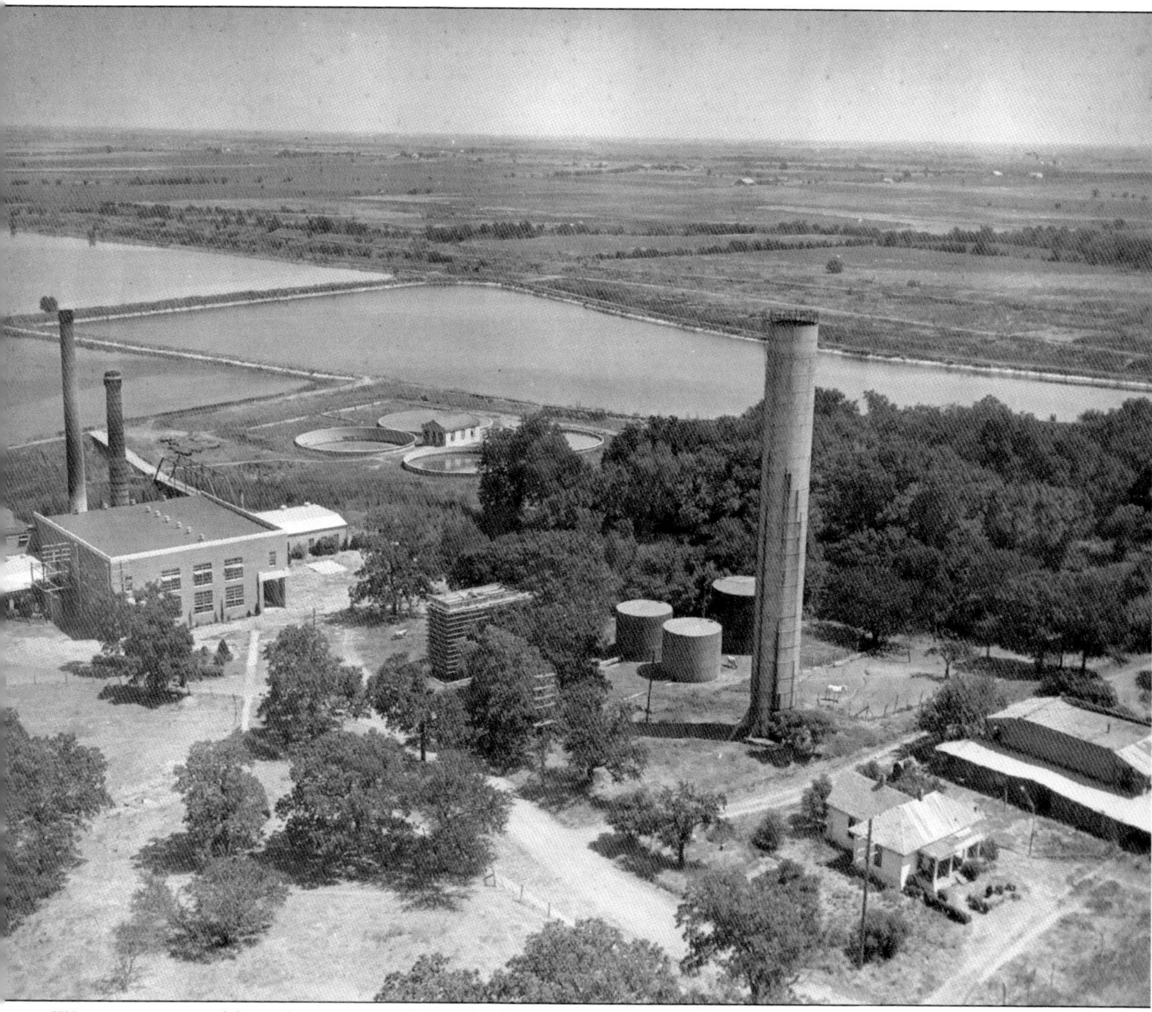

Water was a problem for citizens from the beginning of the town in 1847. Too much rain left roads impassable; too little rain caused the water source in the Sabine River to dry up. Citizens were then forced to share the small water holes with livestock and wild animals. One pioneer wrote that he wanted a good glass of water more than the finest whisky in the world. In 1889, J. M. Cook was awarded a contract to dam the Sabine River on the northern edge of town. Cook built this standpipe, 137 feet tall and 15 feet in diameter. Water flowed out by gravity into homes, businesses, and fire hydrants. The City of Greenville purchased the facility in 1908 for $92,500. The city council created a large reservoir that supplied Greenville with water until the 1920s when more reservoirs were built. In the 1960s, Lake Tawakoni was created on the Sabine River south of Greenville, thereby assuring citizens of a consistent supply of water. (Courtesy of GEUS.)

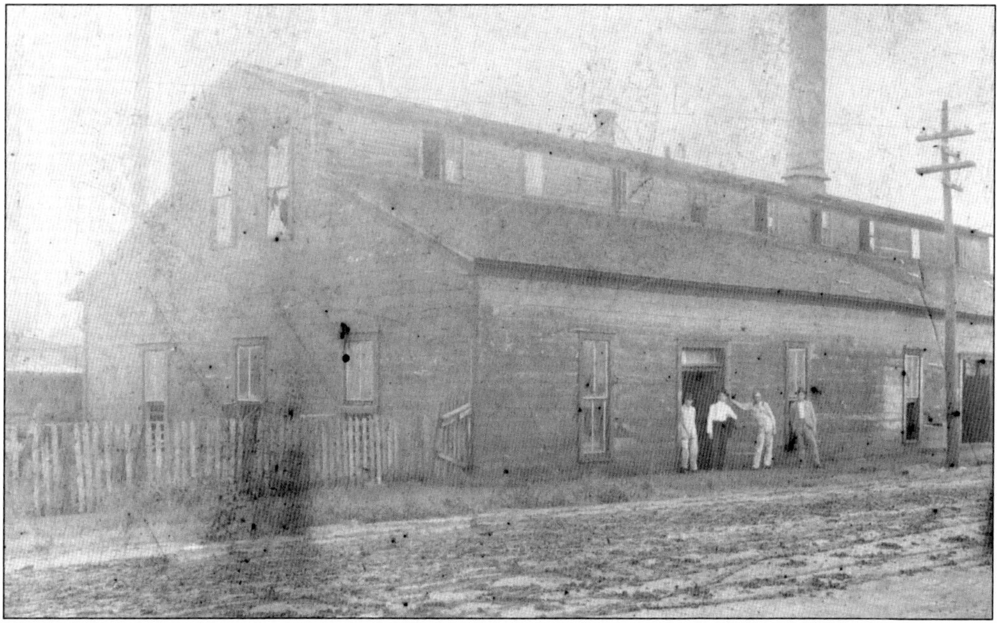

The lights went on in Greenville at dusk on March 4, 1891, when the Greenville Electric Light Company went into operation. Built by Wayne Electric Company, the plant has been continually owned and operated by the City of Greenville since that time. Until 1909, electricity was produced only at night; although, for a special fee, afternoon lighting could be arranged. (Photograph by E. L. Adams; courtesy of GEUS.)

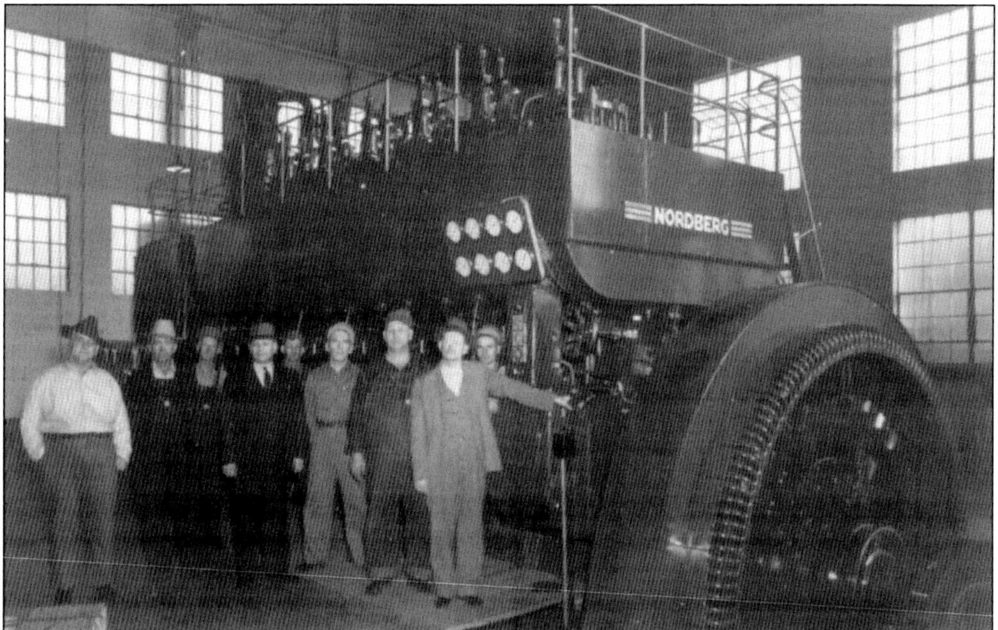

As the Army Air Corps airfield south of Greenville became operational in 1942, the city council realized additional demands would be made on the city-owned electric plant. This six cylinder, 2,400-horsepower, gas-burning Nordberg Diesel was added to three oil-burning units at the new power plant, which was located adjacent to the Greenville Water Plant. (Courtesy of GEUS.)

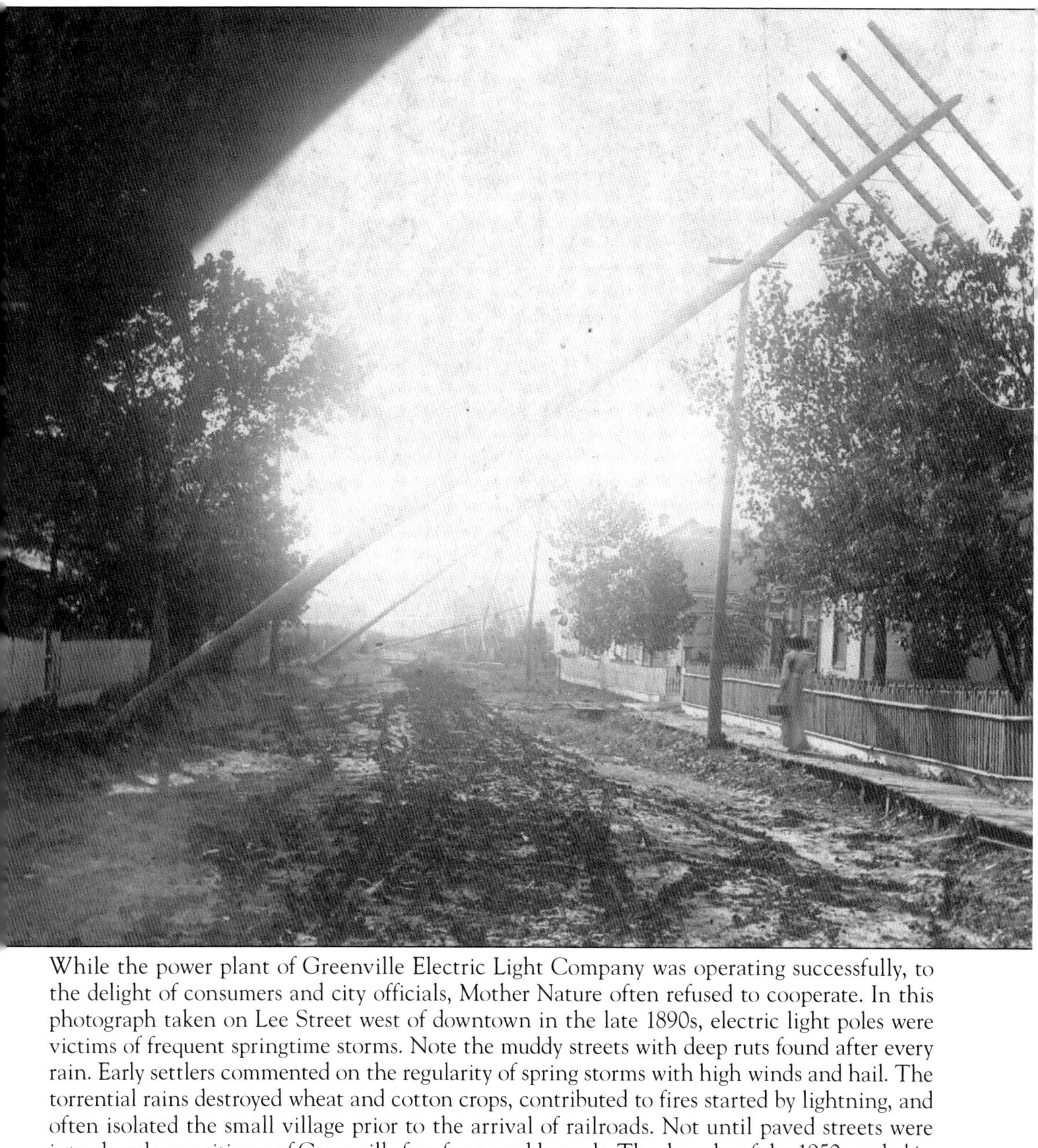

While the power plant of Greenville Electric Light Company was operating successfully, to the delight of consumers and city officials, Mother Nature often refused to cooperate. In this photograph taken on Lee Street west of downtown in the late 1890s, electric light poles were victims of frequent springtime storms. Note the muddy streets with deep ruts found after every rain. Early settlers commented on the regularity of spring storms with high winds and hail. The torrential rains destroyed wheat and cotton crops, contributed to fires started by lightning, and often isolated the small village prior to the arrival of railroads. Not until paved streets were introduced were citizens of Greenville free from muddy roads. The drought of the 1950s ended in the spring of 1957. That year saw a record 75.24 inches of rainfall in the city, often accompanied by high winds and flooding. A state-of-the-art warning system now warns residents of impending bad weather. (Courtesy of GEUS.)

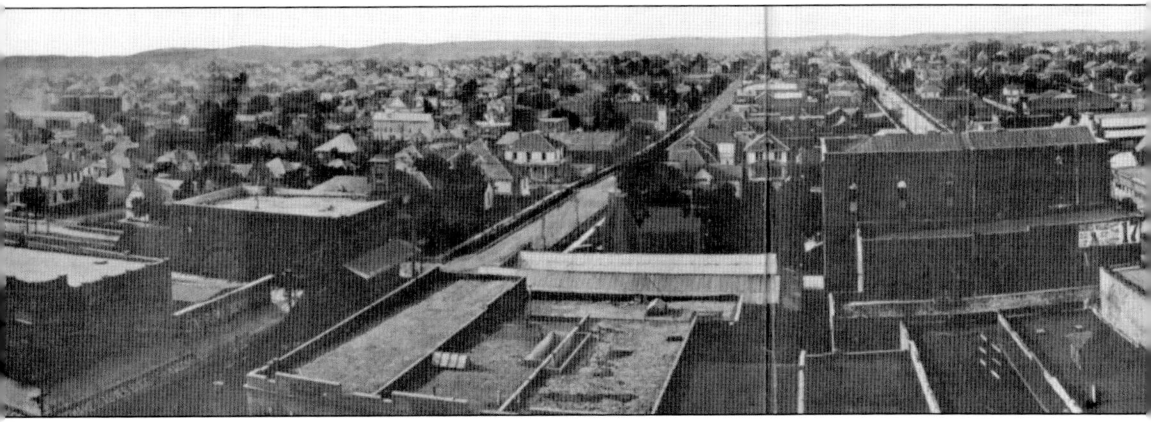

Panorama photographs were all the rage in the early years of the 20th century, and Greenville residents prided themselves for being in on the latest fad. Here is a shot taken from the roof of the courthouse c. 1912 looking south and southwest. In the lower left corner was the Armistead-Ende Store selling hardware, stoves, buggies, and wagons. Two doors south was the Central Fire Station with a large awning. The tall building in the center of the photograph

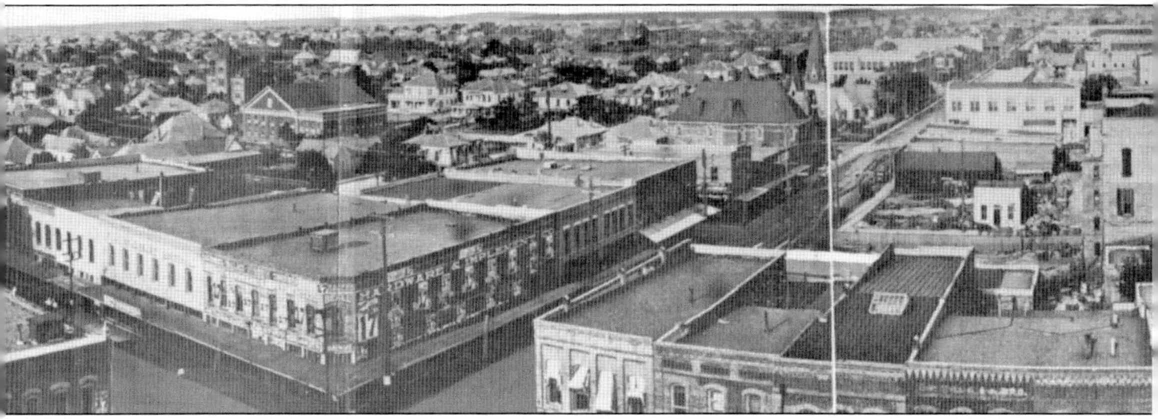

was the new Masonic Lodge. Across Stonewall Street was J. M. Raike Furniture Store. In the same block was Beall Brothers Hardware, one of the largest in East Texas. Near the upper right corner was Central Christian Church, built in 1899. The white building in the upper right corner was the new Knights of Pythias Hall. (Courtesy of Jack Horton.)

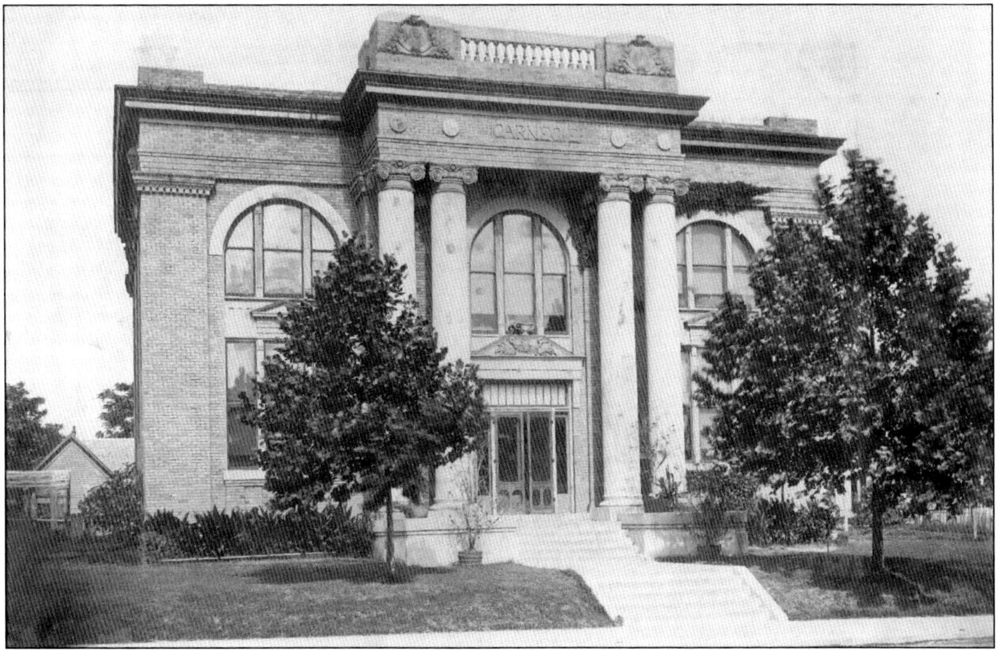

The Carnegie Library in Greenville was opened in February 1904. Andrew Carnegie donated $15,000 to the Women's Review Club to build and equip the facility. The ladies worked in tandem with the City of Greenville to operate and maintain the library until 1954. Longtime residents have delightful memories of visiting the library. (Courtesy of the author.)

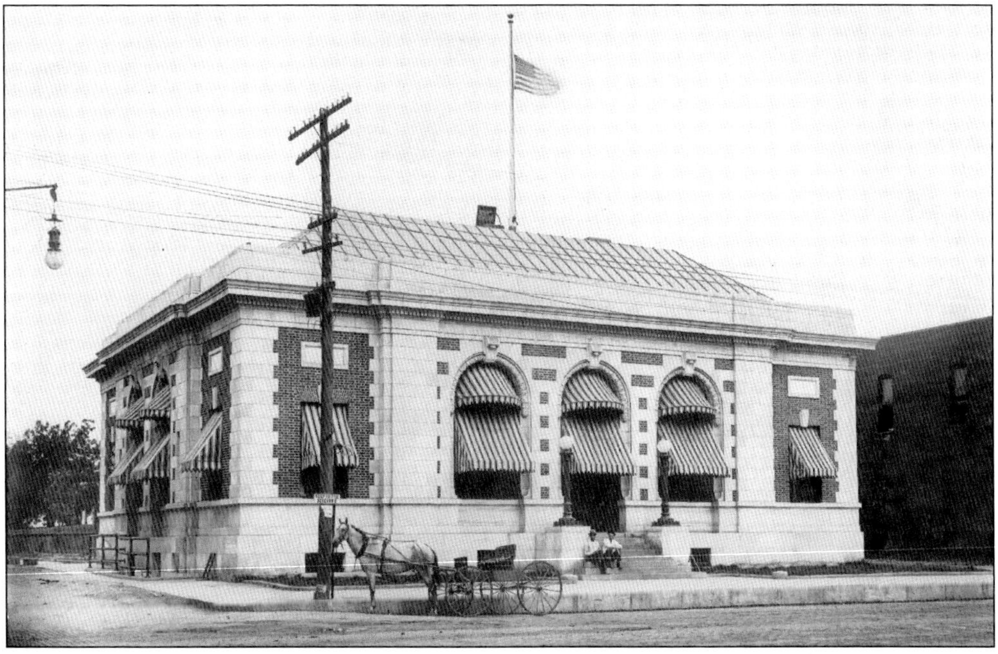

The Greenville Post Office, constructed by Fell and Ainsworth of Waco, opened on April 14, 1910. A second floor was added in 1927, as shown in this 1928 photograph. The Renaissance Revival–style building housed IRS offices, army recruiters, and various New Deal administrations. It is most famous as the site where World War II hero Audie Murphy enlisted in the army. (Courtesy of the author.)

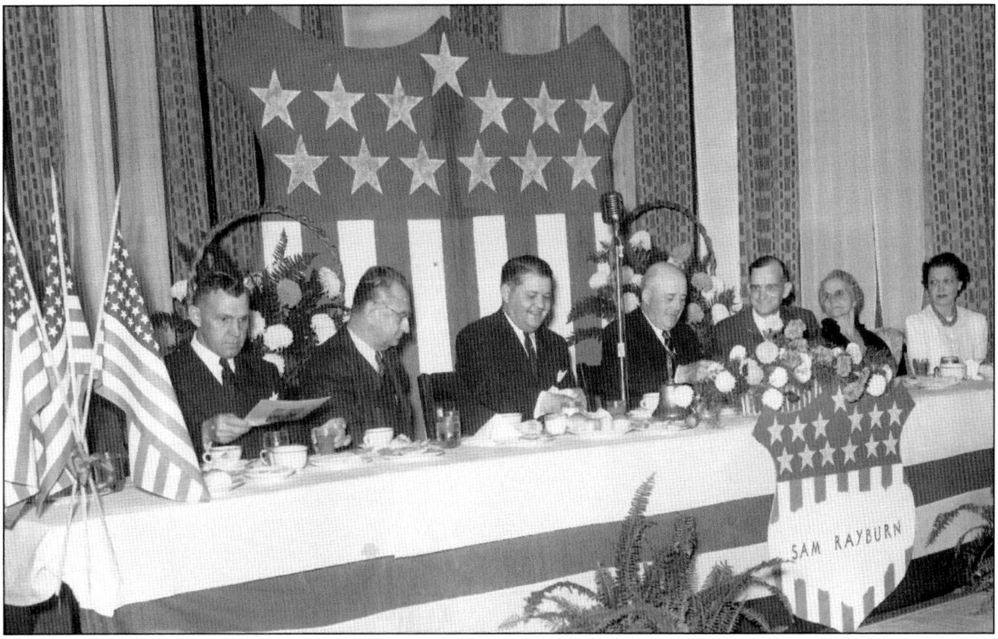

Congressman and Speaker of the U. S. House of Representatives, Sam Rayburn (1882–1961), fourth from left, was reared in Fannin County, north of Greenville. Throughout his political career he was a friend and strong supporter of Greenville. Among the many internal improvements in Greenville that Rayburn assisted with funding were the building of a new city hall, a new elementary school, and Majors Air Field, which was the site of an Army Air Corps training field in Greenville during World War II. City hall, shown below, was designed by local architect W. R. Ragsdale and featured a large auditorium, something the townspeople had wanted for many years. The smaller attachment on the right was the new central fire station. Rayburn spoke at the 1941 Chamber of Commerce Banquet held at the Beckham Hotel. (Both courtesy of W. Walworth Harrison Public Library.)

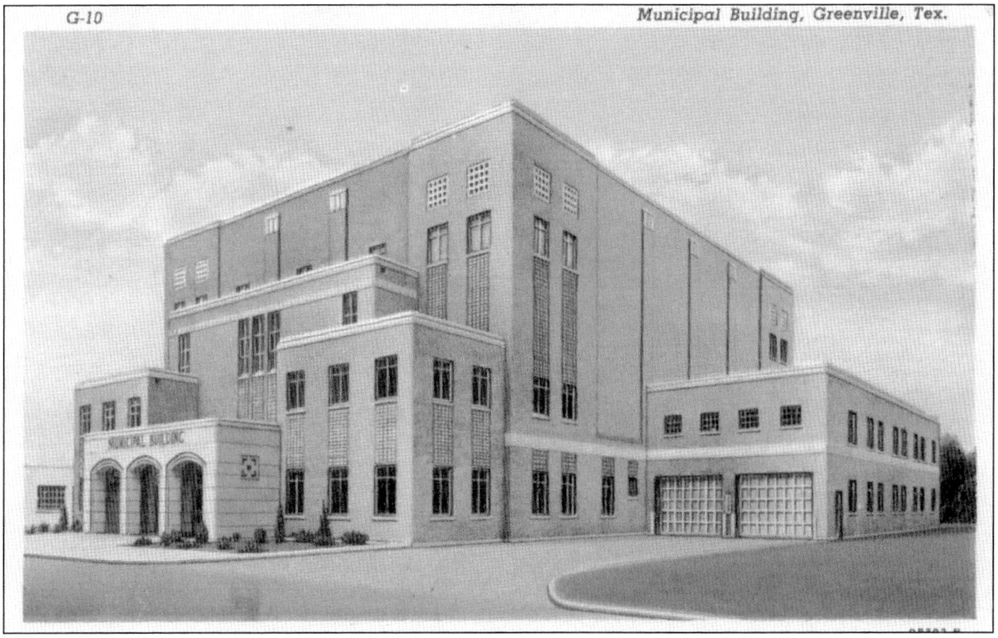

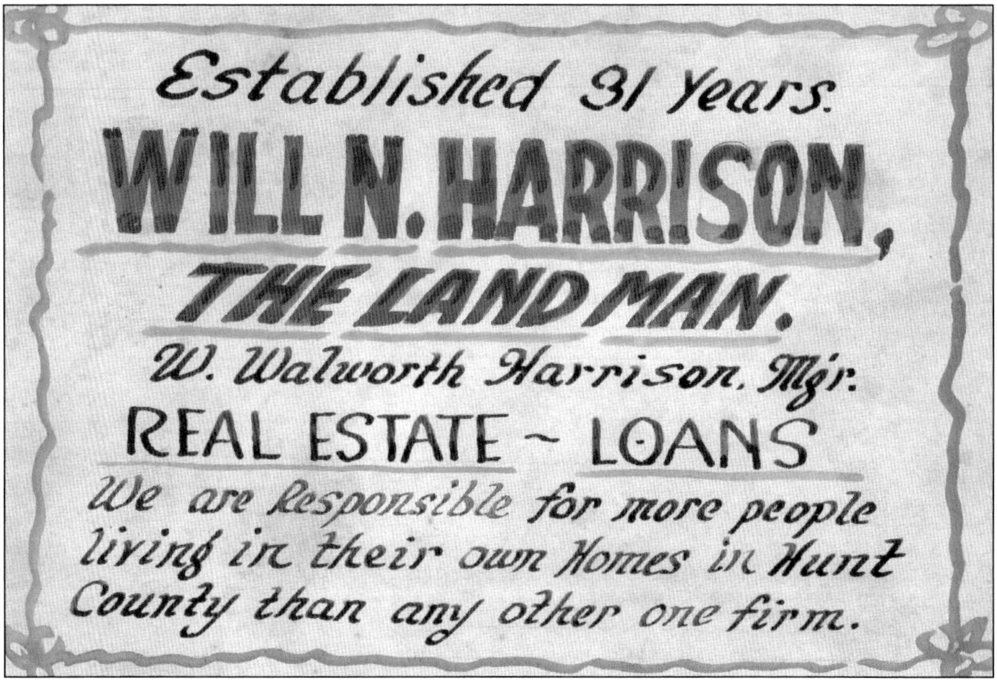

Will N. Harrison (1860–1916) was known for many years as the "Land Man." Sometime before 1912, Harrison invented the following new slogan: "Welcome to Greenville, Blackest Land and Whitest People." The double meaning caught the eye of president-elect Woodrow Wilson in 1912, who voiced his approval. Harrison and his two sons were leaders in the Greenville Booster Club and later the local chamber of commerce. When Harrison died in 1916, friends and city officials decided to hang the sign shown below over the entrance to the downtown business district between the railroad depot and the bus station. Locals believed that the word white was synonymous with nice. However, others believe it reflected the antebellum planter method of using the word to control white middling and lower classes. The sign was removed at the request of Gov. John Connally in the 1960s. (Both courtesy of W. Walworth Harrison Public Library.)

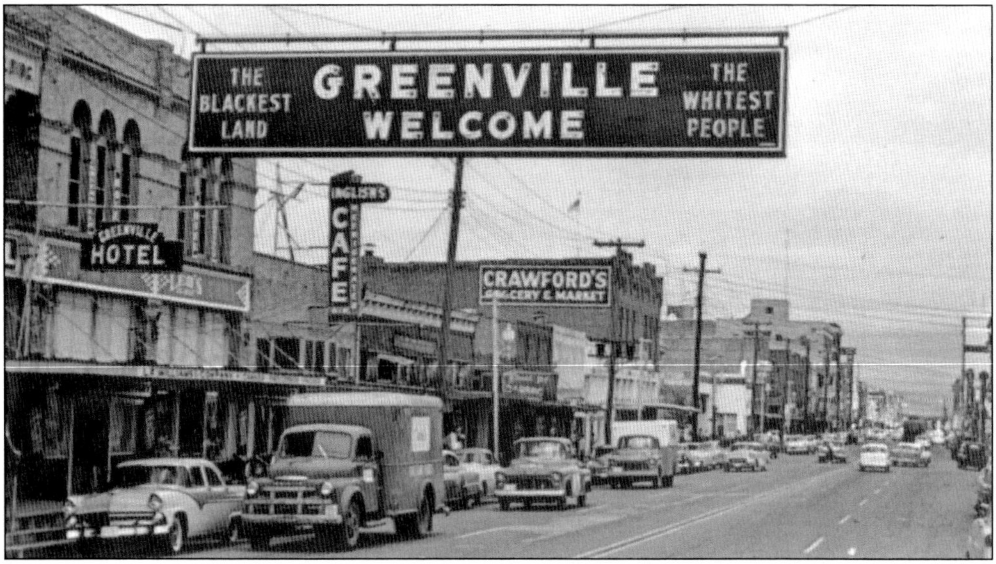

Three

Market Center

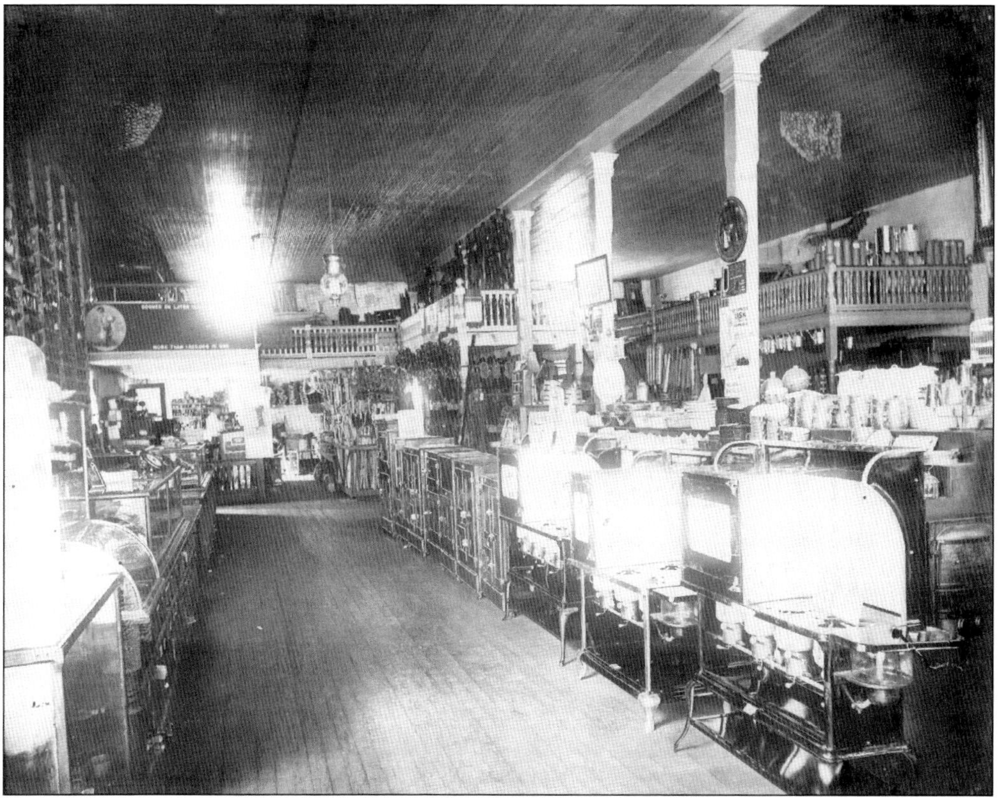

With the arrival of the railroads beginning in 1880, merchants had access to more goods to sell. One of the most prosperous merchants was the firm of Armistead-Ende Store. Here buyers could purchase anything from the latest in cookstoves to shiny new watering cans. The firm occupied the southeast corner of the public square as early as the 1850s. (Courtesy of W. Walworth Harrison Public Library.)

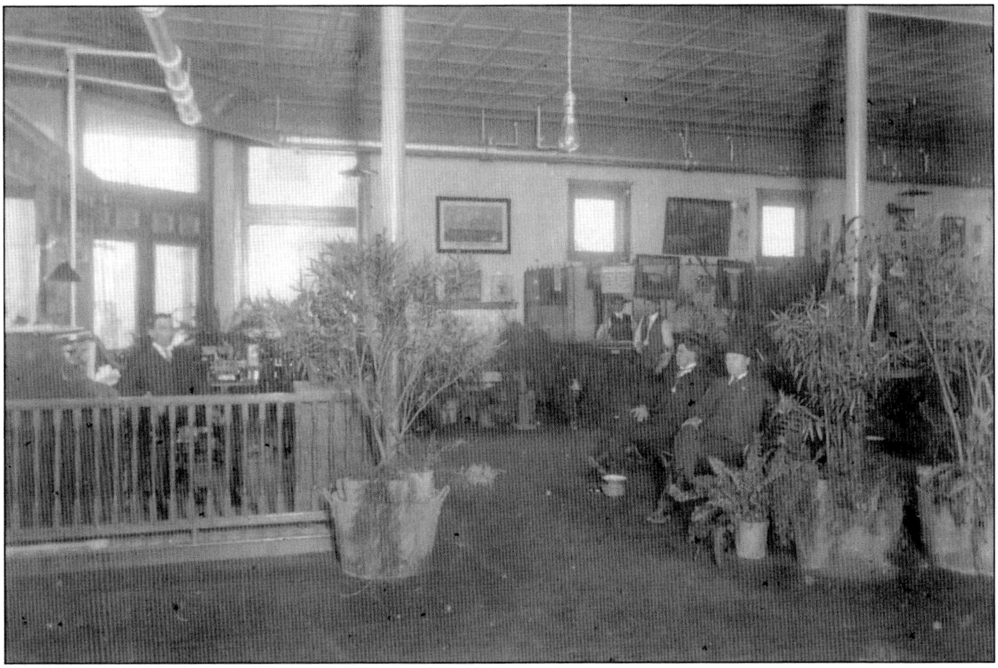

American Express functioned as one of the leading businesses in Greenville for many years. The company primarily dealt in transporting freight on the railroads and from railroad depots to merchants and private consumers. Prior to World War I, vaudeville troupes moved sets, costumes, and performers by American Express. The offices were located near the Beckham Hotel, where most performers stayed, and a short distance from the Missouri, Kansas, and Texas depot and the King Opera House. Greenville merchants frequently booked business travel to Chicago and New York through American Express. Posters and plants added a sophisticated touch to the office. (Both courtesy of Hunt County Historical Commission.)

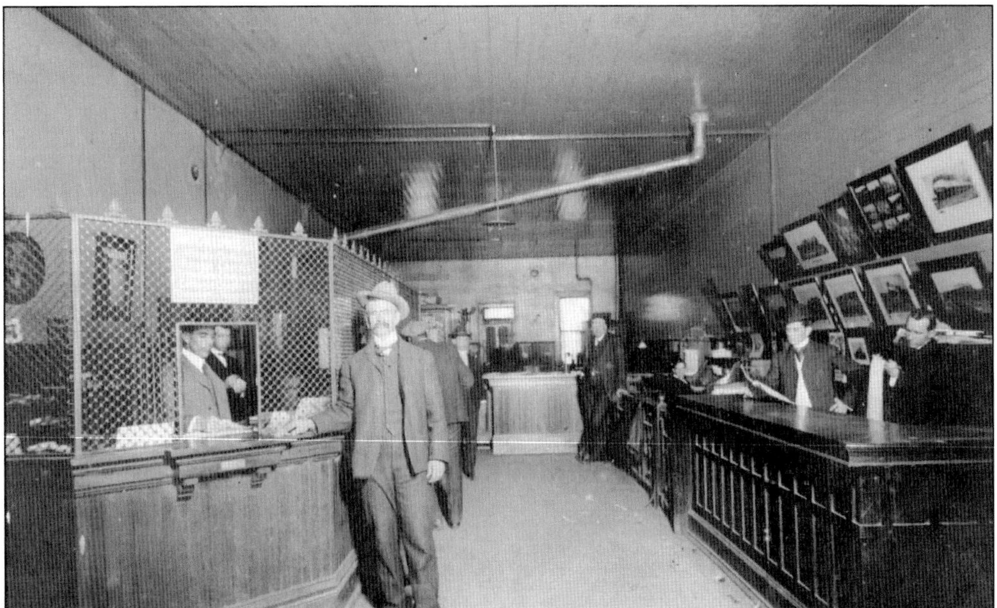

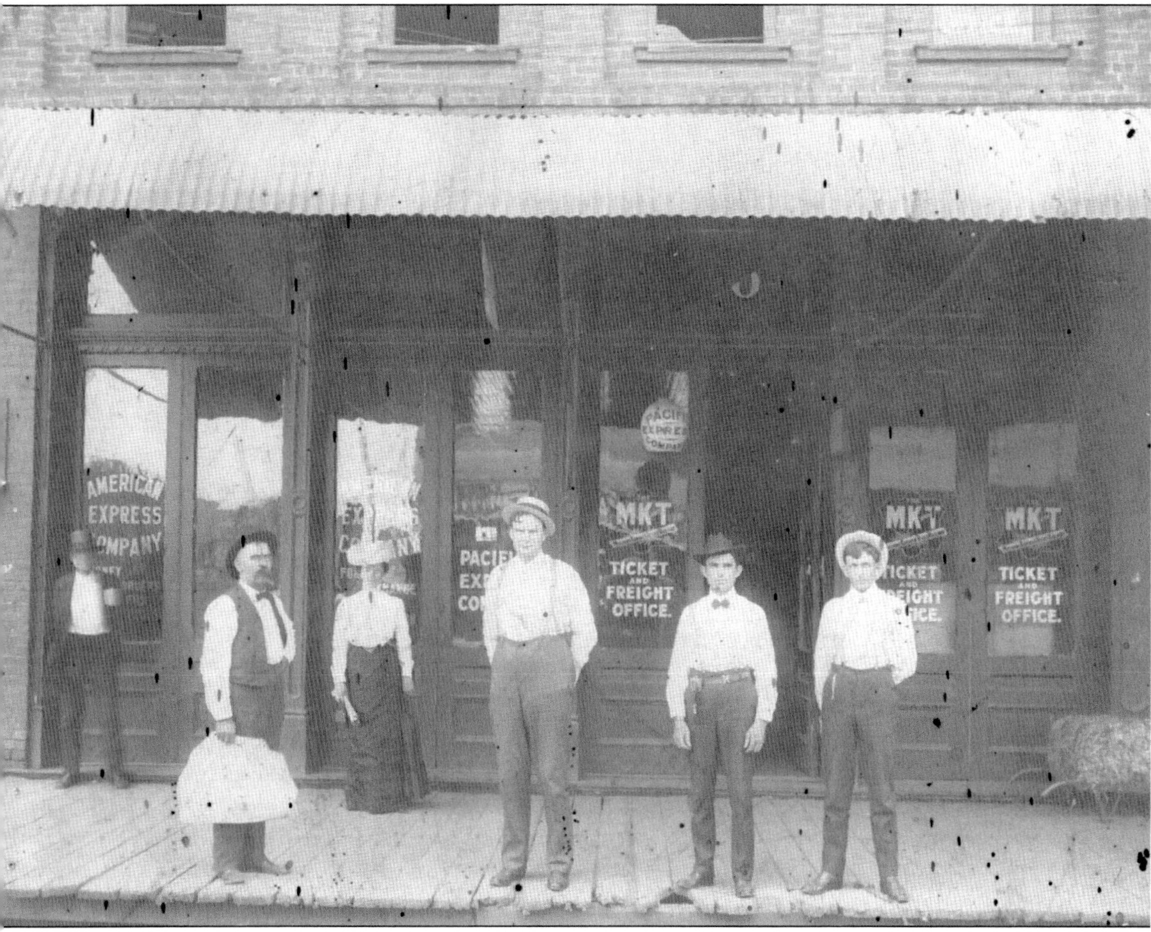

By 1900, nine railroad outlets met in Greenville with 22 passenger trains providing rail service night and day. Outgoing freight included great quantities of cotton bales, cattle, and items manufactured in Greenville, such as brooms, bee hives, and saddles. The Cotton Belt Railroad and the Texas Midland line shared a depot on the east side of town across the way from the large Greenville Cotton Compress. Most cotton was shipped from that depot. The American Express Company shared offices with the Pacific Express Company and the Missouri, Kansas, and Texas Railroad on West Lee Street near the Katy depot. In February 1910, Greenville citizens were startled by an explosion on Lee Street. After an extensive investigation, it was determined that a heavy American Express freight wagon ran over a 32-caliber cartridge, causing the explosion. No damage was reported. (Courtesy of W. Walworth Harrison Public Library.)

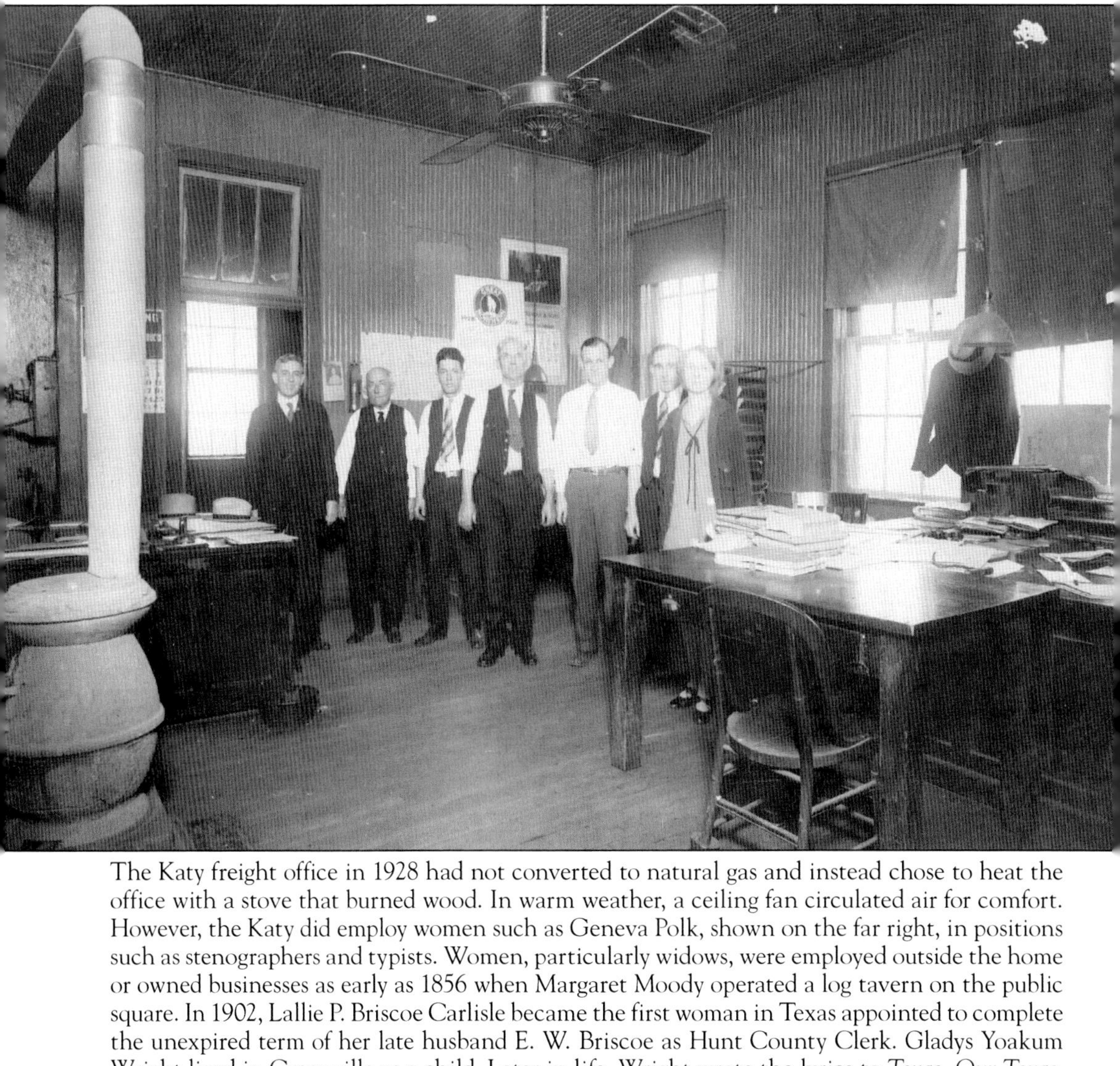

The Katy freight office in 1928 had not converted to natural gas and instead chose to heat the office with a stove that burned wood. In warm weather, a ceiling fan circulated air for comfort. However, the Katy did employ women such as Geneva Polk, shown on the far right, in positions such as stenographers and typists. Women, particularly widows, were employed outside the home or owned businesses as early as 1856 when Margaret Moody operated a log tavern on the public square. In 1902, Lallie P. Briscoe Carlisle became the first woman in Texas appointed to complete the unexpired term of her late husband E. W. Briscoe as Hunt County Clerk. Gladys Yoakum Wright lived in Greenville as a child. Later in life, Wright wrote the lyrics to *Texas, Our Texas*, which is the official state song. The Greenville Banner hired Ollie Coon as the woman's editor. She held this position 60 years until her death in 1968. (Courtesy of the author.)

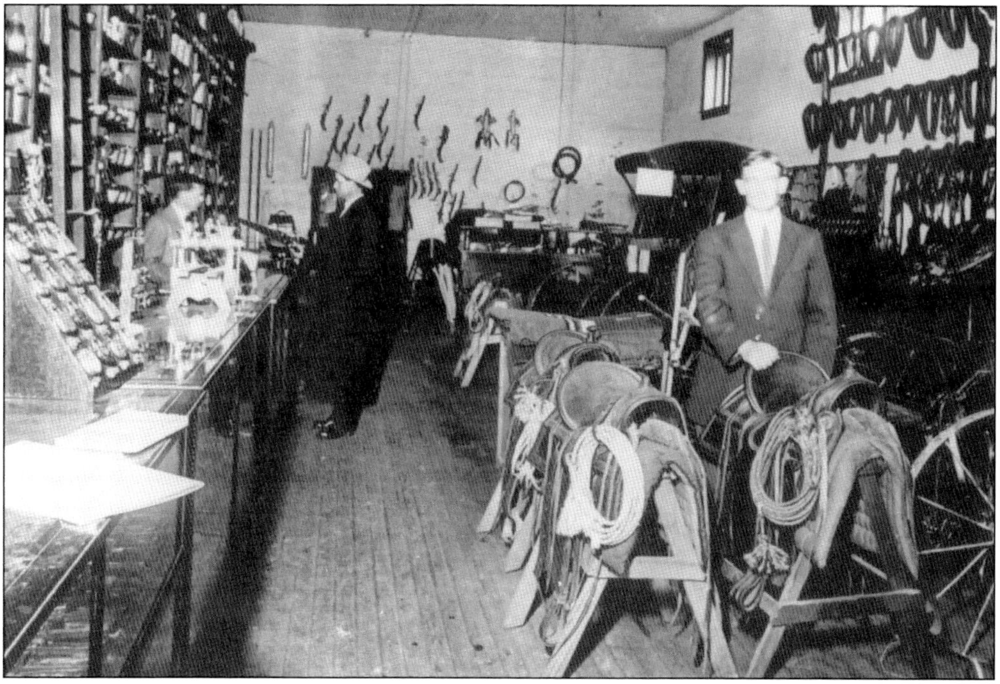

Greenville was primarily a farming and cattle-raising community from its founding in 1847 until World War II. As a result, saddle making became a local industry that continued into the 21st century. In this unidentified saddle shop, the customer could purchase handmade saddles, harnesses, and other needed equipment. Buggies were not a local product but sold well to townspeople who preferred not to walk the muddy roads. (Courtesy of the author.)

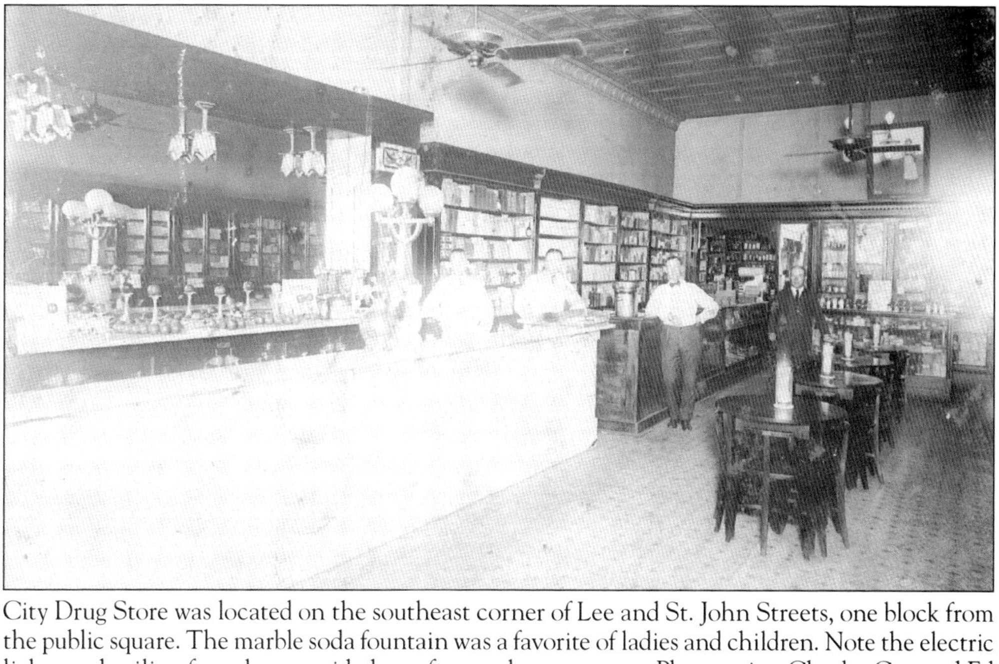

City Drug Store was located on the southeast corner of Lee and St. John Streets, one block from the public square. The marble soda fountain was a favorite of ladies and children. Note the electric lights and ceiling fans that provided comfort to the customers. Pharmacists Charles Gee and Ed B. Williams stand to the right. (Courtesy of W. Walworth Harrison Public Library.)

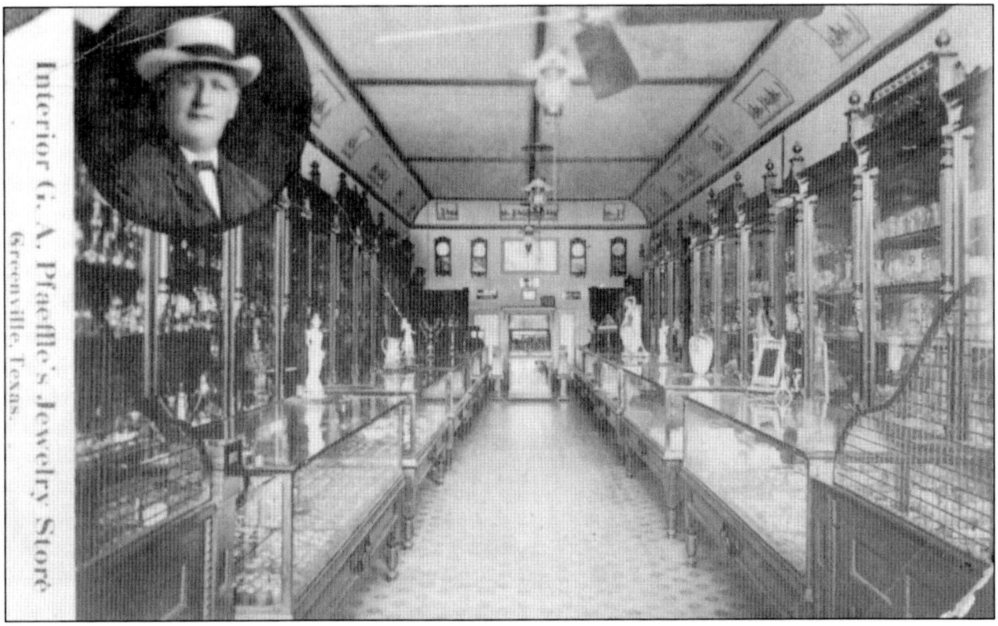

Son of German immigrants, George A. Pfaeffle (1865–1937) arrived in Greenville with very little more than the clothes on his back. He set up shop as a watch repairman. The town's first millionaire was so impressed with Pfaeffle's skill that his reputation was soon established. Even after he opened a larger jewelry store, he kept a large sign featuring a pocket watch for all to see. (Courtesy of Hunt County Historical Commission.)

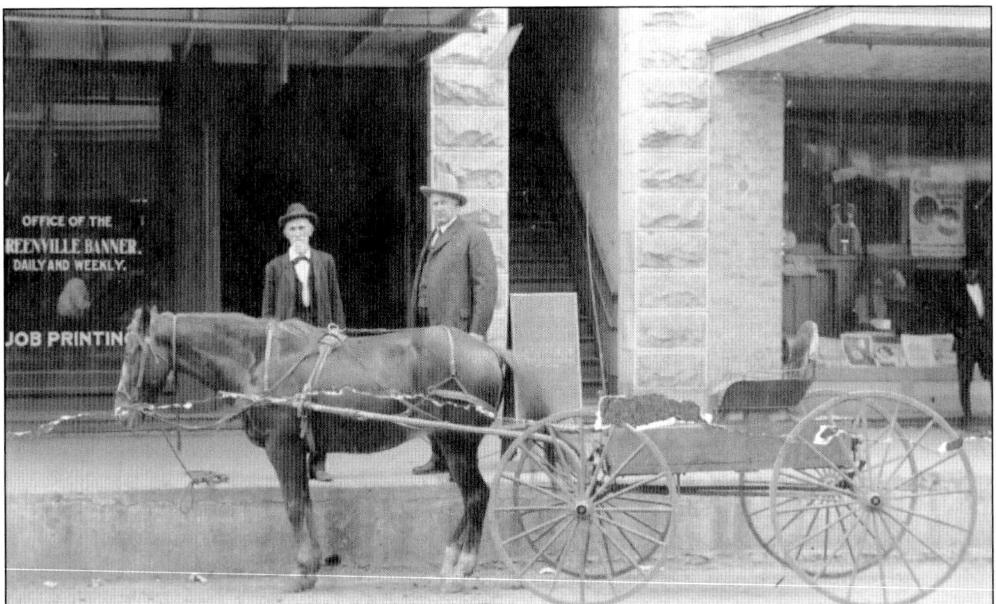

At various times, Greenville was home to numerous newspapers. One of the earliest that is still in business was the *Greenville Banner*. Until 1957, it published an evening edition that carried much of the society news in town. In January of that year, the *Greenville Banner* merged with rival *Greenville Morning Herald* to form the *Greenville Herald Banner*. (Courtesy of W. Walworth Harrison Public Library.)

The first bank in Greenville was the Hunt County Bank, organized in 1879 by John Holt, Cyrus Bivens, and J. W. Rainey of Terrell. On February 14, 1887, it was reorganized and chartered as the Greenville National Exchange Bank. Located on the northeast corner of the public square, the bank prospered, serving merchants and the cotton industry. (Courtesy of W. Walworth Harrison Public Library.)

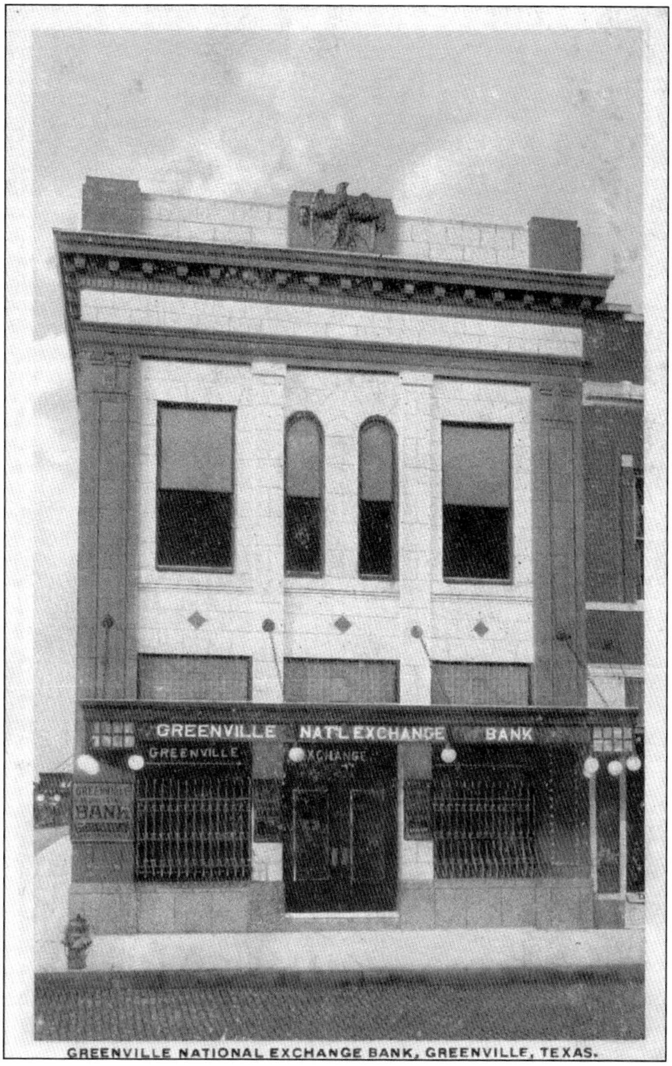

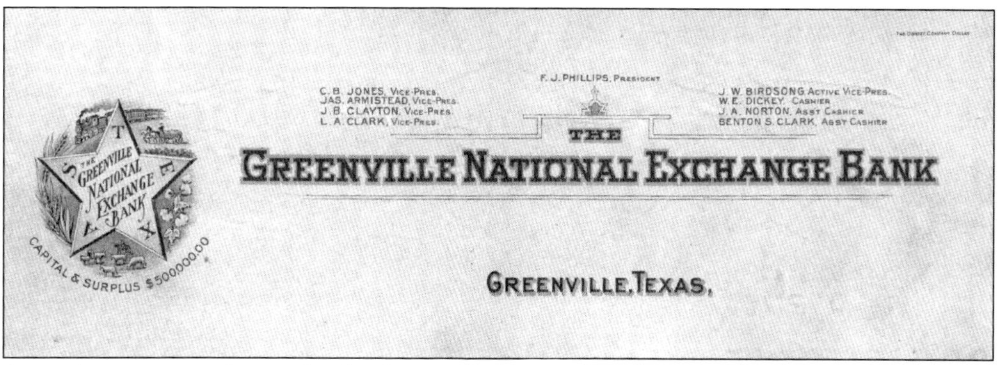

An early promotional piece for the Greenville National Exchange Bank indicated the solidity of the institution. Pres. F. J. Phillips was a noted philanthropist. He and his wife, Eula Lasater Phillips, endowed the athletic department of Greenville High School with a new football field and created a campsite for the YMCA. (Courtesy of W. Walworth Harrison Public Library.)

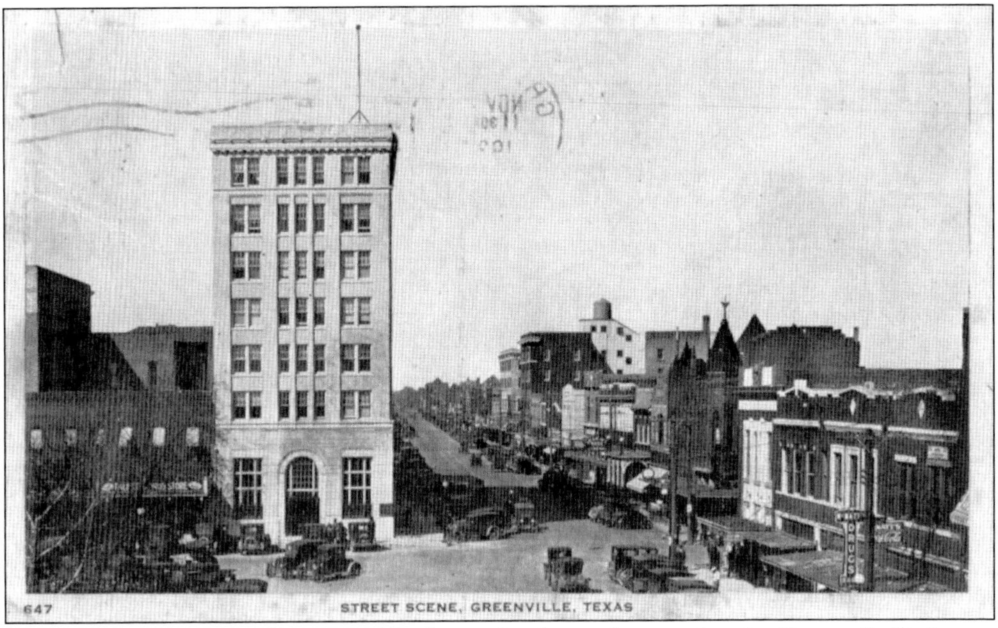

In the 1920s, the Greenville National Exchange Bank was shortened to the Greenville Exchange Bank and moved to the opposite corner of Stonewall and Lee Streets. The new building was designed by Lang and Witchell of Dallas and Lindsey and Kilmer of Greenville. It was the first in a series of new multi-floored buildings that were erected in downtown in the late 1920s. (Courtesy of the author.)

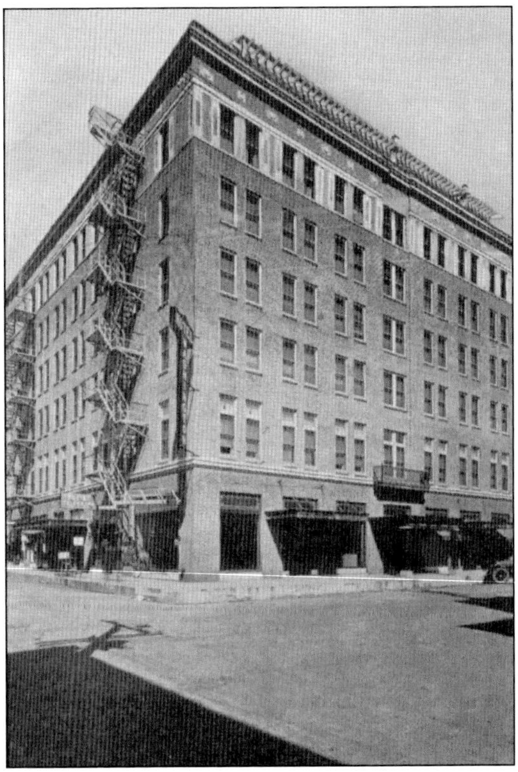

Located at the corner of Washington and St. John Streets, the Washington Hotel was also built during the boom of the late 1920s. The hotel featured a rooftop garden, ballroom, banquet room, and penthouse suites. Every year the hotel sponsored a charity Washington's Birthday Dance led by General and Mrs. Washington, a prominent Greenville couple selected for that honor, in period costume. (Courtesy of Gee Library, Texas A&M University-Commerce.)

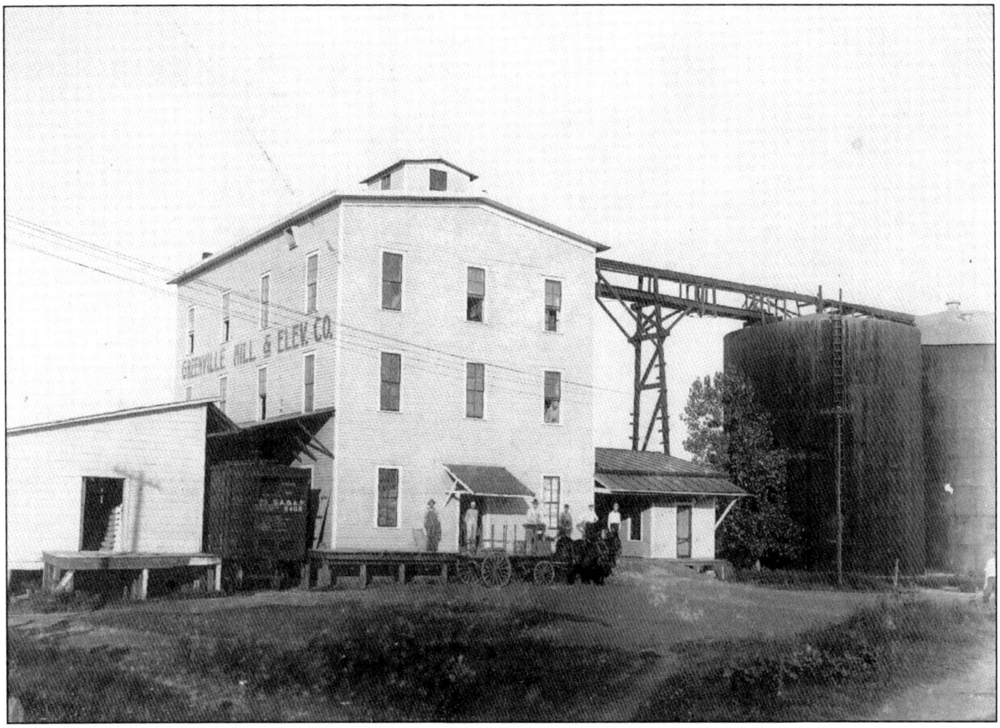

Prior to the arrival of railroads, wheat was the leading cash crop in the Greenville area. A. F. Richter opened the Greenville Mill and Elevator Company in the 1870s to grind and store the local wheat crop. Wheat remained a secondary crop after the rise of cotton production, which allowed Richter to expand his operation. (Courtesy of Hunt County Historical Commission.)

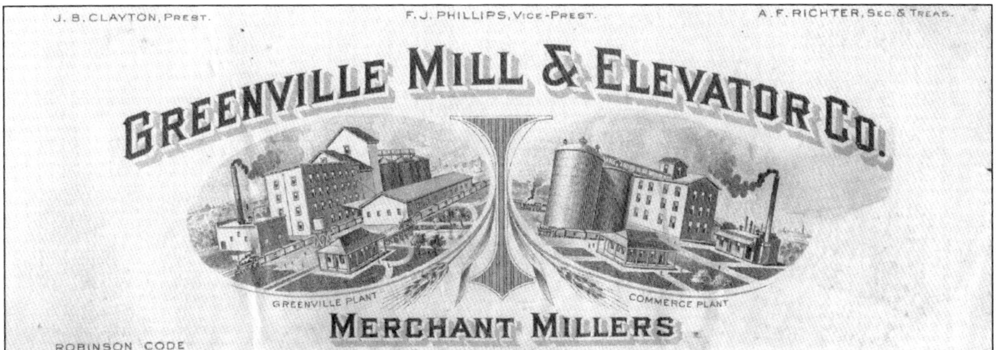

By 1900, Richter had expanded Greenville Mill and Elevator Company to a second operation in nearby Commerce, Texas. Billed as Merchant Millers, neither of the mills was as grand as shown in this promotional piece geared to attract industry to Greenville although both utilized rail transportation. By that time, wheat production was slowly yielding to the popularity of cotton production. (Courtesy of W. Walworth Harrison Public Library.)

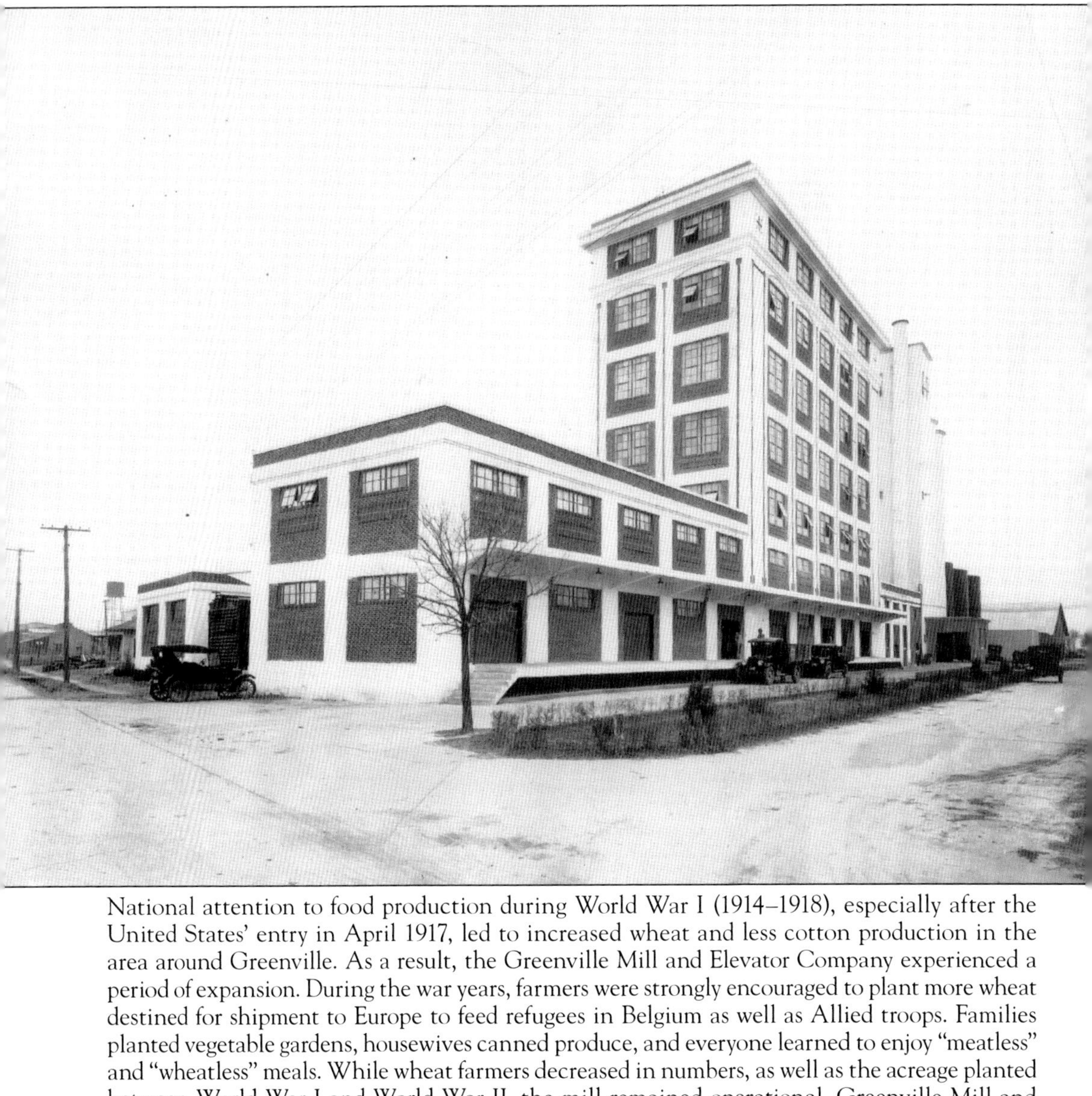

National attention to food production during World War I (1914–1918), especially after the United States' entry in April 1917, led to increased wheat and less cotton production in the area around Greenville. As a result, the Greenville Mill and Elevator Company experienced a period of expansion. During the war years, farmers were strongly encouraged to plant more wheat destined for shipment to Europe to feed refugees in Belgium as well as Allied troops. Families planted vegetable gardens, housewives canned produce, and everyone learned to enjoy "meatless" and "wheatless" meals. While wheat farmers decreased in numbers, as well as the acreage planted between World War I and World War II, the mill remained operational. Greenville Mill and Elevator Company later sold to the Canadian grain giant, Robin Hood Floor, after World War II. The large Robin Hood Flour logo was a landmark to local citizens. (Courtesy of W. Walworth Harrison Public Library.)

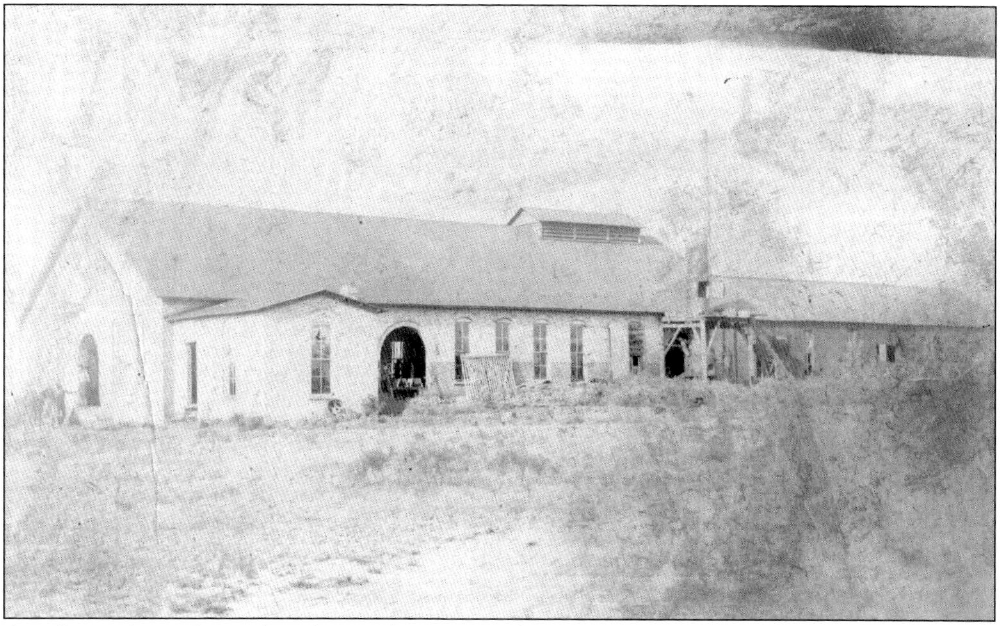

Another industry located in the southeast part of Greenville was the large Greenville Foundry, shown here in the early 1890s. While many of the other attempts at industrial diversification in the area were successful, the Greenville Foundry had difficulty acquiring raw materials during the economic downturn of the mid-1890s. It soon became a victim of the unstable economy. (Courtesy of W. Walworth Harrison Public Library.)

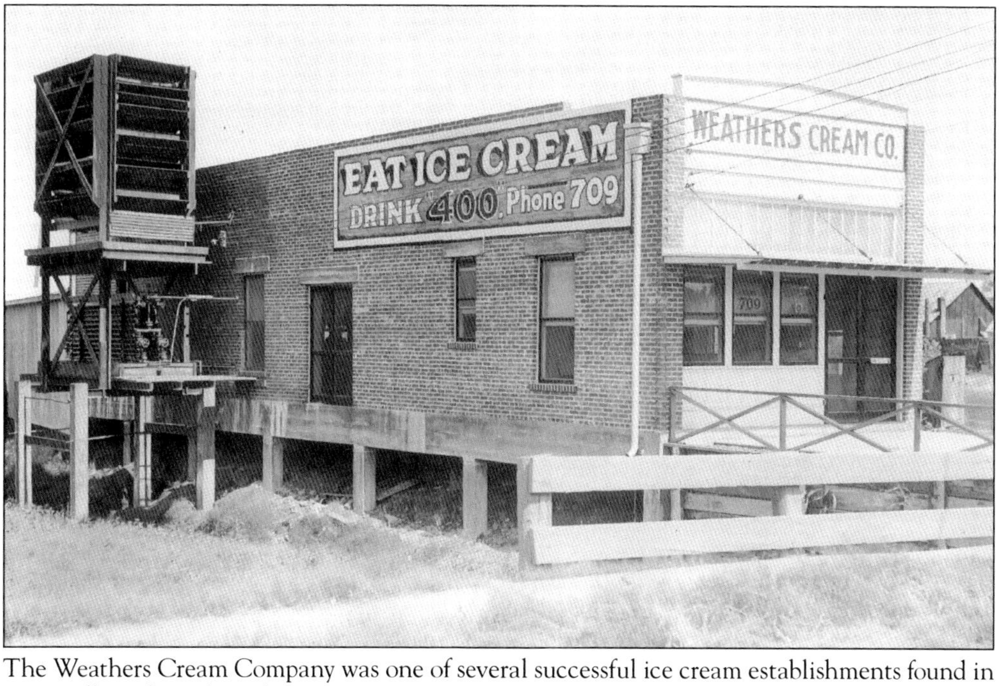

The Weathers Cream Company was one of several successful ice cream establishments found in Greenville in the early 20th century. A "400" was a rich concoction of cream, chocolate syrup, and ice cream. The name denoted the 400 calories each drink was rumored to contain. Adults and children enjoyed a "400" on hot summer days. (Courtesy of Hunt County Historical Commission.)

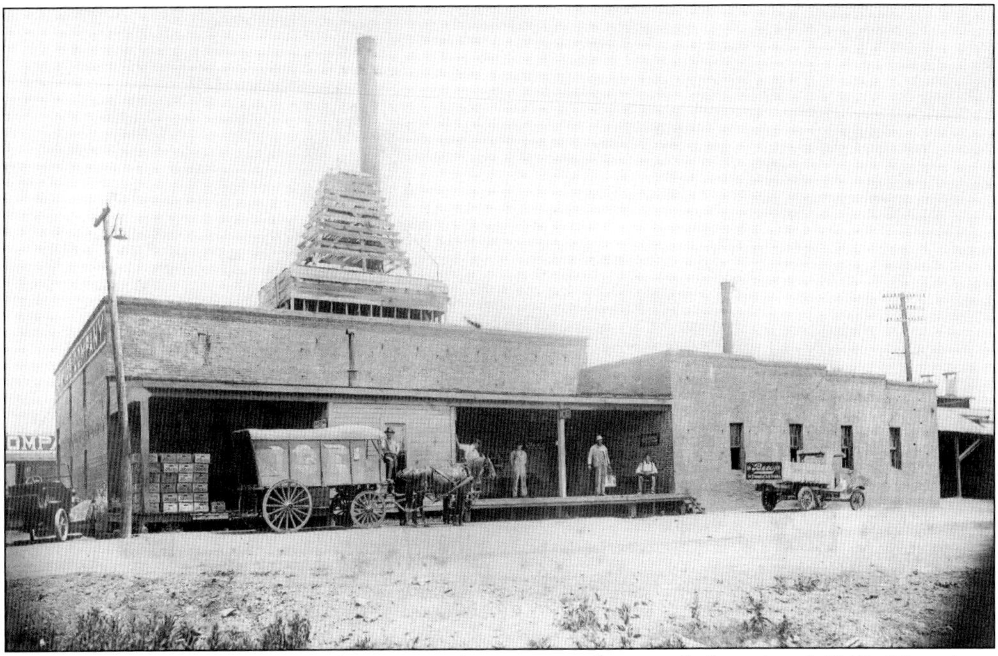

The New Ice Company opened in November 1920 and expanded in April 1922. The plant delivered blocks of ice to homes, restaurants, and hotels. By 1929, it was the sole supplier of ice to the new Washington Hotel with its swanky rooftop garden. The tall, cypress cooling tower was a landmark for Greenville citizens. (Courtesy of the author.)

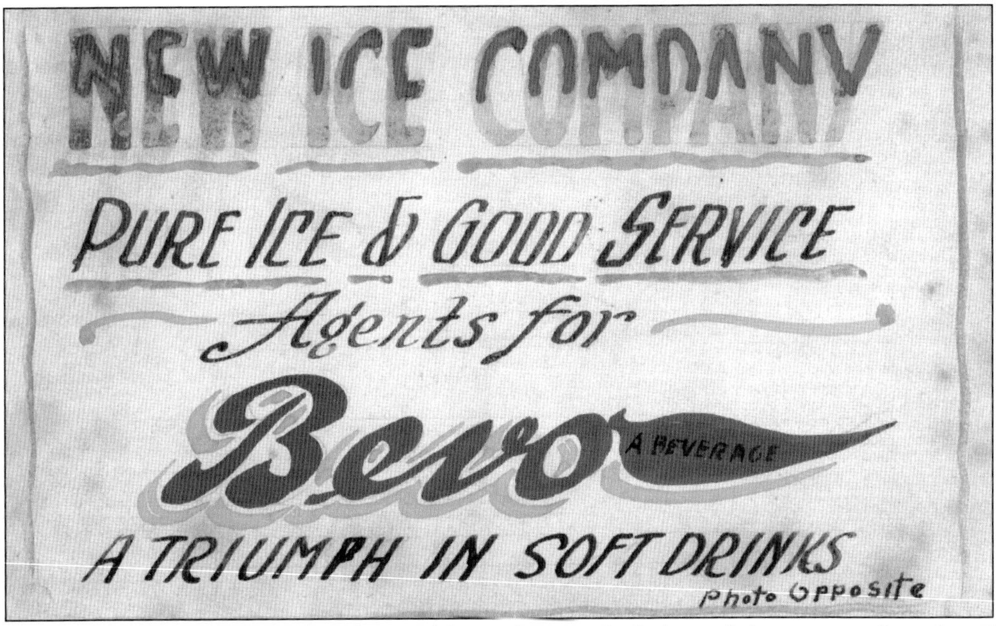

The New Ice Company was distributor of Bevo, the nonalcoholic malt beverage or "near beer" that was manufactured by the Anheuser-Busch Company. Greenville voted for local option and Prohibition in 1902. When Bevo made its appearance in 1916, many in Greenville enjoyed the next best thing to beer. However, Prohibition lasted longer in Greenville than Bevo did. (Courtesy of W. Walworth Harrison Public Library.)

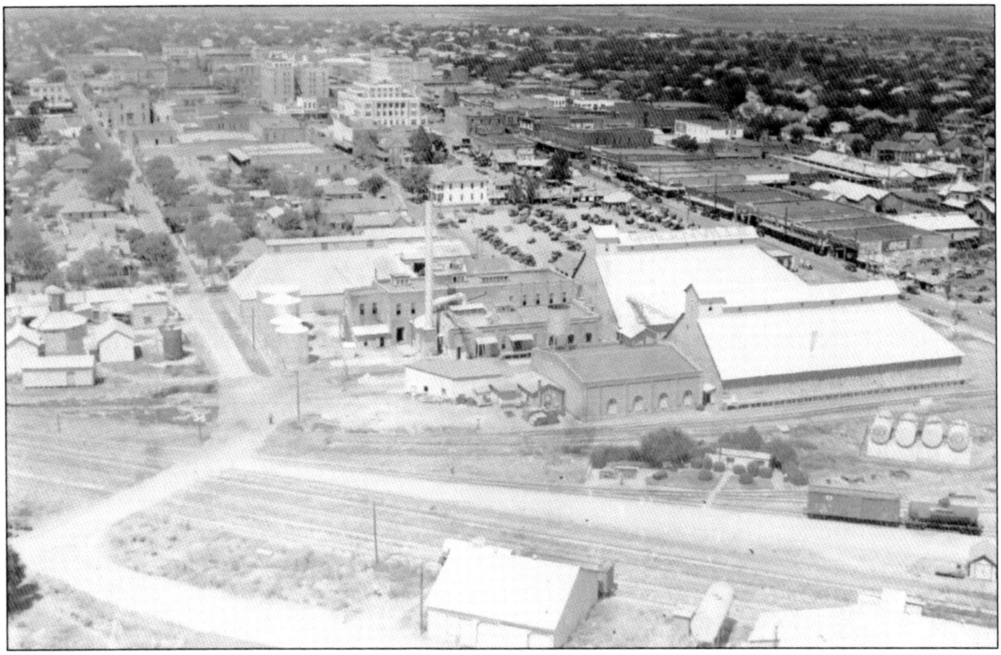

This view of the early agricultural and industrial section of Greenville was taken after 1929. The majority of large buildings in the foreground were part of the Greenville Cotton Oil Mill, which used the oil from cotton seeds in a variety of ways. One of the by-products was Cream of Cotton, a substitute for lard used in baking. (Courtesy of the author.)

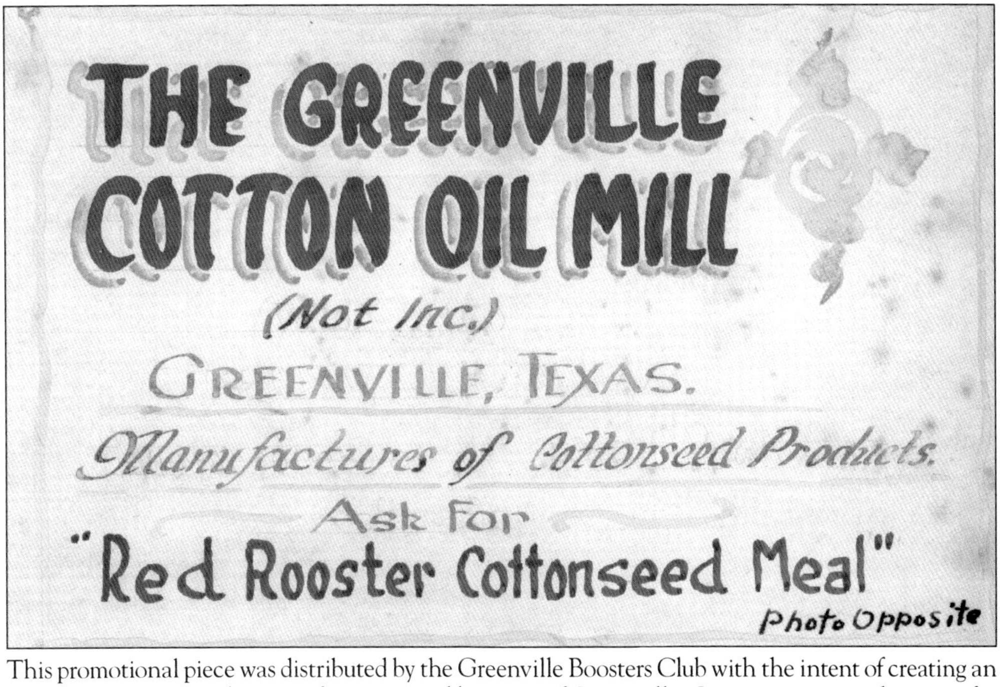

This promotional piece was distributed by the Greenville Boosters Club with the intent of creating an economic interest in the manufacturing and business of Greenville. Cotton was not only grown for its fibers but also for its many by-products. Cottonseed meal has been used as a livestock supplemental food for more than a century. (Courtesy of W. Walworth Harrison Public Library.)

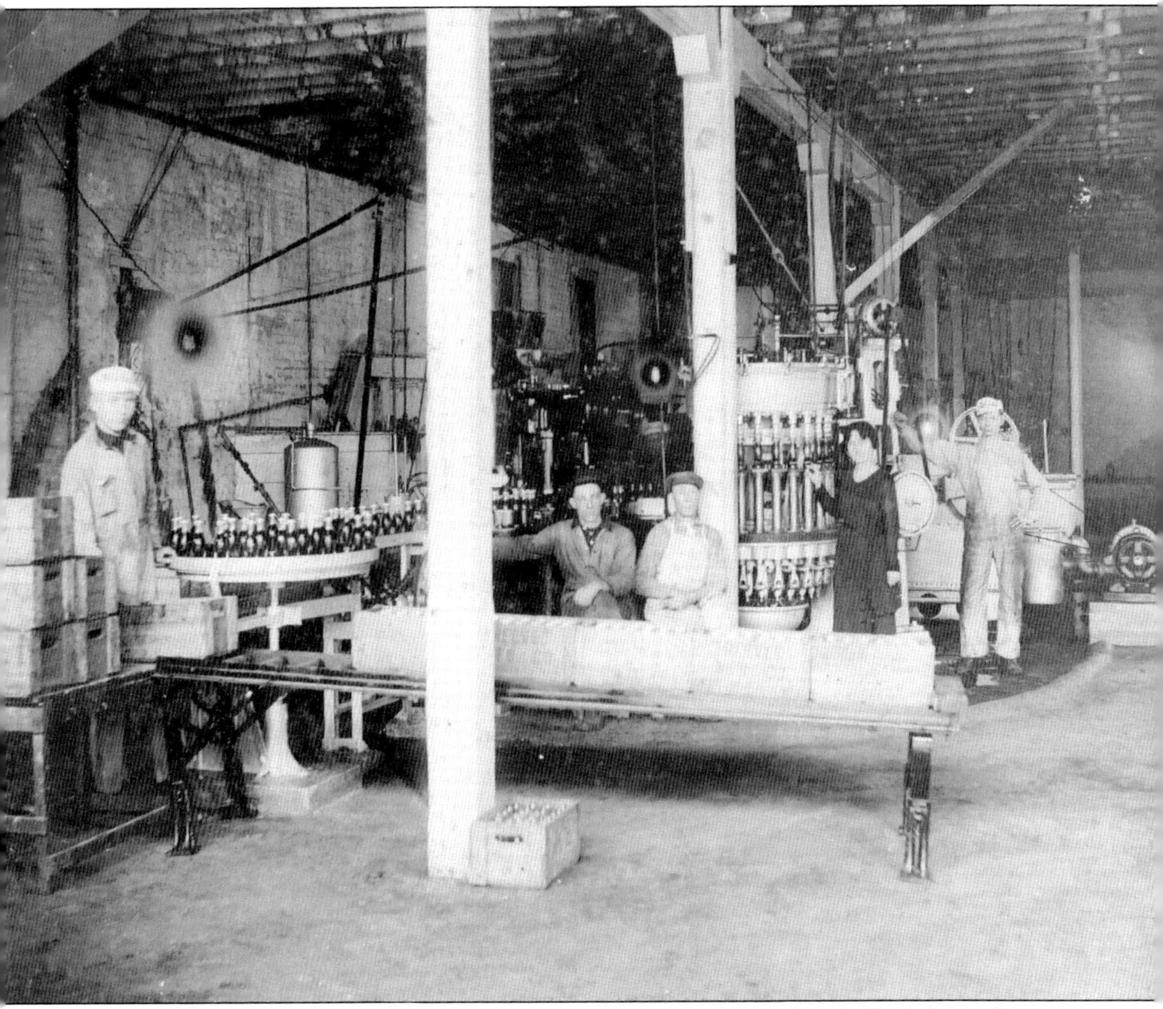

Greenville was the home of two soft drink bottlers during the first half of the 20th century. This photograph shows the interior of the Dr. Pepper Bottling Company, located adjacent to the Missouri, Kansas, and Texas Railroad tracks. Established in 1927 by Rudisell B. and Jessie P. Williams, the plant was first located on West Lee Street with a limited amount of equipment. The operation was moved to the Washington Street location near the Katy tracks in 1937. Demand was so strong for Dr. Pepper that the plant was expanded in 1939 and additional equipment, including a water purification system, was added. The new plant was reputed to be as modern as science could make it. In addition to Dr. Pepper, the plant also bottled Nu-Grape, Two-Way, and Craig's Root Beer. Carbonated and non-carbonated drinks were produced here. By 1950, the plant operated with 10 employees in addition to Rudisell and Jessie Williams. When the plant closed, the building was converted into a home of art deco style. (Courtesy of the author.)

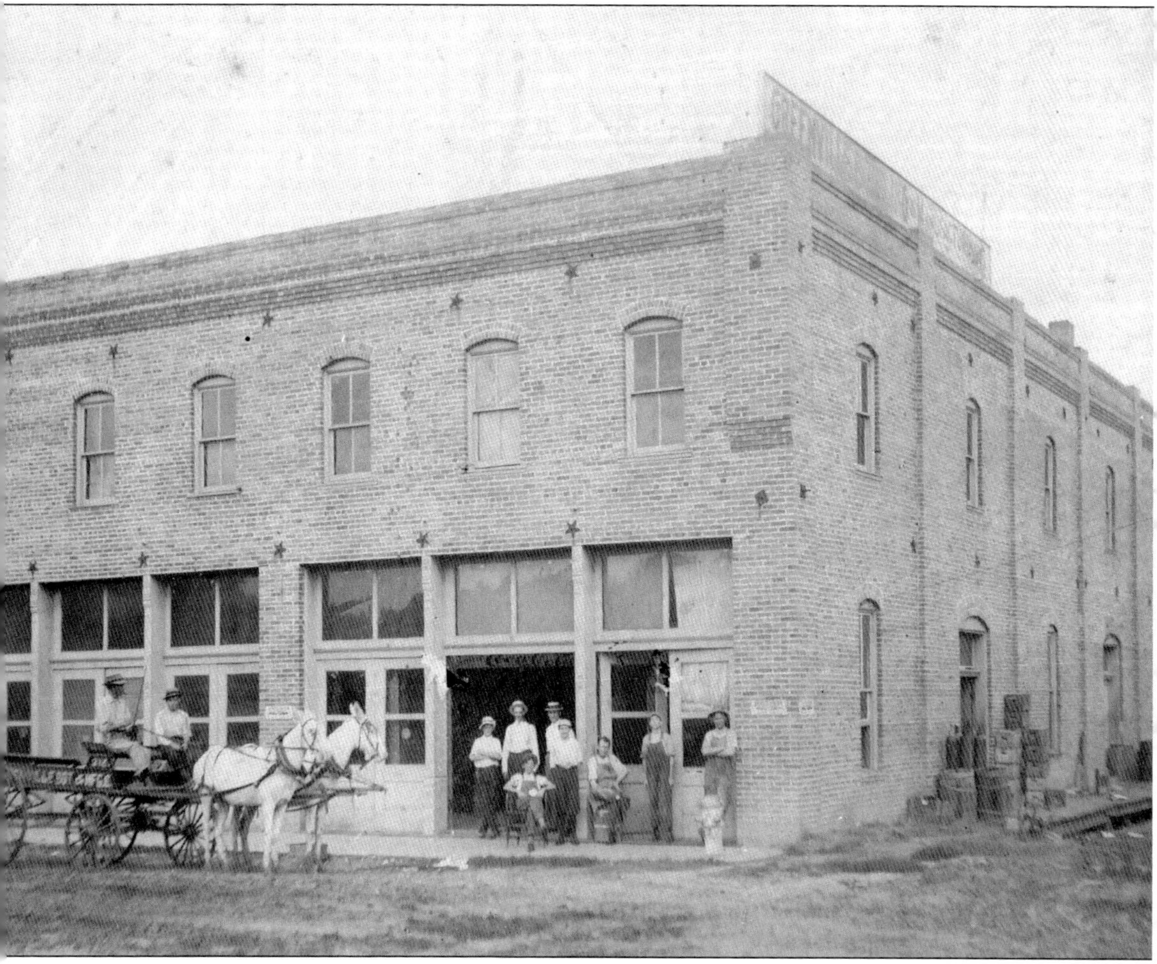

In 1895, Samuel H. Reeves began operation of a soda water plant in a frame building on West Lee Street. The fledgling enterprise was named Star Bottling Company. Three years later, Reeves moved his operations to the corner of Morse and Stuart Streets, which is where it remained for 10 years. During the interim, the business was renamed Reeves Manufacturing Company. In 1908, the business was again moved, this time to the corner of Johnson and Jordan Streets, where it remained for more than 75 years. Prior to the last move, Reeves and his son W. P. Reeves secured the rights for manufacturing and distributing Coca-Cola in this territory. Inside the Johnson Street building shown here is a large Coca-Cola sign with the familiar logo. Mule-driven wagons delivered Coca-Cola to grocery stores and restaurants in Greenville and throughout the northeast Texas area. (Courtesy of the author.)

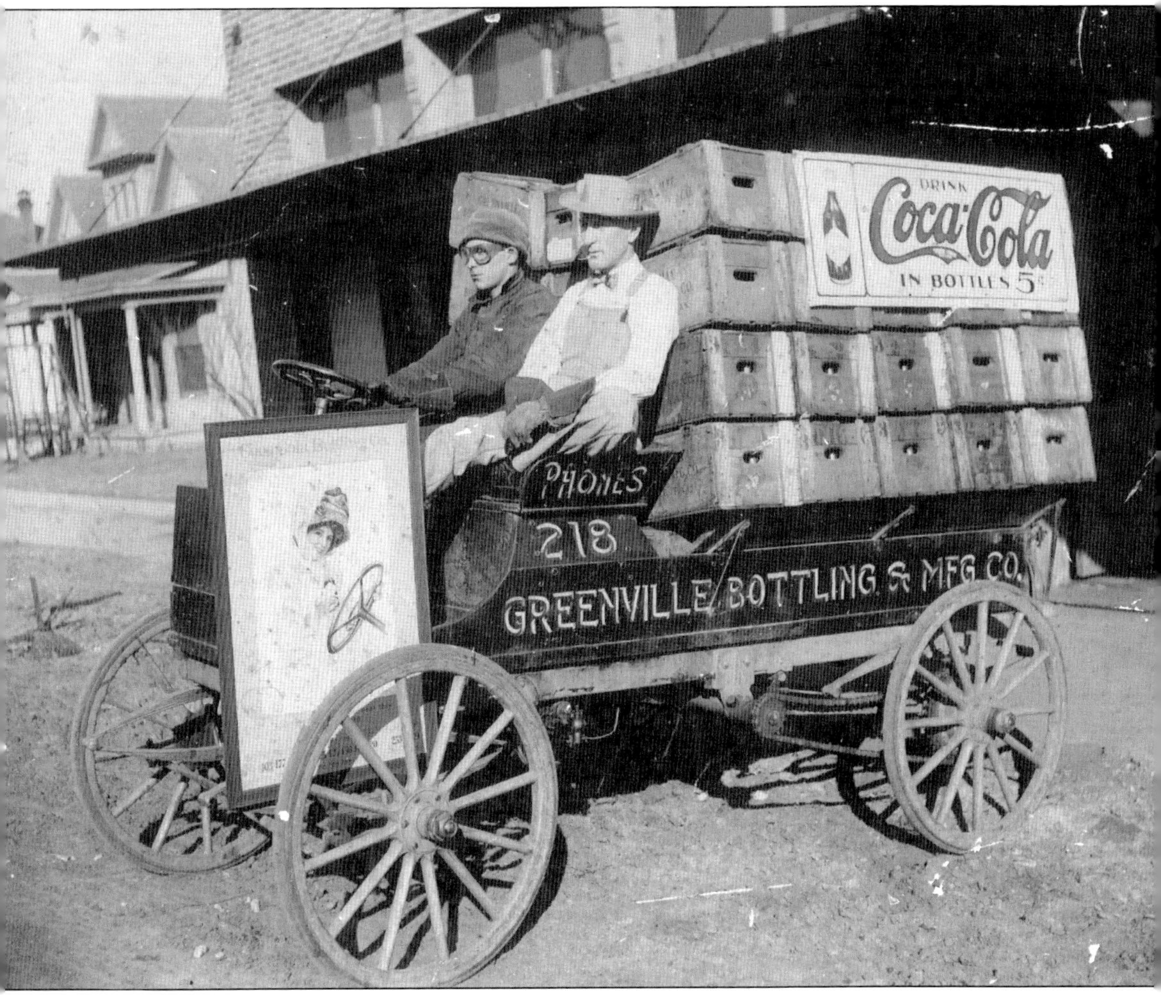

Son of Reeves Manufacturing Company founder Samuel H. Reeves, W. P. Reeves became secretary of the Texas State Bottlers Association in 1902. He held this position for more than 40 years. These nattily dressed young men in the specially built truck delivered Coca-Cola in the 1920s. At the time this photograph was taken, Greenville had two telephone companies. Customers could choose which service to use, but most businesses were connected to both. The telephone companies allowed businesses to use the same number for both systems. Hence, the sign read, "phones 218." In 1940, the company was fitted with the most modern bottling equipment. A renovation was proposed that year to complete an indoor driveway inside the building to allow trucks to be loaded and unloaded in all kinds of weather. When the bottling company was sold to Coca-Cola, Inc., in the 1980s, the owners gave the building to the City of Greenville for use as the city hall annex. (Courtesy of the author.)

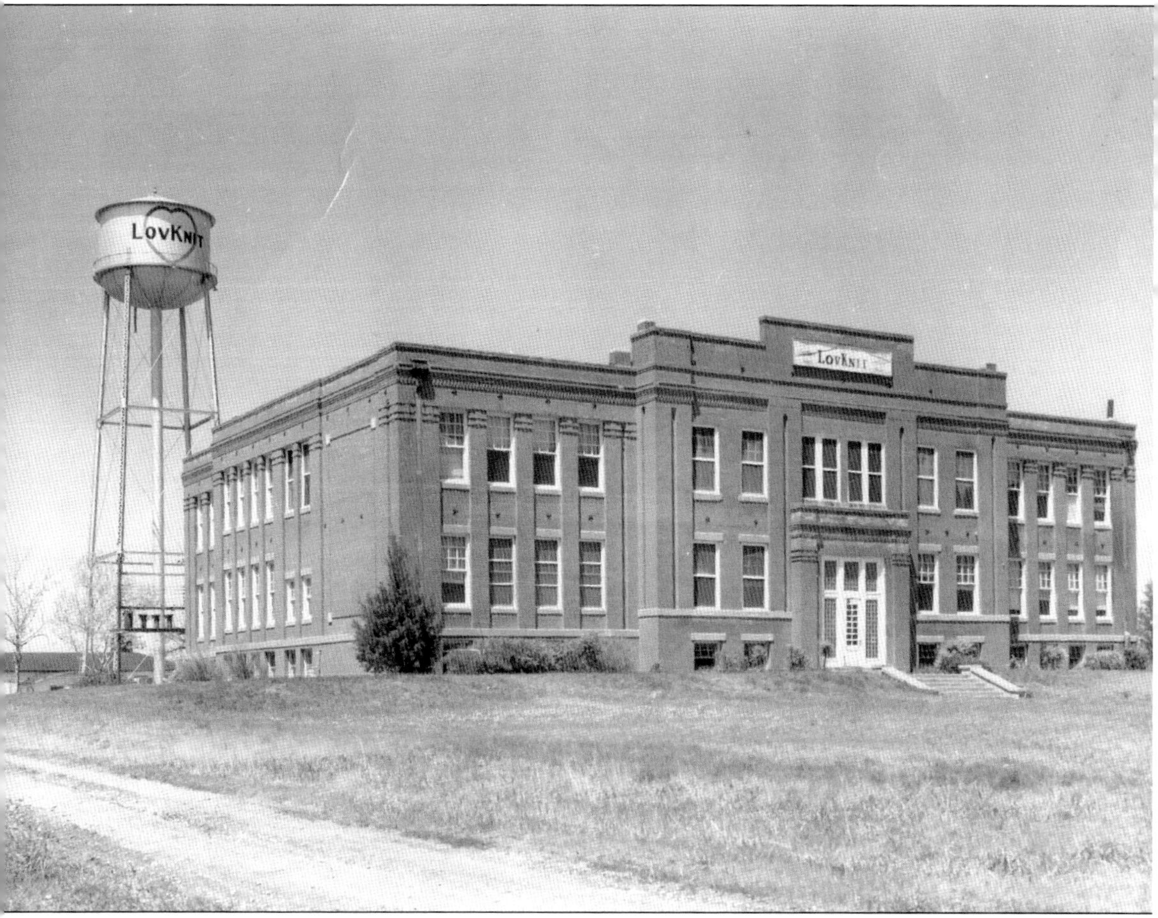

Greenville residents have been quite innovative in reusing older buildings. This structure was best remembered as the administration building at Wesley College. Built in 1912 at an initial cost of $50,000, it housed the office of Wesley College presidents, classrooms, and a performance auditorium. The area was originally proposed as a residential real estate development. However, it would be more than a quarter of a century before that dream was realized. A potent mineral well and pavilion in the neighborhood preceded the college. After the educational facility closed in 1935, the building was converted into offices and manufacturing plant for Love Knit, a locally owned textile company. Later the structure became home to Love Me, a Venetian blind fabricator. Finally, the old administration building was converted into a church furniture plant. It was destroyed by fire in May 2001, nearly 90 years after it was first constructed. (Courtesy of Hunt County Historical Commission.)

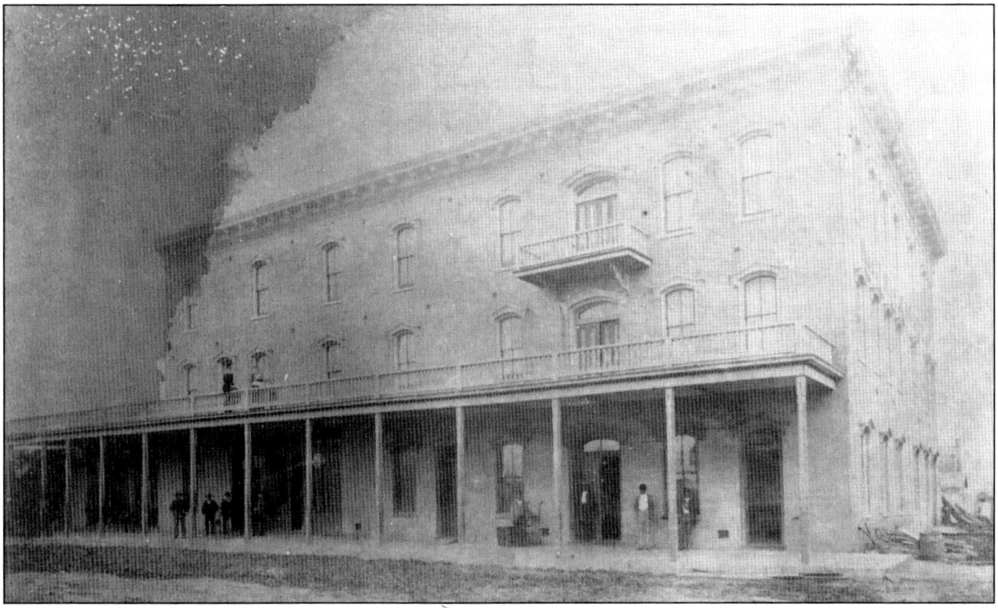

Hotels were a necessity for the first 100 years in Greenville history. Traveling salesmen, vaudeville players, and lawyers appearing at district court sessions needed overnight lodging. In 1885, W. L. Beckham (1855–1923) built the Beckham Hotel on West Lee Street as the premium lodging establishment in Greenville. A local story related that when the hotel was completed, W. L. Beckham opened the dining room with only 50¢ in his pocket. (Courtesy of Hunt County Historical Commission.)

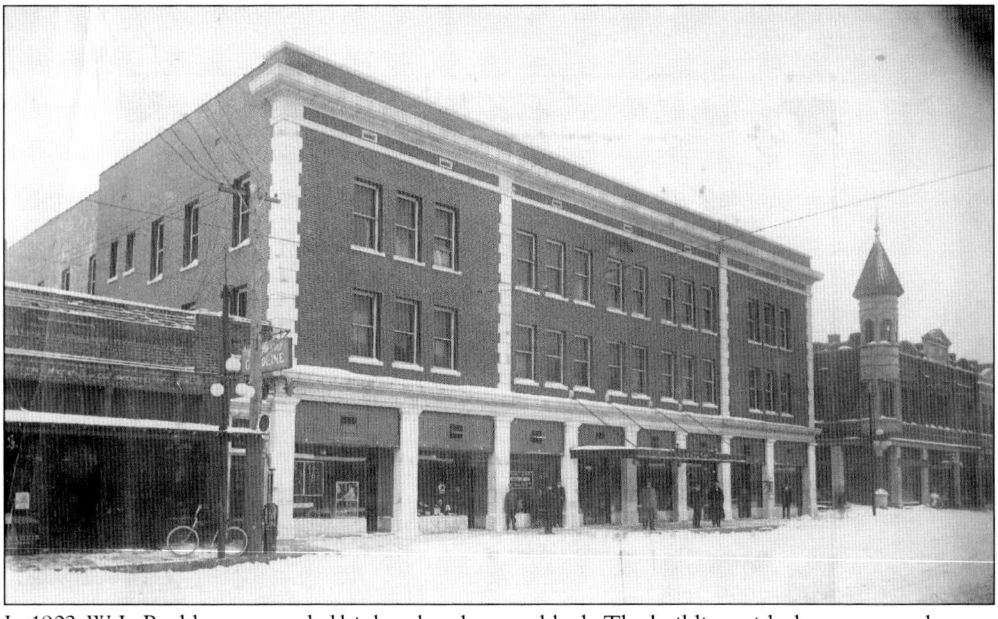

In 1902, W. L. Beckham expanded his hotel to the next block. The building with the turret was known as the Beckham Annex. Guests entered through an overhead bridge connecting the second floors of both buildings. Retail shops rented the ground floor of the annex. In 1914 and 1915, the original Beckham Hotel was renovated into even more elegant lodging. Since the main entry passed by the bar, women entered through a side door. (Courtesy of Hunt County Historical Commission.)

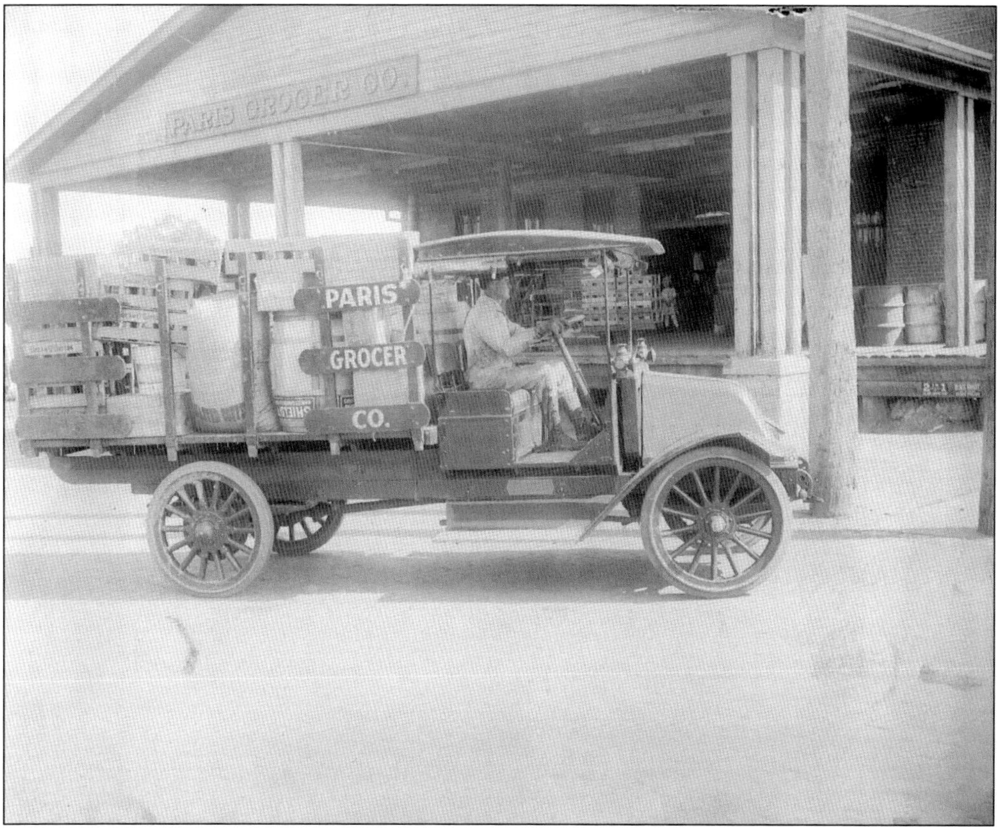

Due to the large railroad connections in Greenville, the town became home to wholesale grocers. Canned goods, fresh produce, and livestock were shipped in several times daily. Then the goods were transported by trucks, such as this one owned by Paris Grocer Company, to smaller stores in town and the surrounding area. (Courtesy of W. Walworth Harrison Public Library.)

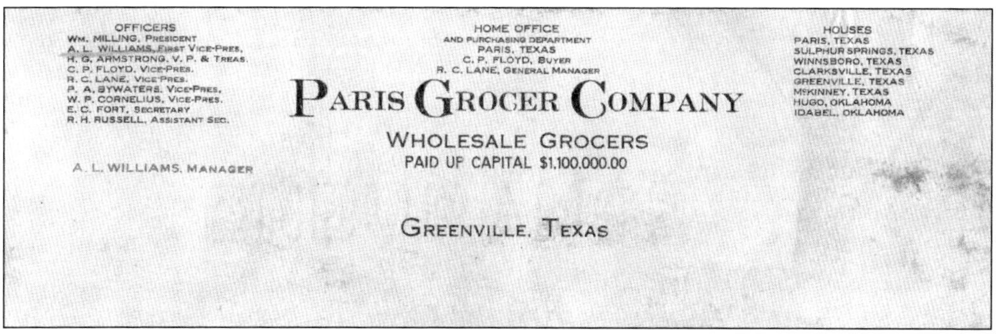

OFFICERS
WM. MILLING, PRESIDENT
A. L. WILLIAMS, FIRST VICE-PRES.
H. G. ARMSTRONG, V. P. & TREAS.
C. P. FLOYD, VICE-PRES.
R. C. LANE, VICE-PRES.
P. A. BYWATERS, VICE-PRES.
W. P. CORNELIUS, VICE-PRES.
E. C. FORT, SECRETARY
R. H. RUSSELL, ASSISTANT SEC.

A. L. WILLIAMS, MANAGER

HOME OFFICE
AND PURCHASING DEPARTMENT
PARIS, TEXAS
C. P. FLOYD, BUYER
R. C. LANE, GENERAL MANAGER

PARIS GROCER COMPANY

WHOLESALE GROCERS
PAID UP CAPITAL $1,100,000.00

GREENVILLE, TEXAS

HOUSES
PARIS, TEXAS
SULPHUR SPRINGS, TEXAS
WINNSBORO, TEXAS
CLARKSVILLE, TEXAS
GREENVILLE, TEXAS
McKINNEY, TEXAS
HUGO, OKLAHOMA
IDABEL, OKLAHOMA

Paris Grocer Company operated local wholesale warehouses throughout north Texas and southeastern Oklahoma. The main warehouse was located in Paris with other locations easily accessible by rail. Paris Grocer Company chose to locate regional warehouses in nearby county seats, including Greenville. By 1900, the company was well established in the area. (Courtesy of the author.)

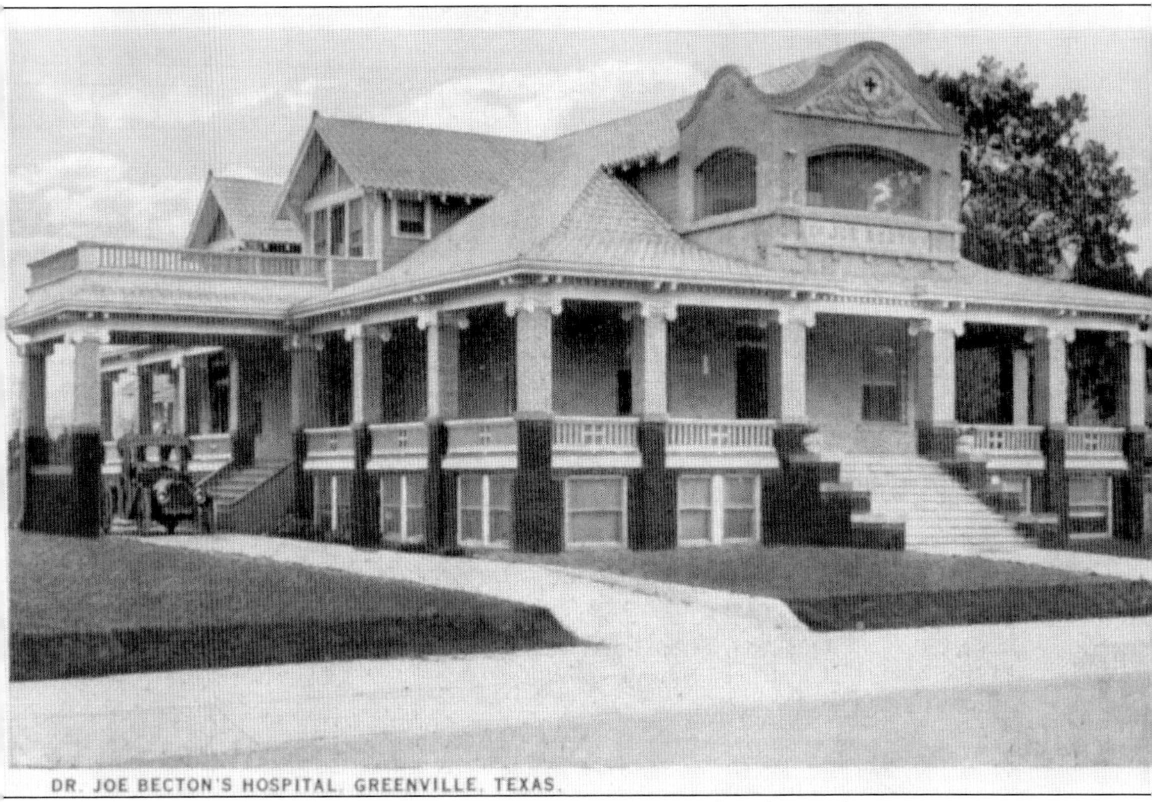

Not only was Greenville a town of wide retail, agricultural, and manufacturing interests, it was home to numerous physicians from its founding in 1847. Doctors at the beginning of the 20th century usually owned their own hospitals where they resided with their families. Dr. Joe Becton Sr. and his brother Dr. Ed Becton first opened a hospital in Greenville in 1908. Dr. Joe Becton Sr. opened this hospital on Oneal Street in 1914 while his brother opened another hospital on Washington Street. Neither of the hospitals had modern x-ray equipment, nor facilities for lab work, nor miracle drugs, but both hospitals progressed and were widely known throughout the northeast Texas region. In 1928, Dr. Joe Becton Jr. became associated with his father in this Oneal Street facility. Dr. Joe Becton Sr., Dr. Ed Becton, and Dr. Joe Becton Jr. were widely regarded as outstanding surgeons. (Courtesy of the author.)

Dr. Joe Becton Sr. died in 1931 while singing in the choir at Kavanaugh Methodist Church next door to the hospital. His son carried on the belief that it was necessary for patients to receive the best care possible but also to recuperate in beautiful and tranquil surroundings. The hospital lawns and gardens were showplaces enjoyed not only by patients but also by the citizens of Greenville, especially those in the Park Street neighborhood south of town. In 1939, Dr. Joe Becton Jr. built a new clinic in connection with the hospital that his father founded. Both father and son were also generous supporters of Greenville and played active roles in promoting the city as a place to live and work. When Dr. Joe Becton Jr. relocated to a new facility on Stuart Street in 1947, Dr. T. C. Strickland operated the Oneal facility through the 1950s. (Courtesy of W. Walworth Harrison Public Library.)

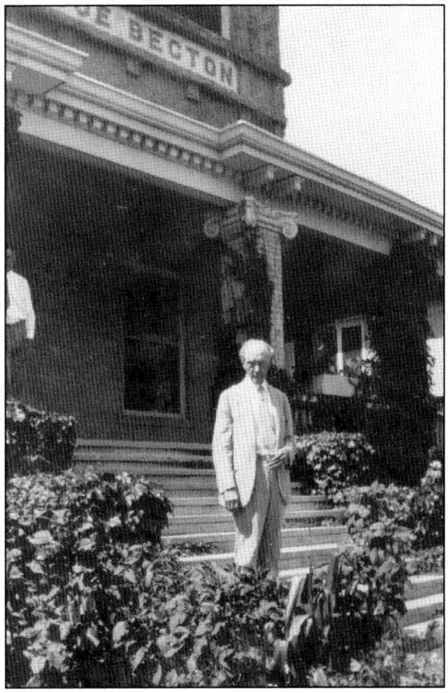

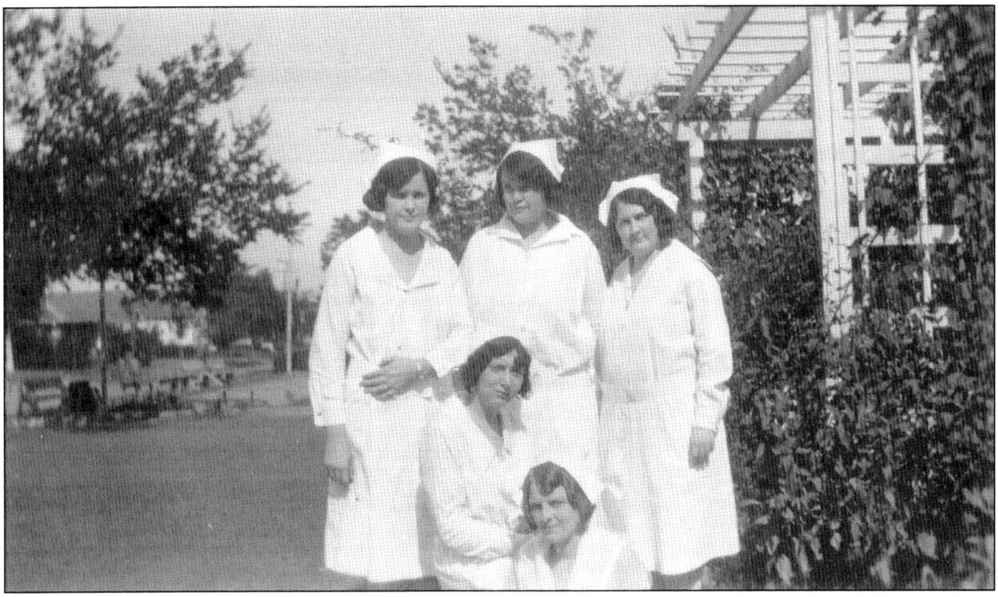

Dr. Joe Becton Jr. operated a training school for nurses as well as a private hospital and clinic. These young women wore the requisite uniforms of white long-sleeved button-down-the-front dresses that were stiffly starched. The starched caps, black shoes, and white stockings were mandatory for nurses and nursing students of the 1930s. Dr. Becton's students received classes in anatomy, physiology, drugs, and solutions, as well as procedures. They were responsible for total care of the patients, including bed baths and keeping the bedside area neat and tidy. Long hours and strenuous studies often caused many nurses to drop out of the program before completion. These five young ladies took a brief respite from their training regimen to enjoy the well-known rose garden and grounds of the Joe Becton hospital. Many would fill positions in doctors' offices in Greenville and other communities in the area. (Courtesy of W. Walworth Harrison Public Library.)

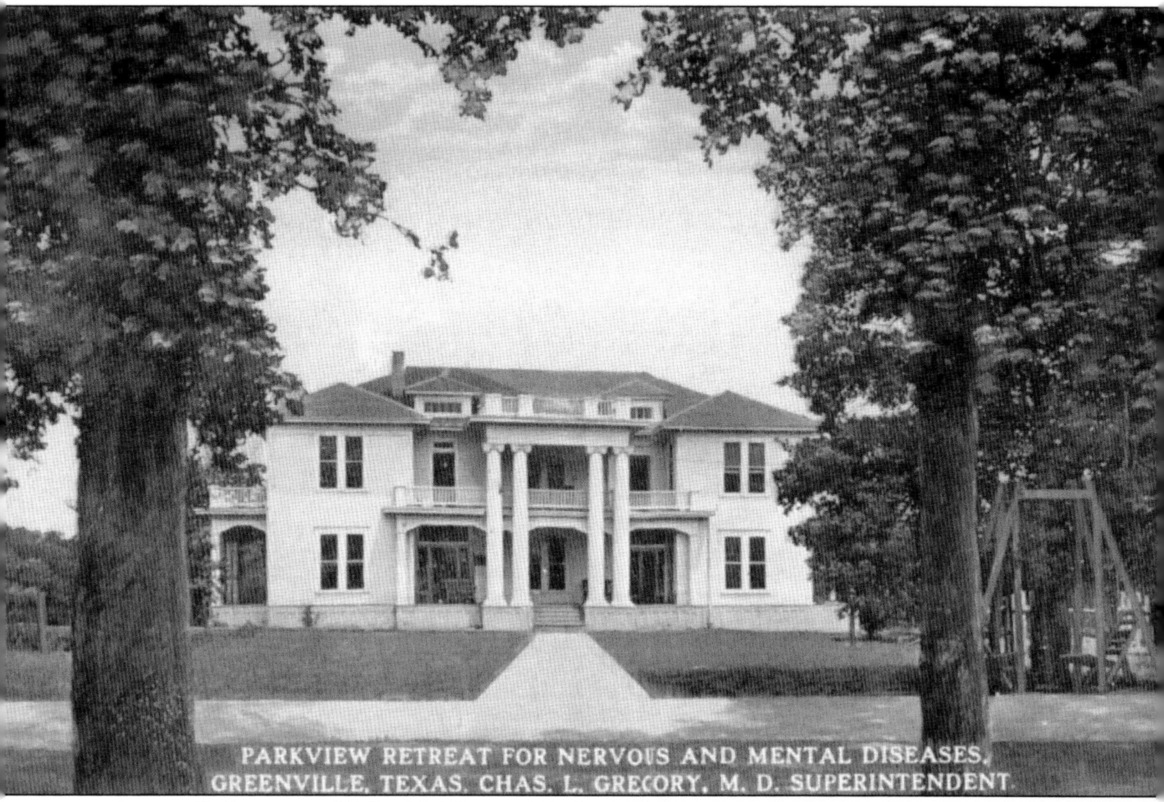

Originally known as McBride's Hospital for Mental Diseases, this medical facility was located across Bee Street (now Sockwell Boulevard) from Graham Park. Owner and attending physician Dr. Albert Sidney McBride (1872–1932) advertised it as a treatment center for "Mental and Nervous Diseases, Drug and Alcoholic Addicts, Home for Aged and Infirm" in the 1928 Greenville City Directory. Dr. McBride was educated in Hunt County schools and attended Henry College in neighboring Campbell before he completed his medical training at the Kentucky School of Medicine in Louisville. He first practiced medicine in Oklahoma and then in the nearby town of Lone Oak before establishing his practice in Greenville in 1911. Many of his patients were women addicted to laudanum. After Dr. McBride died in an automobile accident in 1932, his practice sold to Dr. Charles G. Gregory. Gregory then renamed the residential institution Parkview Retreat. (Courtesy of W. Walworth Harrison Public Library.)

Four

KING COTTON

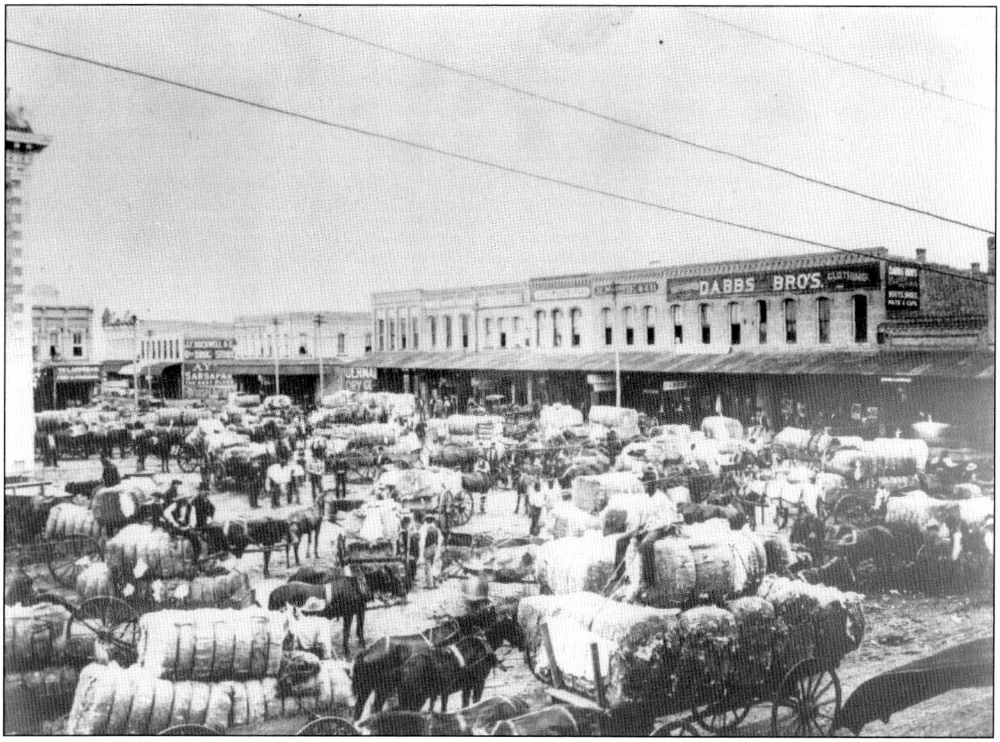

Businessmen, landowners, and cotton buyers in Greenville believed the statement of South Carolina senator James Henry Hammond that "Cotton is King." With the arrival of rail transportation in Greenville, cotton did become king; it dominated the economy for at least 60 years. Every fall, mule-drawn wagons crowded the public square; farmers brought all or a representative portion of the year's crop to sell at the highest price. (Courtesy of the author.)

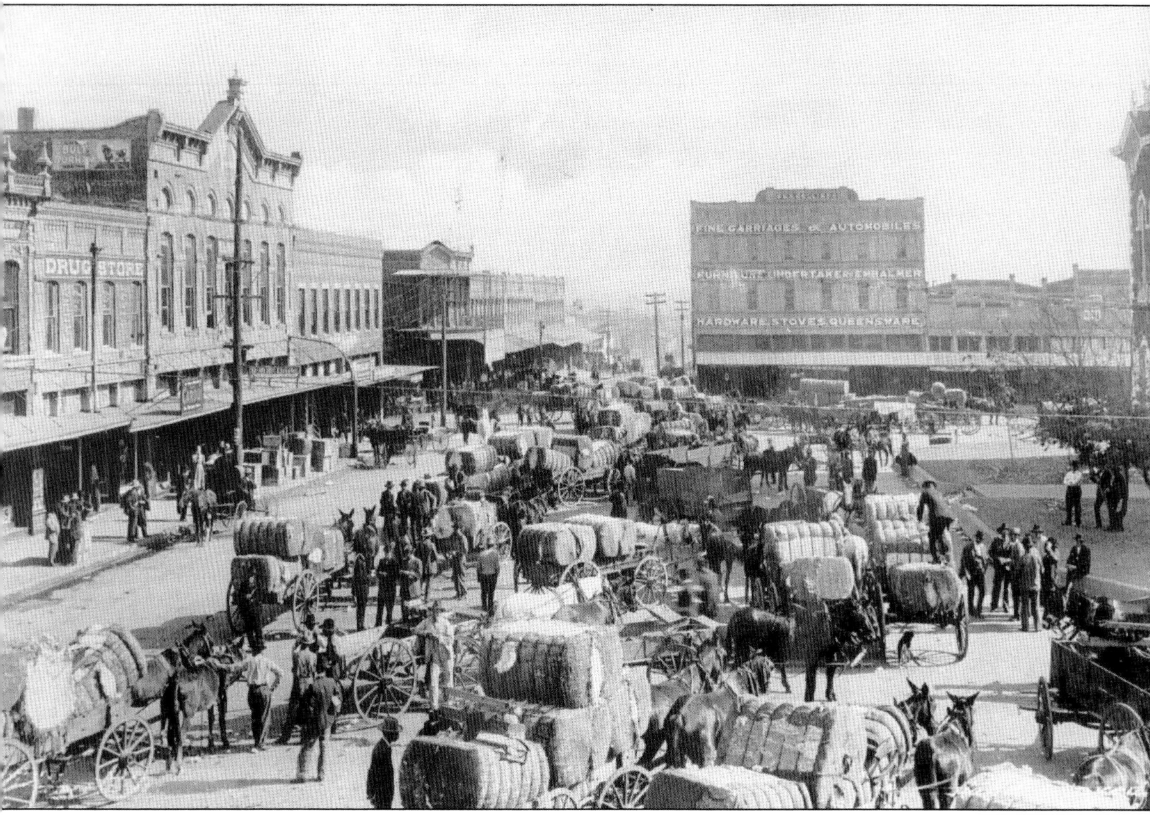

Cotton was the principal cash crop throughout the black land prairie of Texas. It was planted in spring, maintained in summer, and the white bolls picked in the fall of the year. Once the fields were cleared, the cotton was taken to the local gin for removal of trash and seeds. At the gin, the cotton was encased in 480-pound bales for sale. At that point, the farmer or the tenant farmer brought all of his bales or a sample of bales to town for sale on the courthouse square. Since cotton was a one-time crop each year, producers usually bought on credit with a furnishing merchant. In the late 19th century, cotton producers sold to these merchants to pay off debts. Interest on loans made by the furnishing merchants was not regulated. By 1900, Greenville had about one dozen agents from the various cotton-buying firms in New Orleans, New York, and London who purchased the cotton directly from the producer. Here farmers and buyers are negotiating sales. (Courtesy of Jack Horton.)

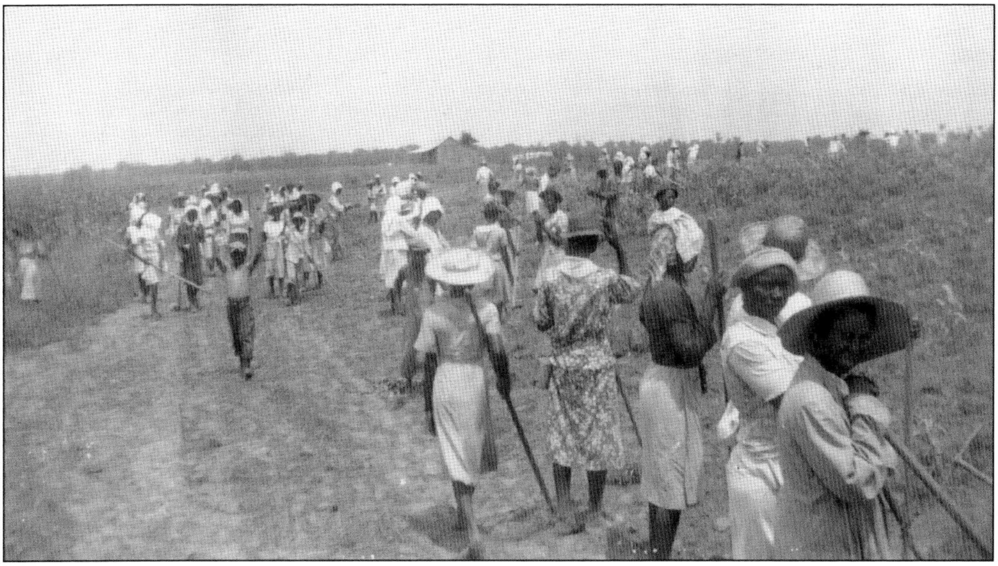

Groups of African Americans and whites were hired to work the cotton fields from the time the cotton began to break through the soil until the fields were picked. It was necessary to hoe cotton continually to keep weeds from extracting valuable moisture in the soil. All work in cotton fields was labor intensive. (Courtesy of W. Walworth Harrison Public Library.)

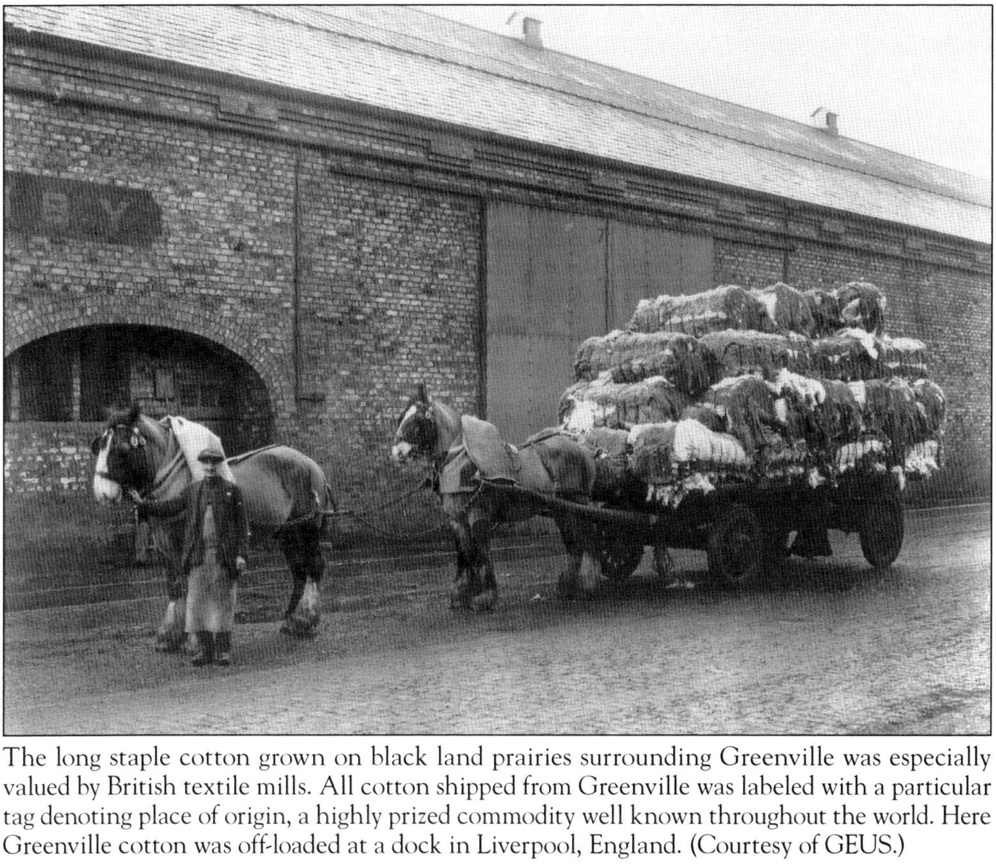

The long staple cotton grown on black land prairies surrounding Greenville was especially valued by British textile mills. All cotton shipped from Greenville was labeled with a particular tag denoting place of origin, a highly prized commodity well known throughout the world. Here Greenville cotton was off-loaded at a dock in Liverpool, England. (Courtesy of GEUS.)

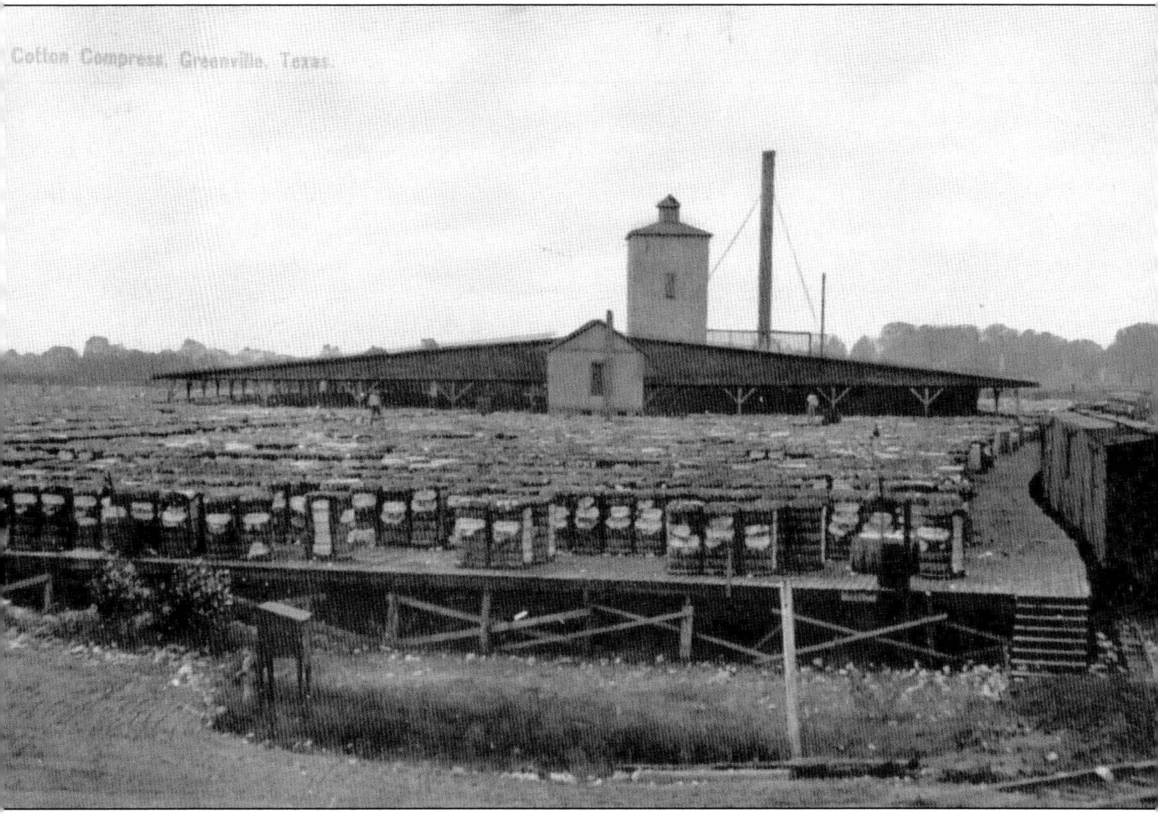

Cotton bales were compressed to smaller, denser size before shipment to European ports. In 1912, the cotton compress in Greenville was the largest inland compress in the world. On September 30 of that year, the workmen at the compress set a world record of 2,073 bales compressed and hand loaded on to freight cars. (Courtesy of the author.)

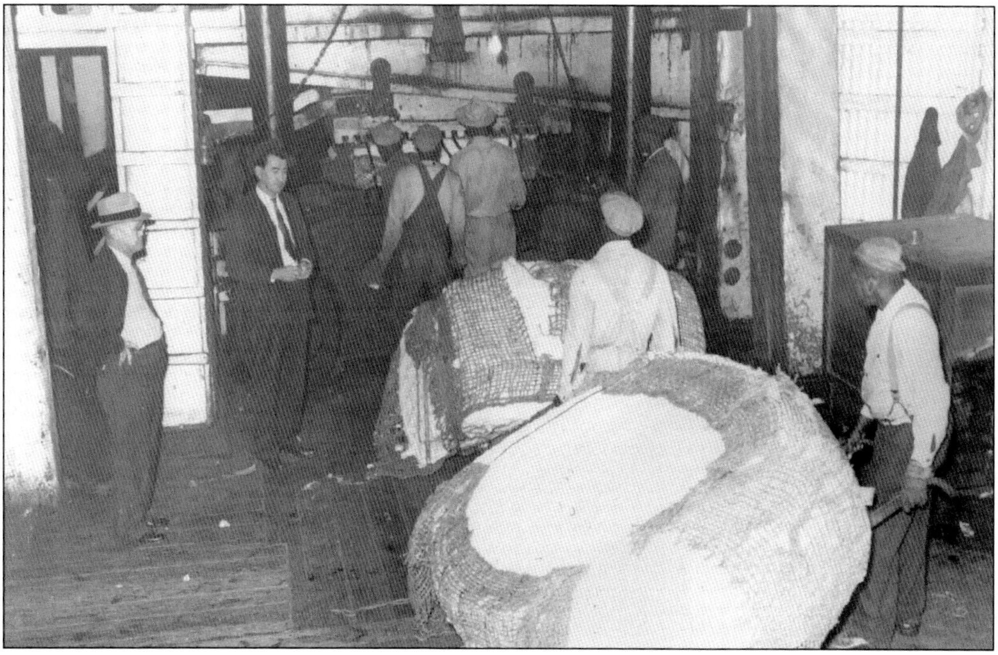

Cotton was first ginned and wrapped into large bales at the cotton gin. After the cotton was sold, it went to the compress to be reduced to a manageable size. Here the ginned cotton bales are hand trucked into the compress, which was where elevator-like machinery used pressure to reduce the size of cotton bales. (Courtesy of Hunt County Historical Commission.)

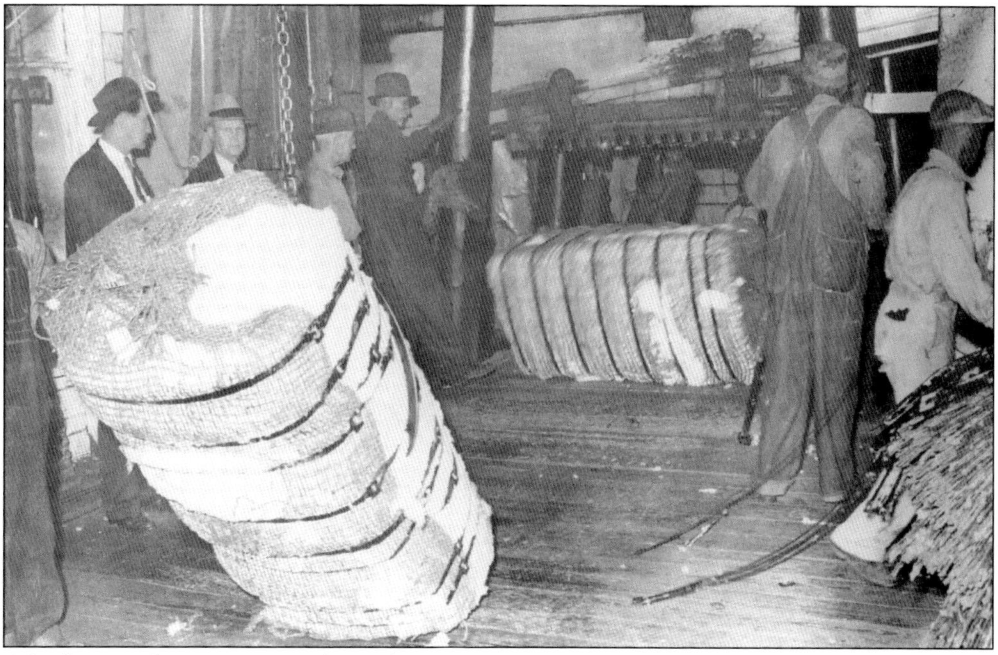

After leaving the compress machine, the cotton was wrapped in burlap, tied with metal strips, and then hand trucked to the loading docks to await shipment. The process was dangerous, hot, and labor intensive. The workmen often sang to make the difficult work bearable. Most of the workmen worked at the compress year after year. (Courtesy of Hunt County Historical Commission.)

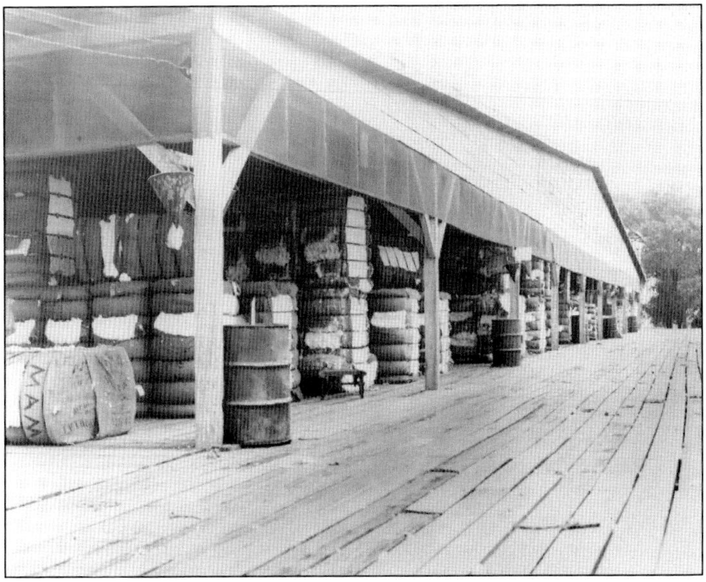

Note the large rain barrels at regular intervals along the loading docks. Hanging at each post were two buckets, specially designed with a pointed bottom to discourage theft. In 1888, the first compress was destroyed by fire. The danger of fire at the compress was real; safety and precautions were the order of the day. (Courtesy of Hunt County Historical Commission.)

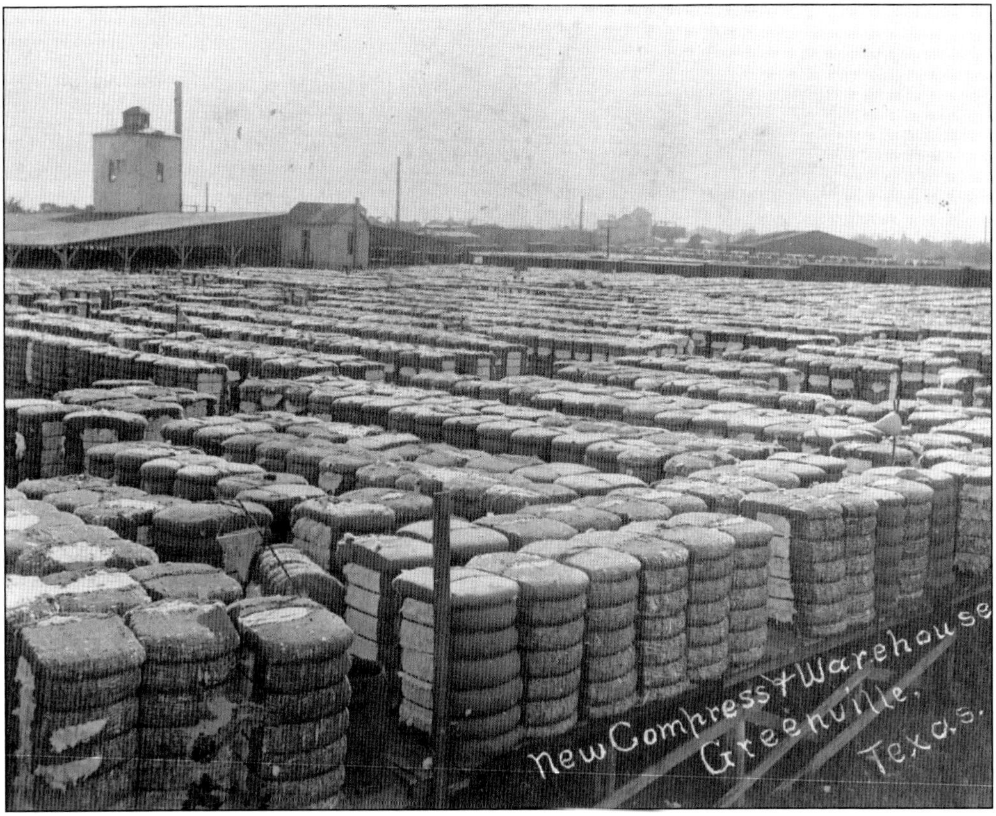

Thousands of bales of compressed cotton sit on loading docks awaiting shipment to Galveston. From there, they will be loaded on ships bound for European or New England textile mills. During World War I (1914–1918), European mills were converted to armament factories, thereby lessening the need for U.S. cotton, including that from Greenville. (Courtesy of Hunt County Historical Commission.)

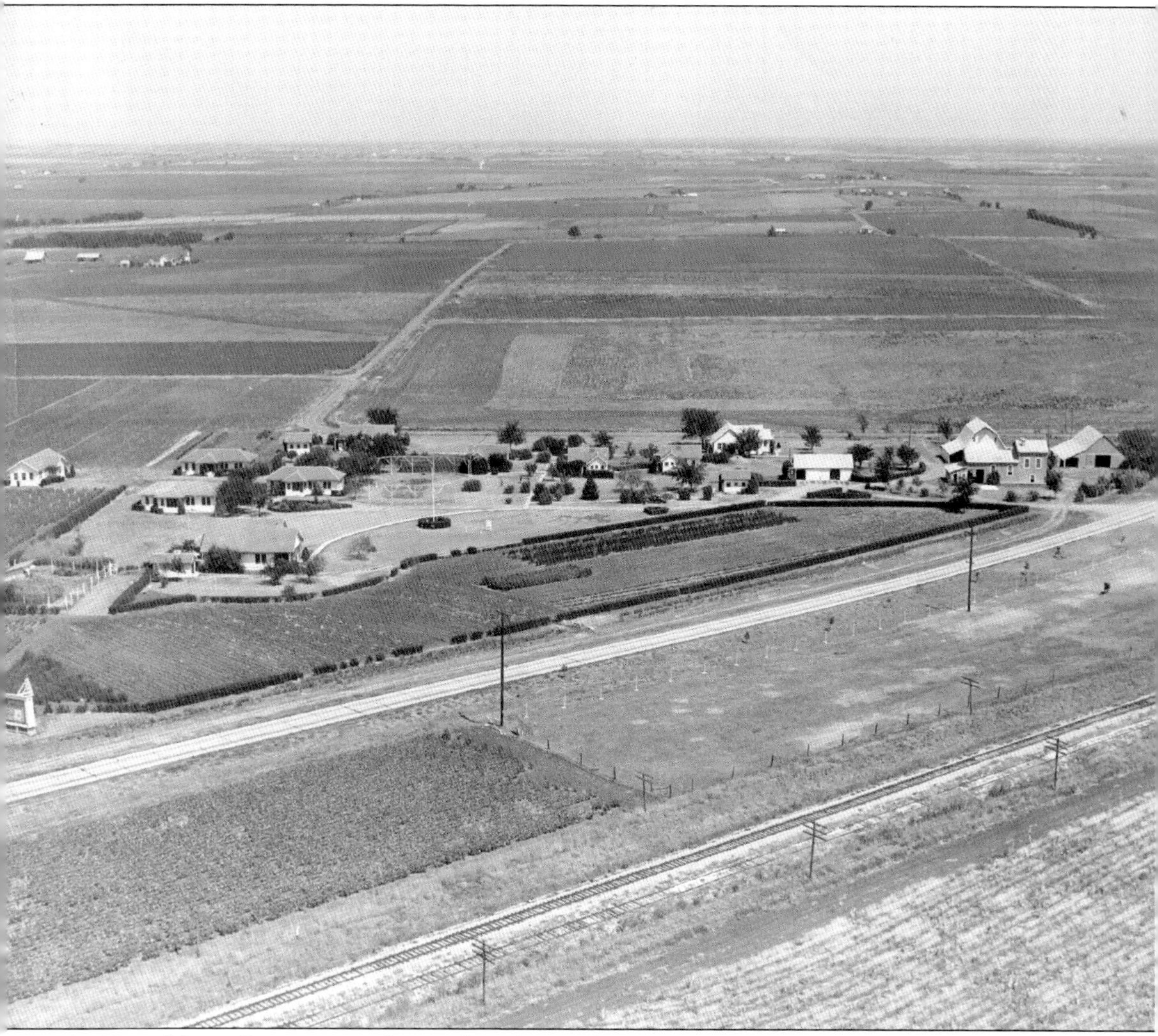

The United States Department of Agriculture (USDA) Field Station located southwest of Greenville was unique in that it was a cooperative venture between the USDA and the local chamber of commerce. It ultimately served a wide region that covered six states. The field station was an outgrowth of early cotton work by the USDA through the efforts of Col. E. H. R. Green, owner of the Texas Midland Railroad, who offered to finance cotton demonstration work in Texas. The field station was transferred to Greenville in 1913 under the direction of Dr. D. A. Saunders. In 1915, a conference of local, state, and federal leaders reached the consensus that the cotton-breeding program should be placed on a more permanent and definite footing. The Greenville Chamber of Commerce furnished 60 acres of land to the USDA under a 99-year lease. (Courtesy of W. Walworth Harrison Public Library.)

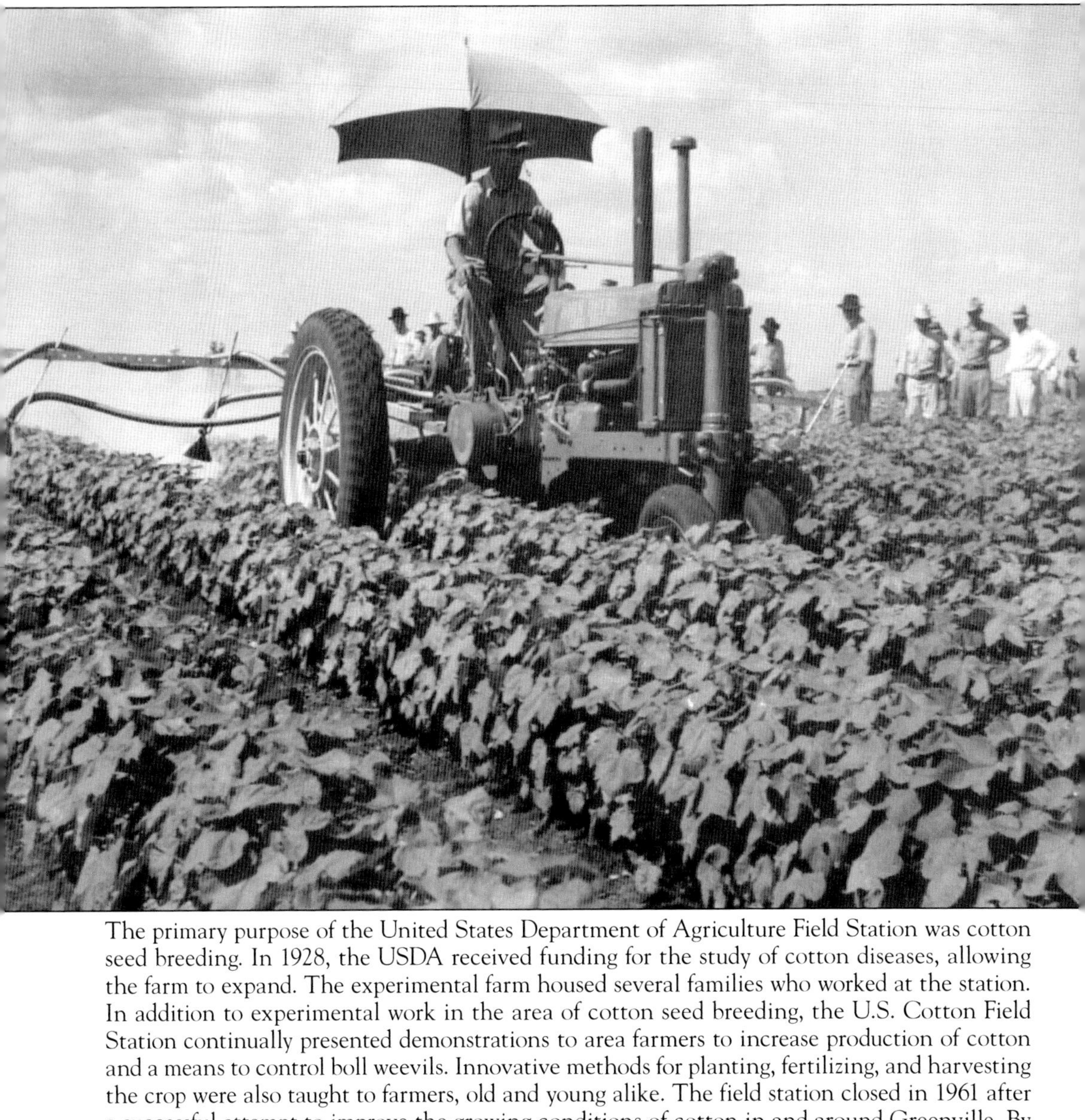

The primary purpose of the United States Department of Agriculture Field Station was cotton seed breeding. In 1928, the USDA received funding for the study of cotton diseases, allowing the farm to expand. The experimental farm housed several families who worked at the station. In addition to experimental work in the area of cotton seed breeding, the U.S. Cotton Field Station continually presented demonstrations to area farmers to increase production of cotton and a means to control boll weevils. Innovative methods for planting, fertilizing, and harvesting the crop were also taught to farmers, old and young alike. The field station closed in 1961 after a successful attempt to improve the growing conditions of cotton in and around Greenville. By that time, industry was on the way to replacing agriculture as the main source of employment on the black land prairie. (Courtesy of W. Walworth Harrison Public Library.)

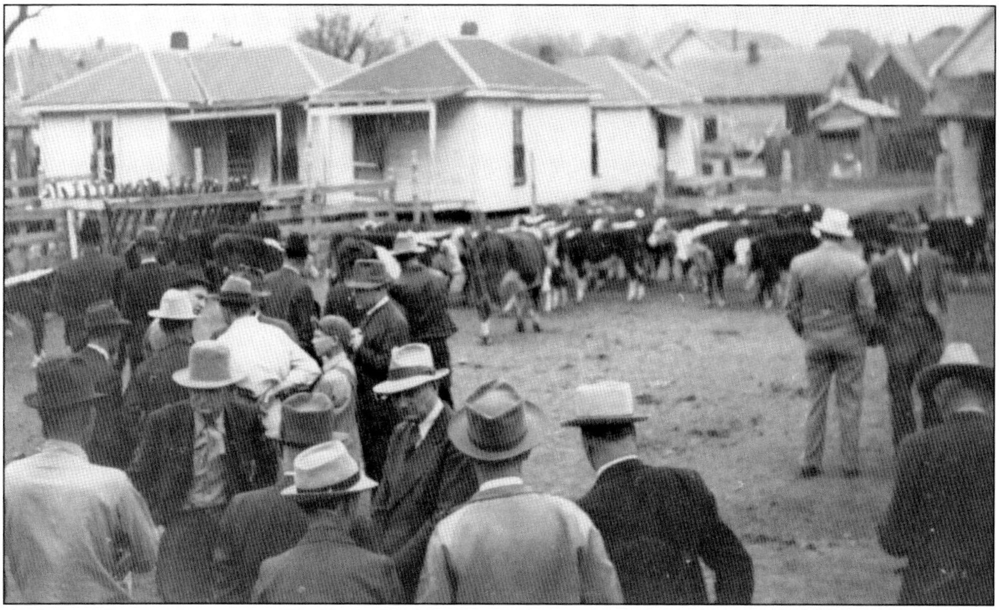

Just west of the Missouri, Kansas, and Texas freight depot and roundhouse were the West Yards. It was in these pens that cattlemen brought herds of beef and dairy cattle to be loaded on freight cars for shipment to eastern markets. It was not unusual for one cattleman to fill 10 to 20 cars with cattle at one time. (Courtesy of the author.)

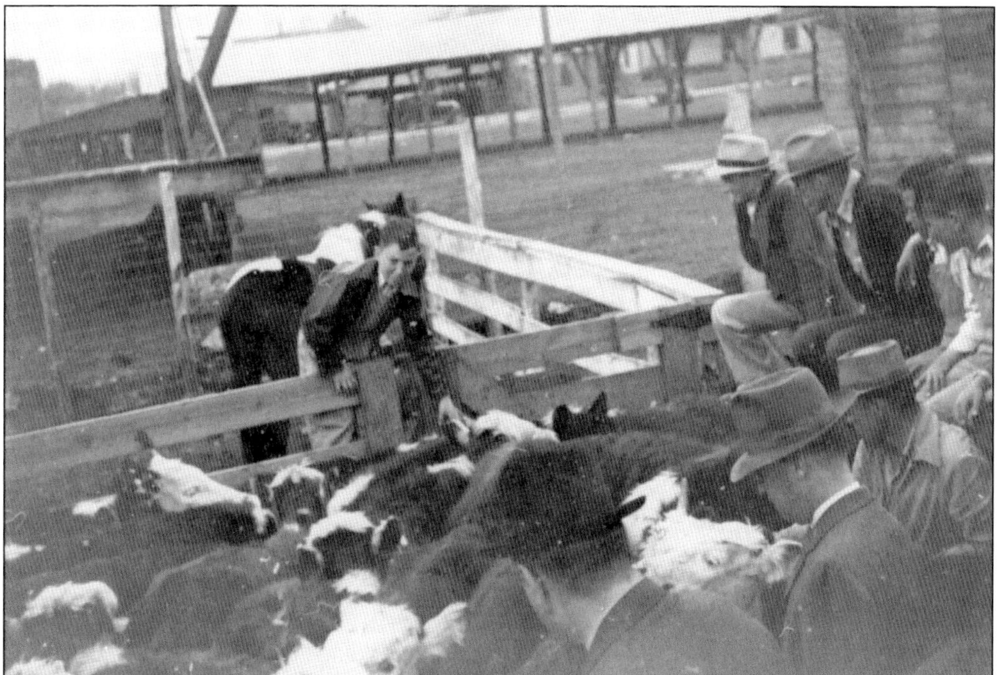

At the West Yards, livestock commissioners or buyers bought the cattle before they were shipped to markets. One of the dangers that cattlemen faced was the risk that stray dogs in the neighborhood might be rabid, thus infecting a herd that must then be destroyed. Dairy cattle were as prevalent as beef cattle in the area. (Courtesy of the author.)

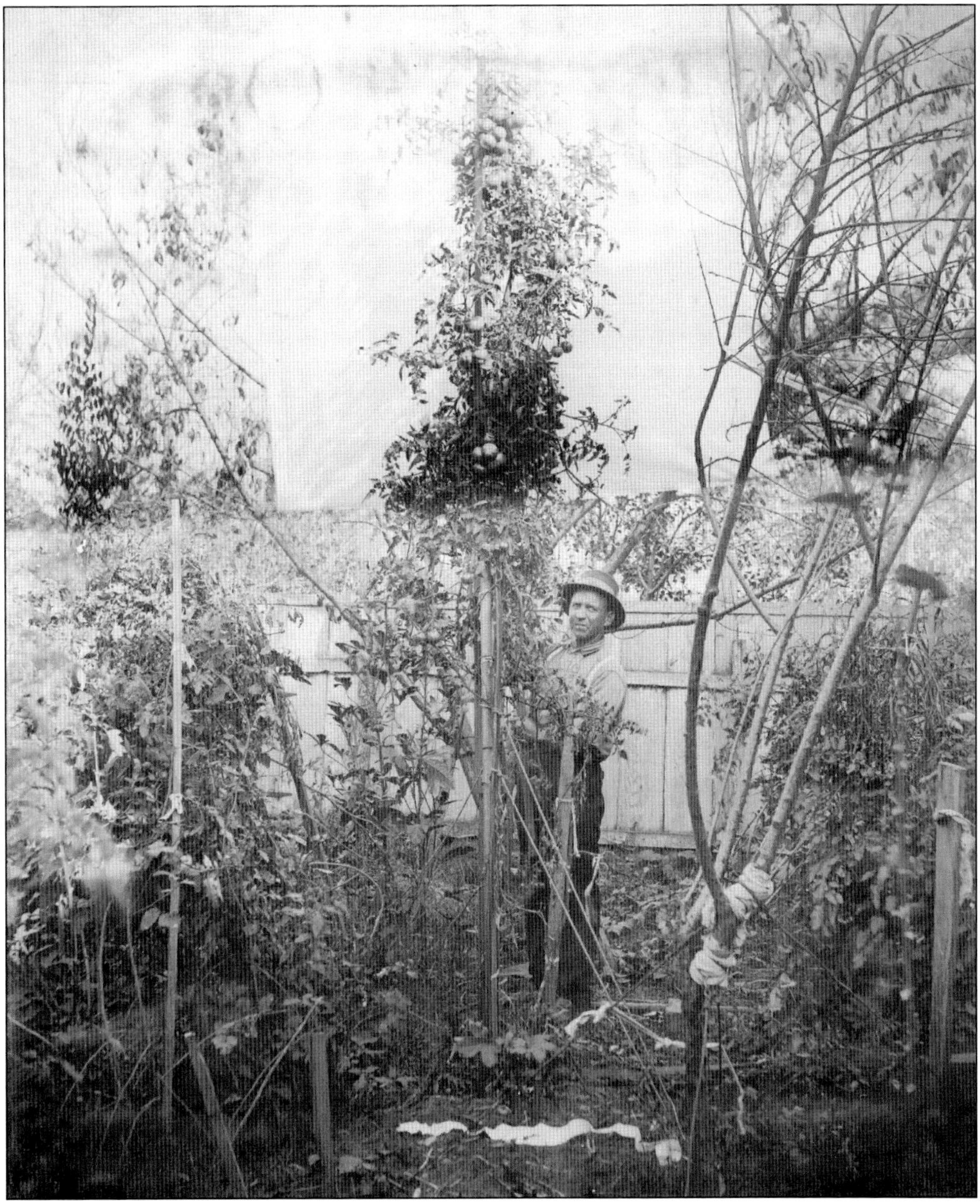

Cotton and cattle were not the only agricultural interests in Greenville. When the United States entered World War I, a nationwide movement began to encourage families to cultivate gardens in order to help solve the problem of feeding the nation and its troops. The slogan "food will win the war" resonated throughout Greenville and the surrounding area. Victory gardens sprang up in church yards, neighborhoods, and on school grounds. The Cotton Belt Railroad allowed anyone who did not have room for a garden at home to turn the railroad right-of-way into a vegetable garden. Women were taught how to safely preserve the produce. Even men and children were urged to join the food conservation effort. The few local truck farmers were encouraged to become canners. This gentleman seemed to have been extremely successful with his victory garden, especially with tomatoes that produce well in the black land prairie soil. (Courtesy of W. Walworth Harrison Public Library.)

Five

Ox Teams to Commuter Trains

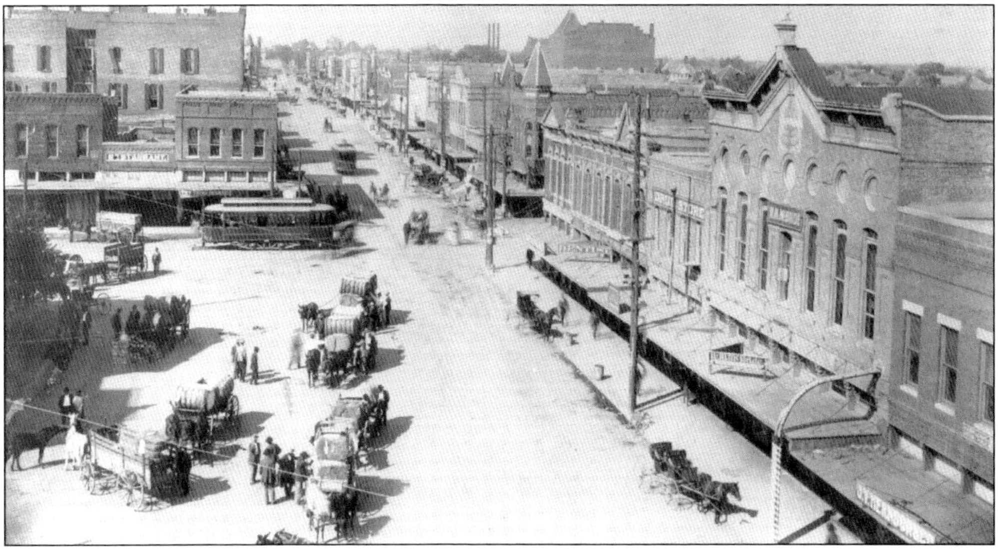

In the early years of the 20th century, Greenville was a city of farm wagons, buggies, horses, streetcars, and the occasional automobile. On either end of Lee Street were the railroad depots of the Missouri, Kansas, and Texas; the Cotton Belt Railroad; and the Texas Midland. Transportation changed Greenville from an inland village surrounded by a sea of mud into a thriving market center in less than 40 years. (Courtesy of the author.)

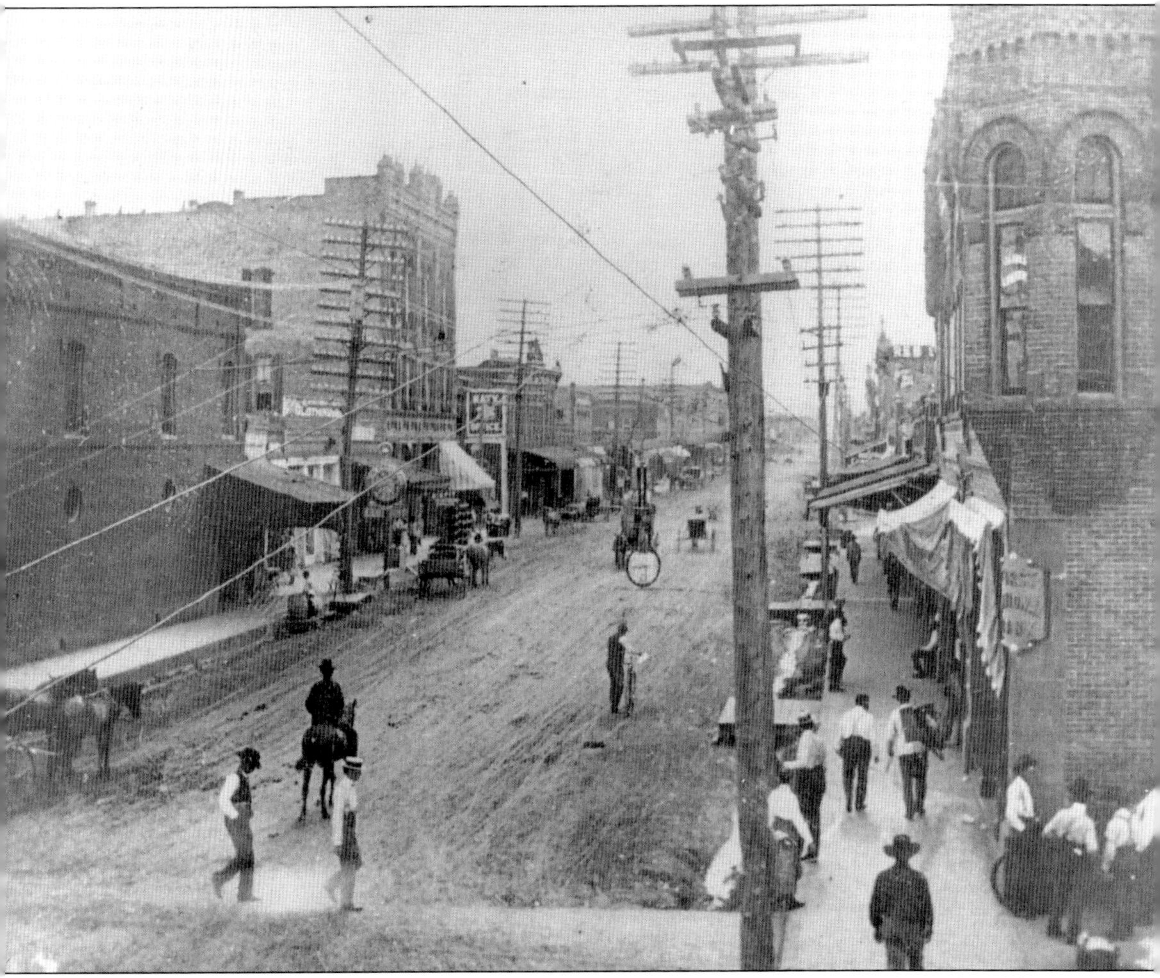

Prior to the spring of 1891, the downtown business district was lit at night with oil-burning streetlamps. With the introduction of electricity generated by the municipally owned power plant south of the public square on Town Branch, the downtown, as well as many homes, cast oil-burning lights aside in favor of incandescent lighting. In this photograph, the circle in the middle of the image is actually one of the new electric streetlights dangling from overhead wires. Note the absence of women in the street scene. The dusty streets and number of saloons prevented well-bred ladies from patronizing the area. The building on the right was the First National Bank. On the left side of Lee Street was the large pocket watch that marked the first location of George A. Pfaeffle's Watch Repair and Jewelry Store. (Courtesy of the author.)

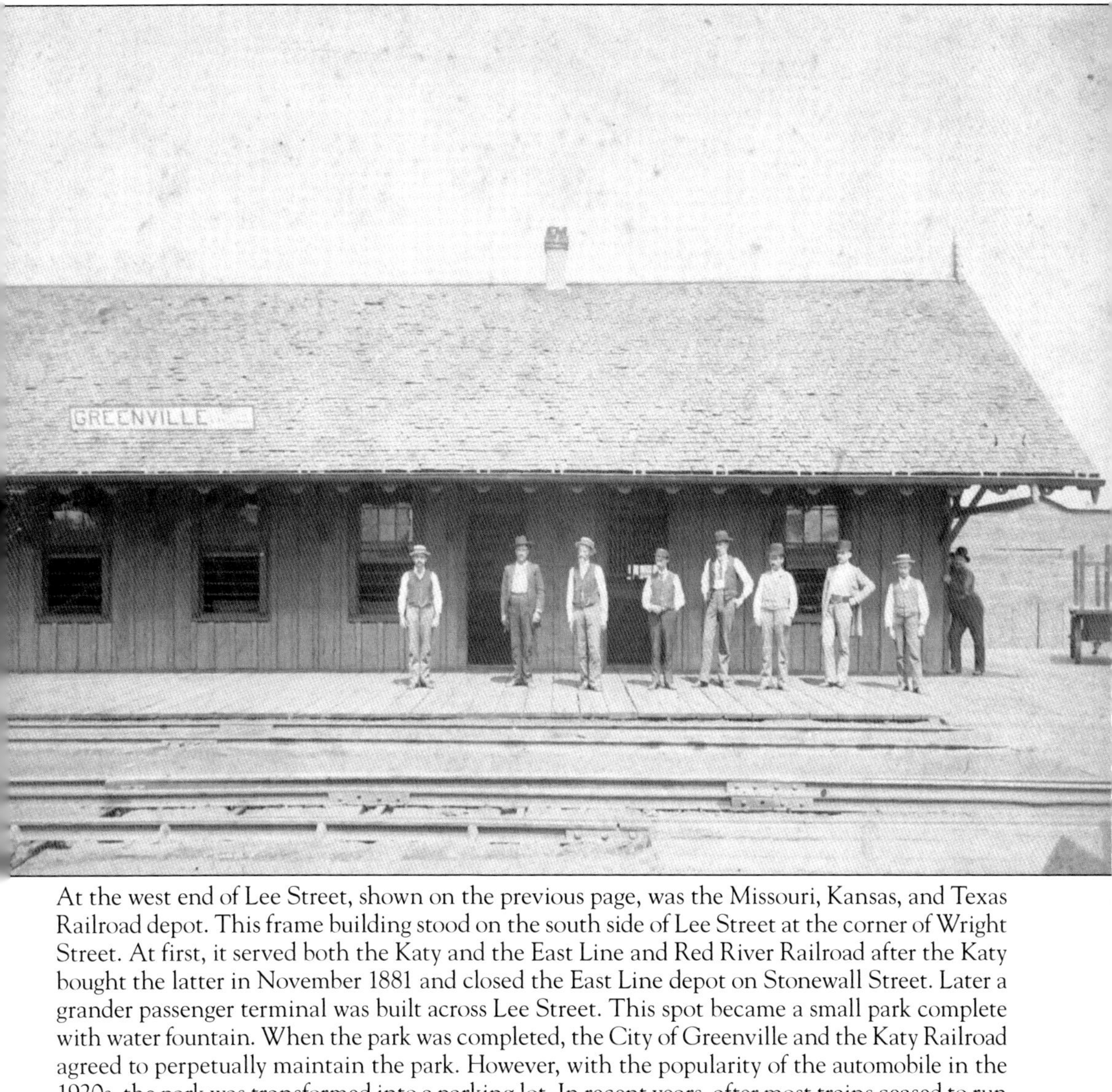

At the west end of Lee Street, shown on the previous page, was the Missouri, Kansas, and Texas Railroad depot. This frame building stood on the south side of Lee Street at the corner of Wright Street. At first, it served both the Katy and the East Line and Red River Railroad after the Katy bought the latter in November 1881 and closed the East Line depot on Stonewall Street. Later a grander passenger terminal was built across Lee Street. This spot became a small park complete with water fountain. When the park was completed, the City of Greenville and the Katy Railroad agreed to perpetually maintain the park. However, with the popularity of the automobile in the 1920s, the park was transformed into a parking lot. In recent years, after most trains ceased to run through Greenville, private citizens re-created Katy Park as a monument to the colossal impact the railroads had on the growth and development of the city. (Courtesy of the author.)

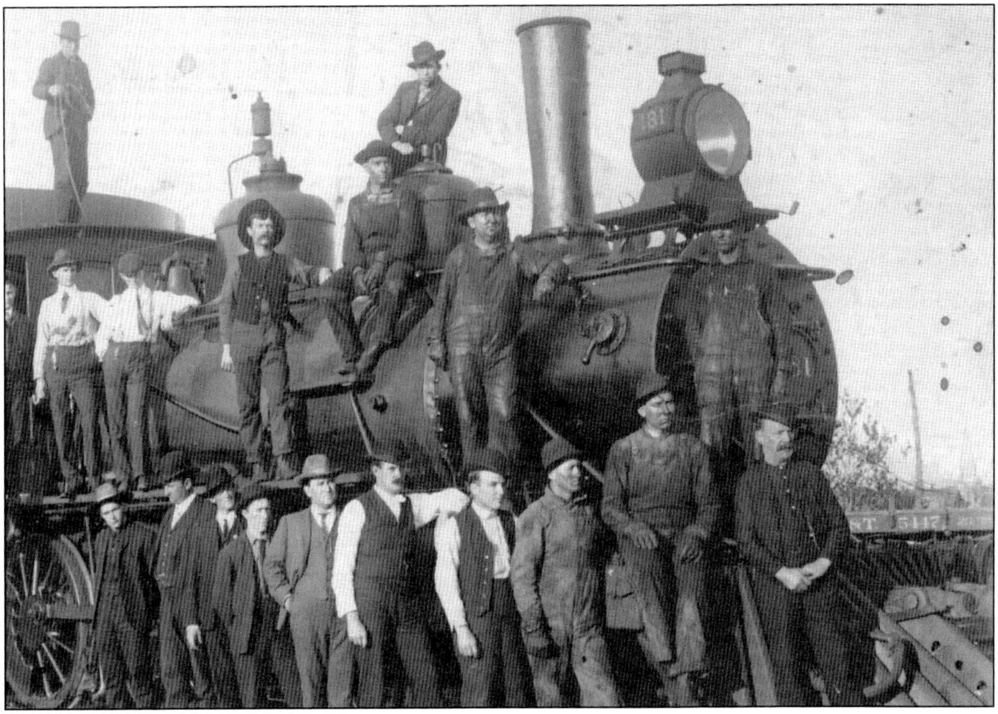

The Missouri, Kansas, and Texas Railroad maintained a roundhouse to the south of the freight depot for a number of years. After it was destroyed by fire, the railroad moved the facility to Denison, Texas. Many residents of the area adopted the policy of those in other areas of the country and sued the railroads, seen as a source of wealth for frivolous reasons. (Courtesy of the author.)

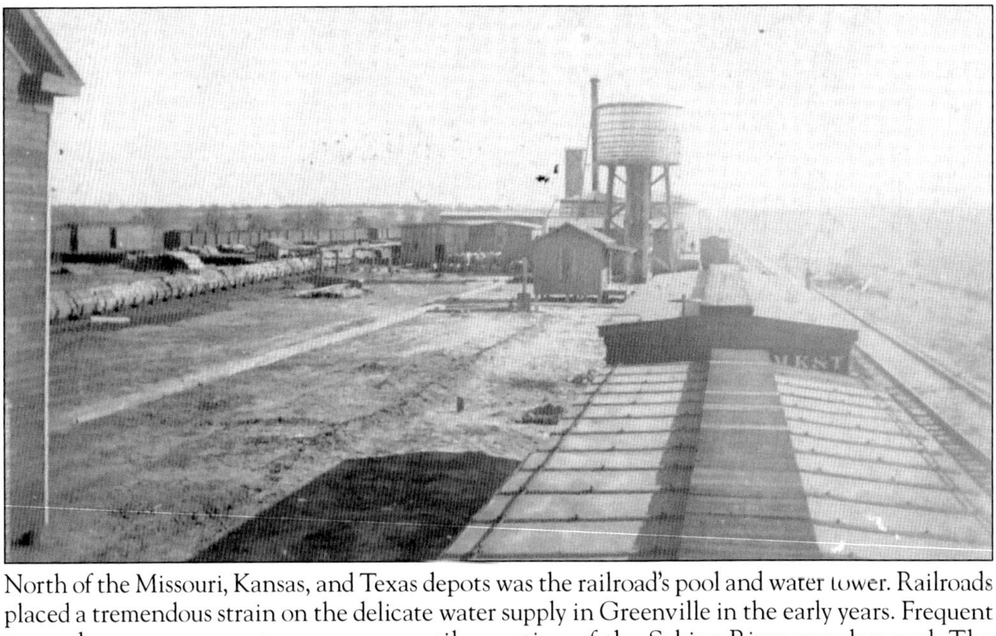

North of the Missouri, Kansas, and Texas depots was the railroad's pool and water tower. Railroads placed a tremendous strain on the delicate water supply in Greenville in the early years. Frequent water shortages were not uncommon until a portion of the Sabine River was dammed. The railroads hauled water into Greenville in wooden barrels on flatcars for their own use and that of the citizens. (Courtesy of the author.)

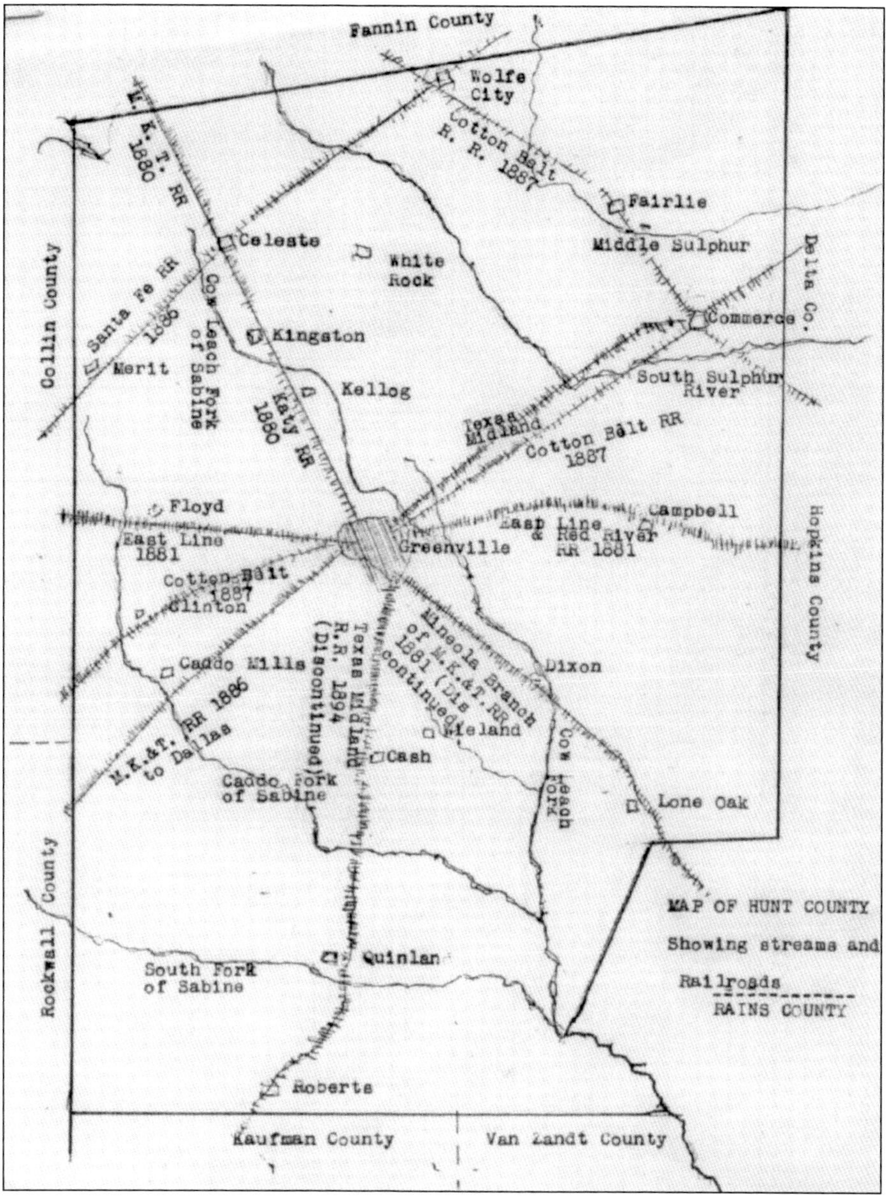

Serious effort was made in 1873 to bring railroads into the county when the Texas Legislature chartered the Paris, Greenville, and Cleburne Railroad. However, the plans were aborted by the Panic of 1873. In 1879, Greenville supposedly offered the East Line and Red River Railroad $10,000 to build tracks to the town that followed old freight wagon trails. The Katy Railroad received free right-of-way through the county northwest to southeast, depot grounds, and cattle pen grounds in Greenville plus $5,000 cash, if the road was completed in eight months with rolling stock in place. The first train arrived with moments to spare on Friday, October 1, 1880, an occasion for grand celebration. The line on to Mineola was completed the following year. The East Line and Red River arrived in February 1881. The Cotton Belt arrived in 1887 with the Texas Midland following in 1894. Women in surrounding communities boarded trains for shopping in Greenville when their children went to school and returned before school was out for the day, which was considered an early commuter system. (Courtesy of the author.)

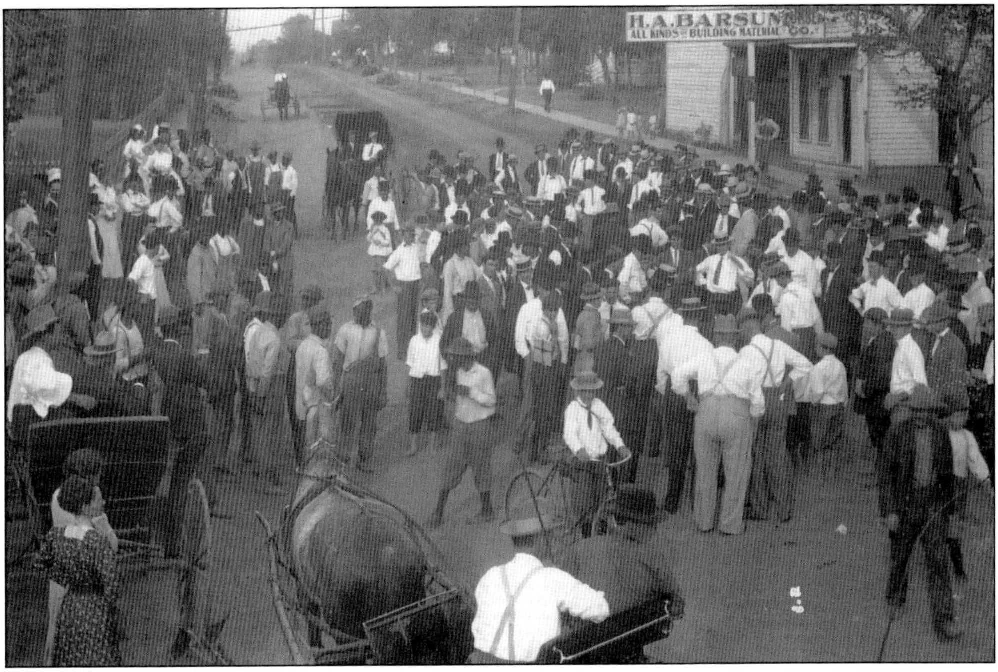

Citizens gathered to witness the first spike driven in the electric street railway line in 1910 just west of the Missouri, Kansas, and Texas depot on Lee Street. The rather eclectic crowd demonstrated the wide interest that the streetcars drew. Not everyone was in favor of them, fearing they would make crossing streets dangerous. (Courtesy of the author.)

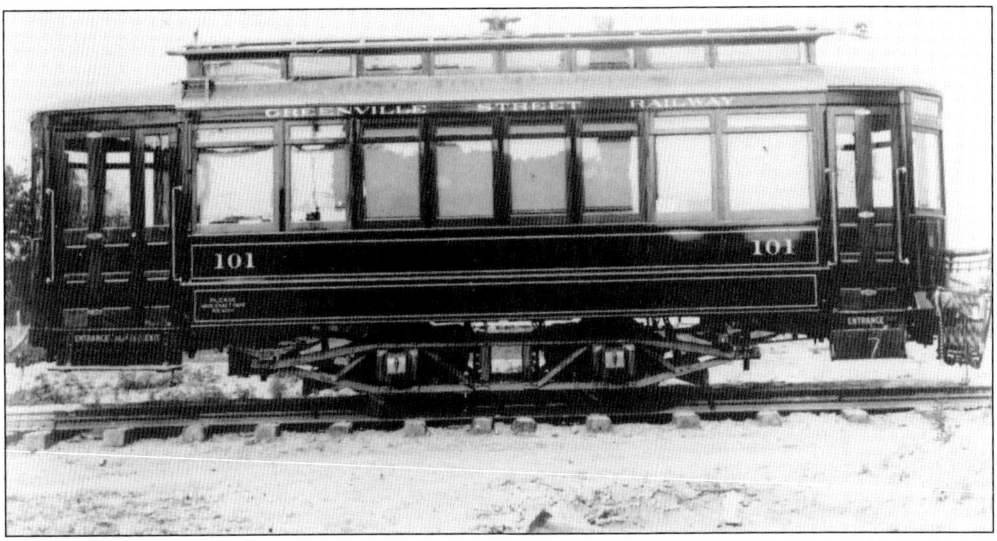

In July 1910, voters approved the contract with Dayton Electric Company to allow additional lines provided that the city would build the tracks. This particular streetcar line traveled to within one block of Burleson College, located in the western part of Greenville. Local students could easily reach the campus for classes. (Courtesy of the author.)

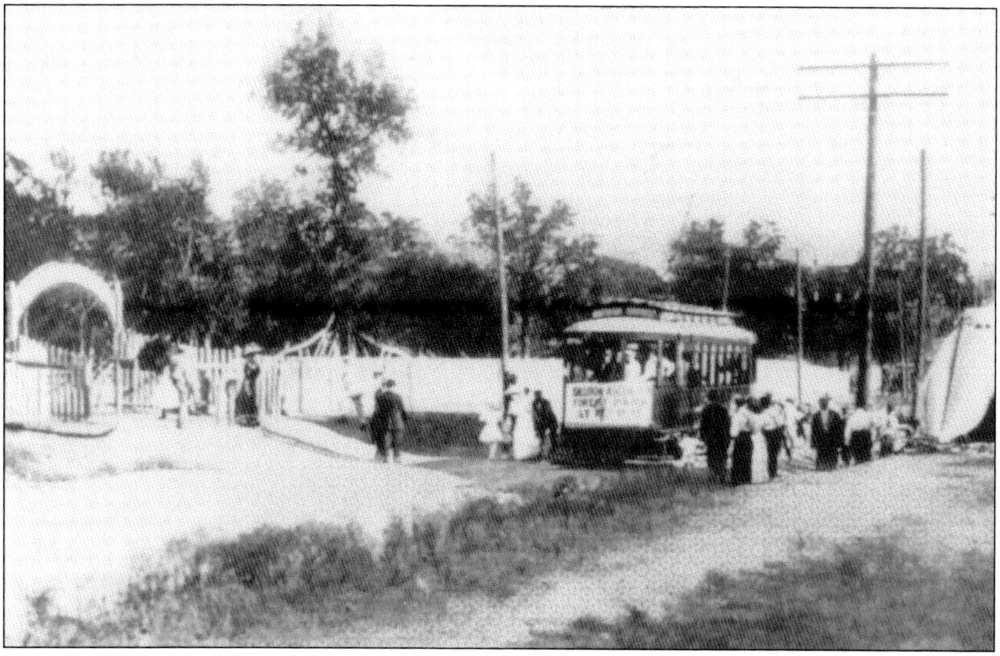

The streetcar company leased the city park located at the northern terminus of the line to encourage ridership. Added to the park were a band shell, dance pavilion, bowling alley, skating rink, a zoo, playground equipment, and a 600-seat auditorium with large stage. Electric lights were provided by the municipally owned electric plant. (Courtesy of W. Walworth Harrison Public Library.)

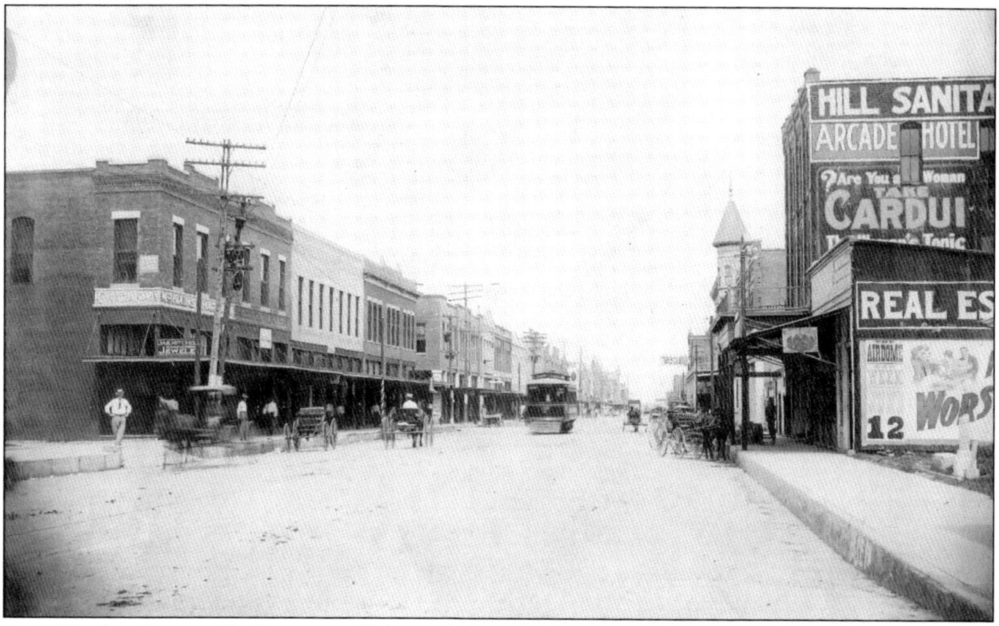

In 1912, the Greenville Boosters Club used this photograph in a promotional piece. It featured Lee Street looking east toward the courthouse. On the right, a poster advertises the Airdome, an open-air summer theater on the vacant lot between the Arcade Hotel and the Beckham Annex. The Airdome played a summer stock company featuring melodramas. Note that buggies were driven on both left and right sides of the street. (Courtesy of the author.)

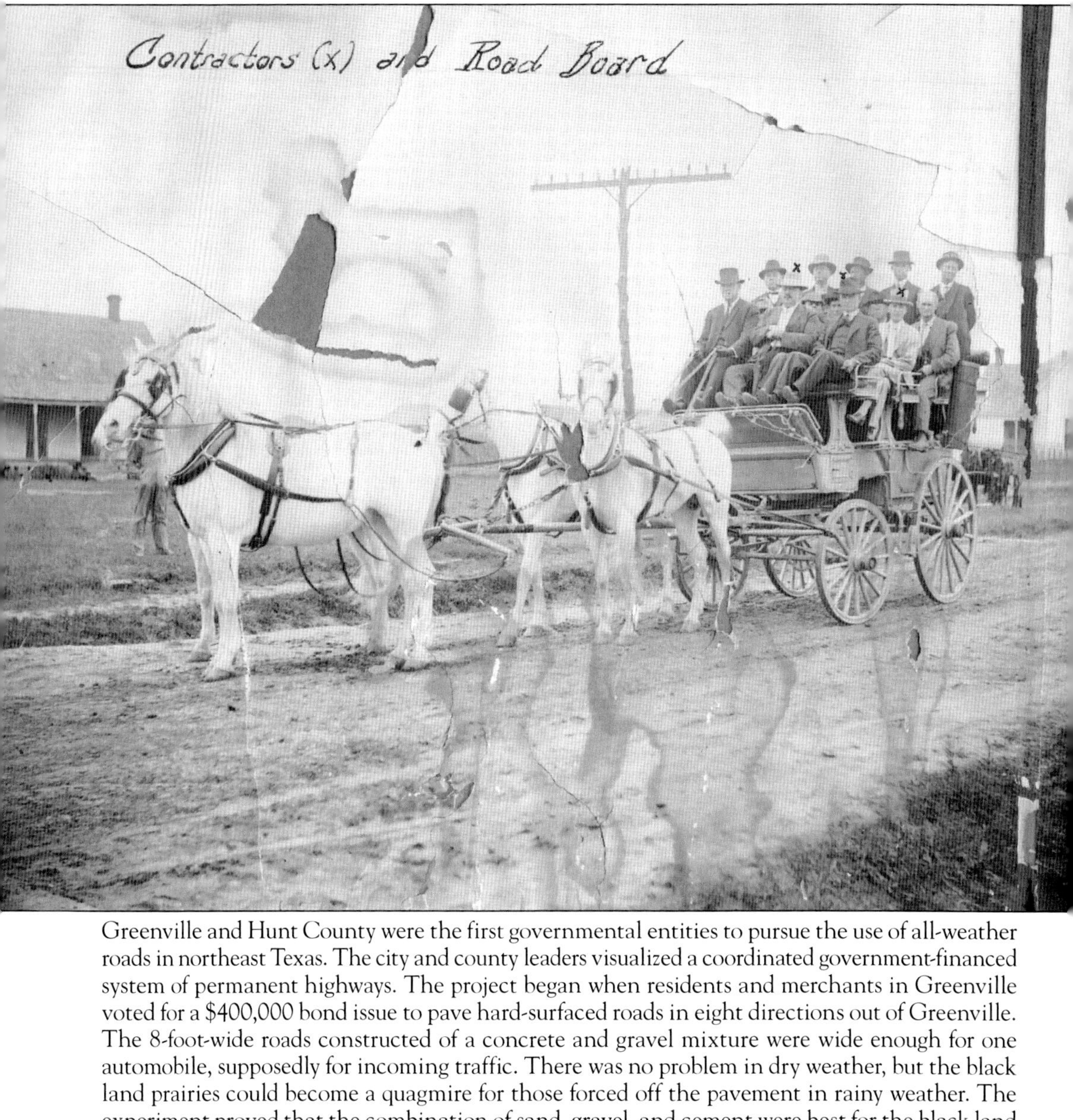

Greenville and Hunt County were the first governmental entities to pursue the use of all-weather roads in northeast Texas. The city and county leaders visualized a coordinated government-financed system of permanent highways. The project began when residents and merchants in Greenville voted for a $400,000 bond issue to pave hard-surfaced roads in eight directions out of Greenville. The 8-foot-wide roads constructed of a concrete and gravel mixture were wide enough for one automobile, supposedly for incoming traffic. There was no problem in dry weather, but the black land prairies could become a quagmire for those forced off the pavement in rainy weather. The experiment proved that the combination of sand, gravel, and cement were best for the black land prairies of Texas. Here members of the Good Road Board arrived at the groundbreaking ceremony in an elegant coach drawn by four white horses; perhaps symbolic of the transition from old to new transportation means. (Courtesy of the author.)

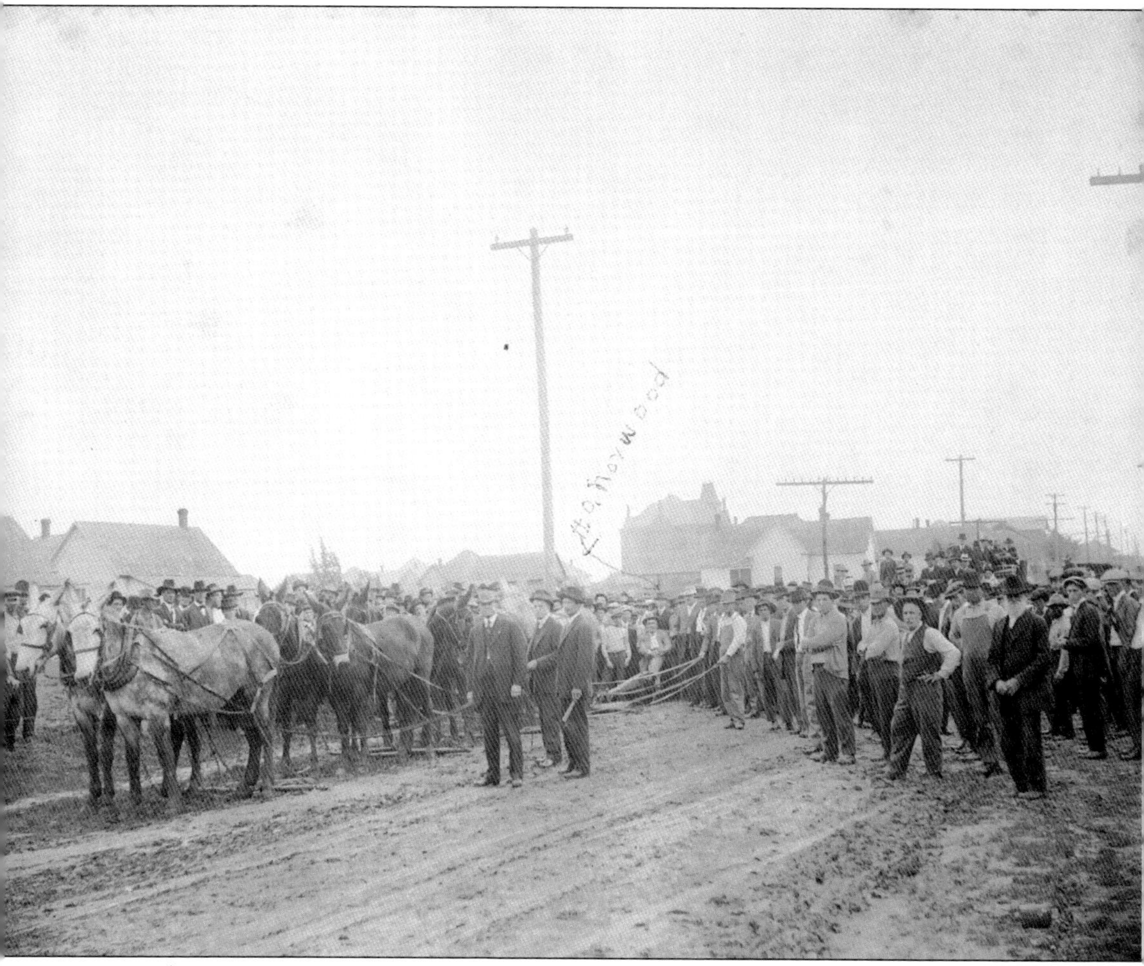

In 1919, a $2 million campaign for a county wide hard surface road system was passed by a substantial vote. The groundbreaking of a new paved road leading into Greenville from the west was ceremoniously marked with dignitaries, local citizens, and a variety of spectators. The drag line was driven by the county judge H. O. Norwood for this promotional photograph. The large structure in the background is the administration building at Burleson College. The movement for good roads eventually included the Broadway of America Highway passing through downtown Greenville as well as portions of the noted Bankhead Highway. While the progressive attitude of Greenville and Hunt County merchants and civic leaders may have been in part a means to further business revenues, both town and rural residents benefited from the good roads projects as much as they did with the coming of the railroad, electricity, a more adequate source of water, and other projects. (Courtesy of the author.)

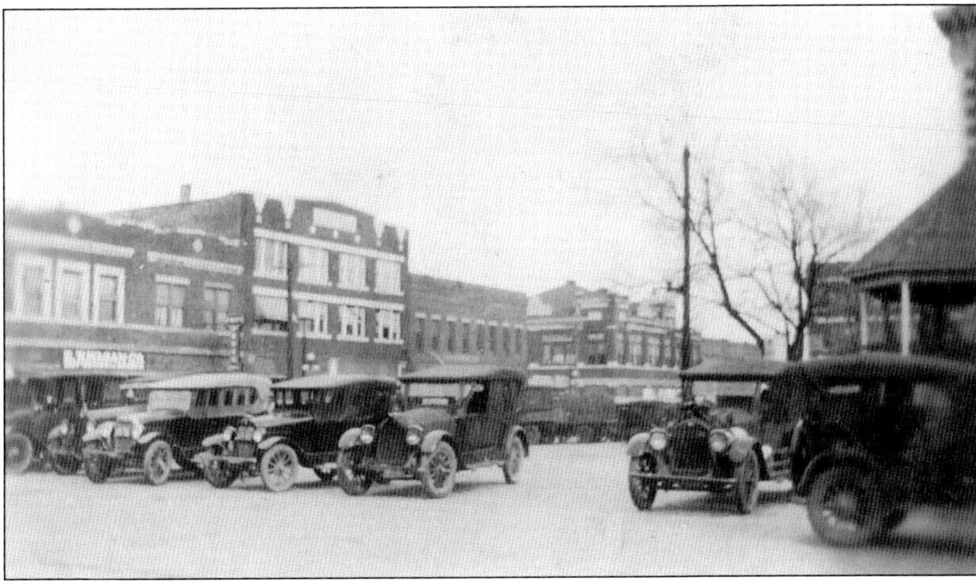

Early automobiles parked around the courthouse square indicated the acceptance automobiles received by the citizens of Greenville. The Booster Club often drove in long caravans to other towns and communities in the area to promote to virtues of Greenville. The large building on the left was McBride's, a local department store with the slogan "Meet Me at McBride's." (Courtesy of W. Walworth Harrison Public Library.)

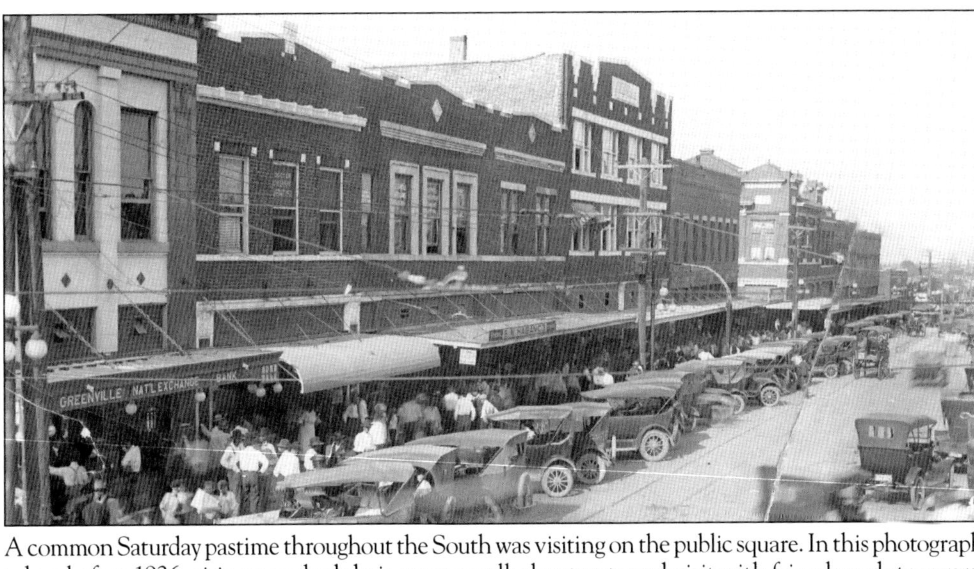

A common Saturday pastime throughout the South was visiting on the public square. In this photograph taken before 1926, citizens parked their cars to walk the streets and visit with friends and strangers. While men and boys usually walked up and down the sidewalks, women tended to remain in cars and visit with other women in their cars. (Courtesy of W. Walworth Harrison Public Library.)

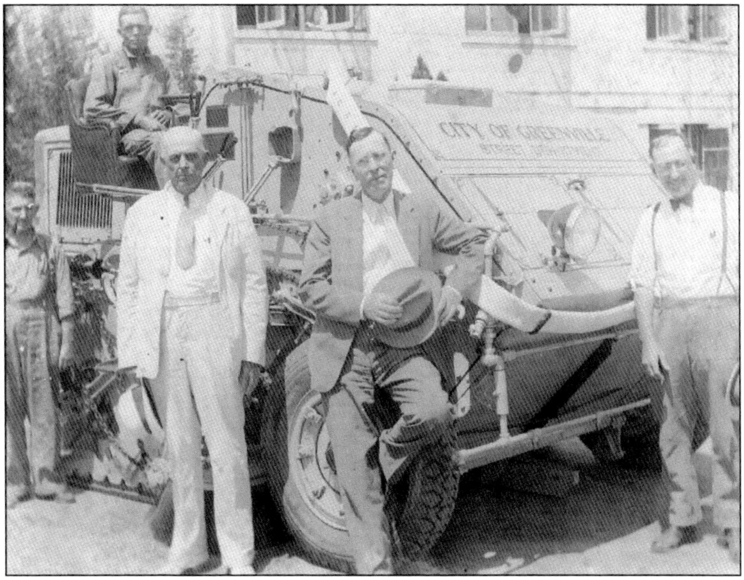

In August 1935, the City of Greenville had enough paved streets to warrant the purchase of a new street sweeper, shown here in front of the 1929 Hunt County Courthouse. The event sparked the interest of employees in the courthouse who often called out to pedestrians on the street from open windows. (Courtesy of W. Walworth Harrison Public Library.)

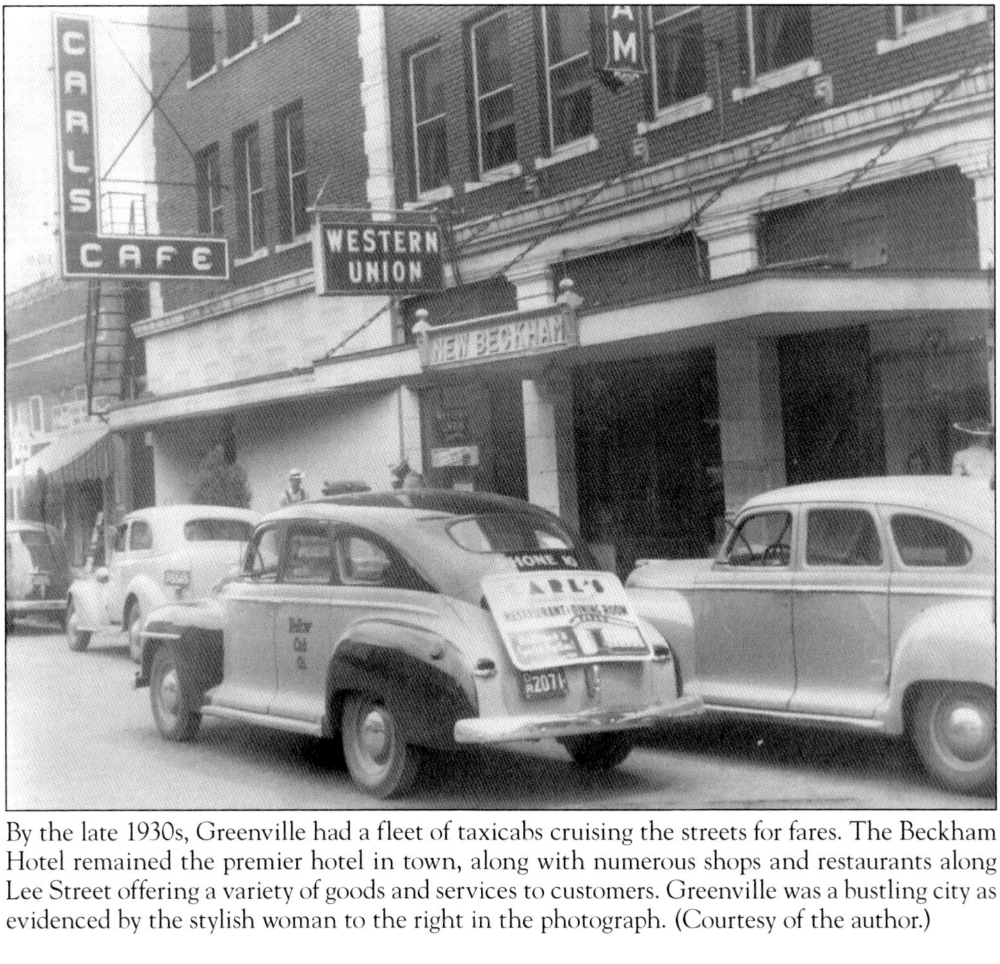

By the late 1930s, Greenville had a fleet of taxicabs cruising the streets for fares. The Beckham Hotel remained the premier hotel in town, along with numerous shops and restaurants along Lee Street offering a variety of goods and services to customers. Greenville was a bustling city as evidenced by the stylish woman to the right in the photograph. (Courtesy of the author.)

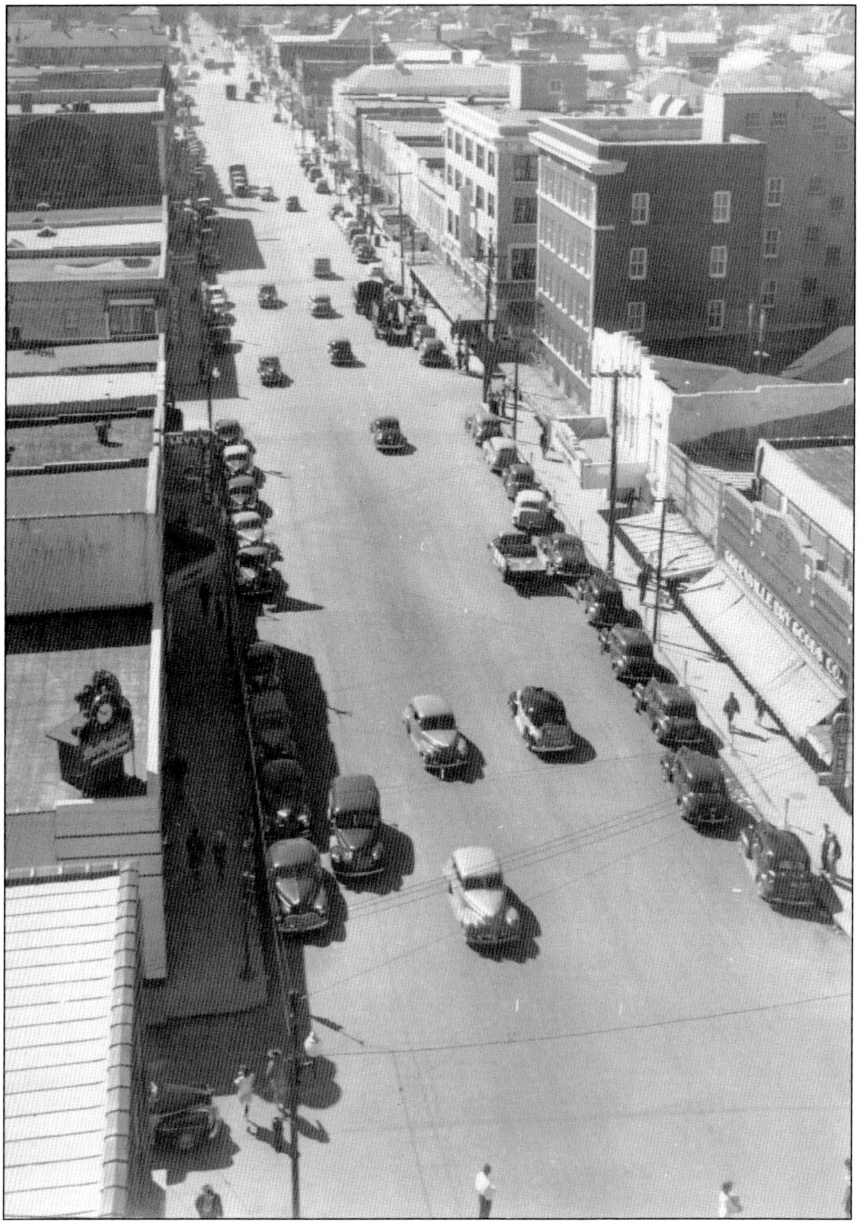

Following the end of World War II, Greenville retained its claim as a market center in northeast Texas. Parking spaces were hard to find, stores were bustling with shoppers, and the city enjoyed financial success. Such innovations as the clock on the roof of a local men's store, parking meters, and clean streets brought visitors in from the rural areas to shop, attend movies, and dine at restaurants. Elvis Presley appeared at the Municipal Auditorium at least once. After the show, he ate dinner in one of the downtown restaurants. The Medical Arts Center, housed in a red brick building with white stone trim, provided local doctors with offices in one central location. To the left was Sears Department Store located in the Graham-Fagg Building. Unfortunately, to avoid traffic congestion within the downtown area, Interstate 30 would soon be built south of town. This soon lured new retail out of downtown, which gradually lessened the opportunities for growth downtown. (Courtesy of the author.)

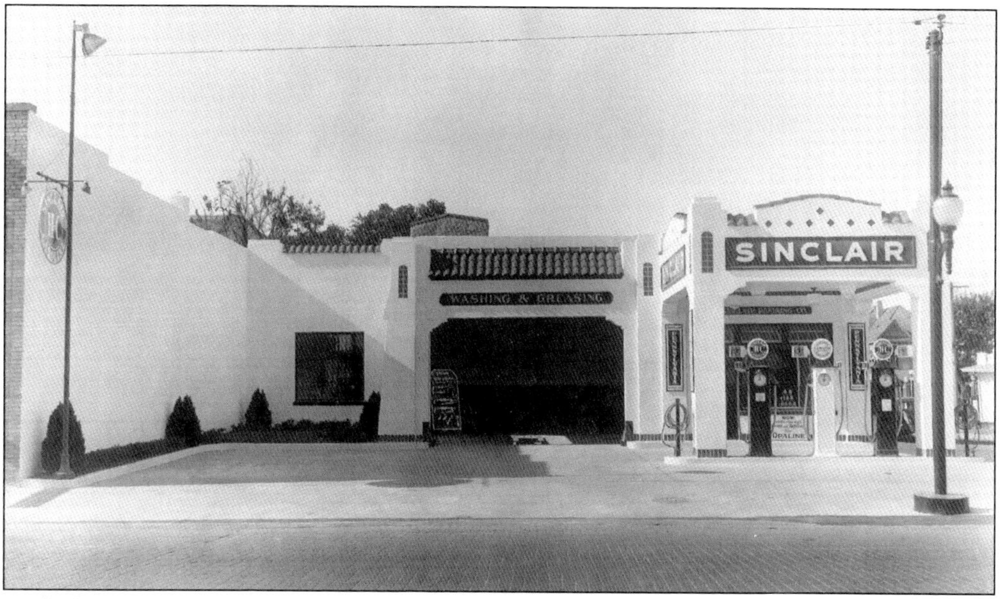

With the mass acceptance of the automobile came businesses that catered to cars and drivers. The Sinclair gas station on West Lee Street was immaculate when opened. Attendants filled the car with gas, washed the windshield, and checked air pressure in tires before wishing the driver a good day as he or she drove away. (Courtesy of W. Walworth Harrison Public Library.)

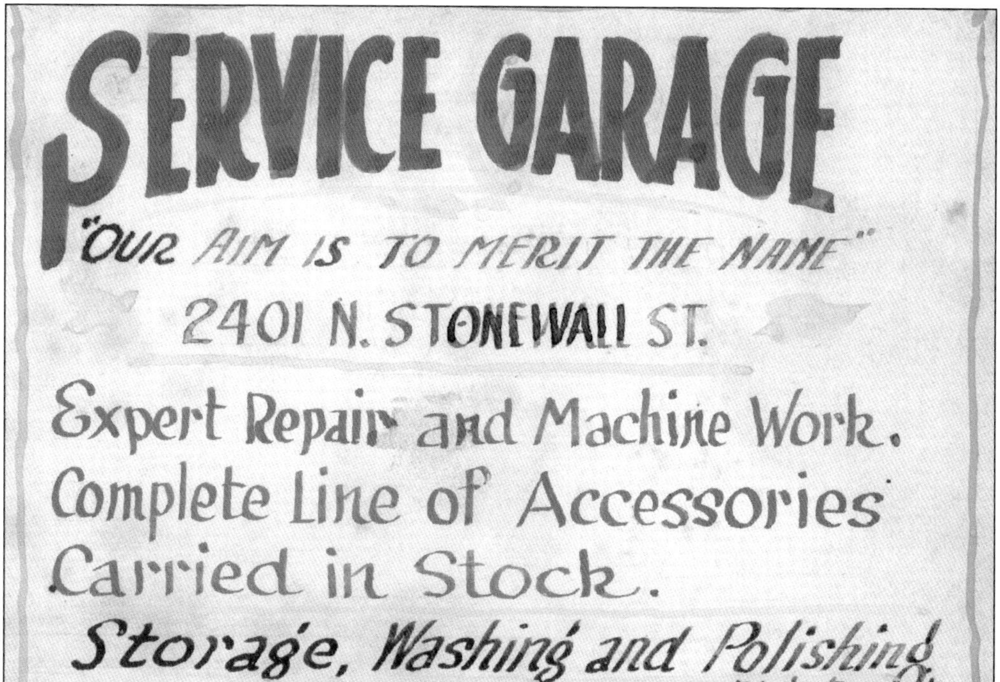

This promotional piece appeared in a Booster Club brochure in the early 1900s when the automobile was new to Greenville. Billed as garages, the businesses promoted the availability of parts and accessories for cars. Since very few homes had a place to store the new car out of the elements, the garages offered storage as well. (Courtesy of W. Walworth Harrison Public Library.)

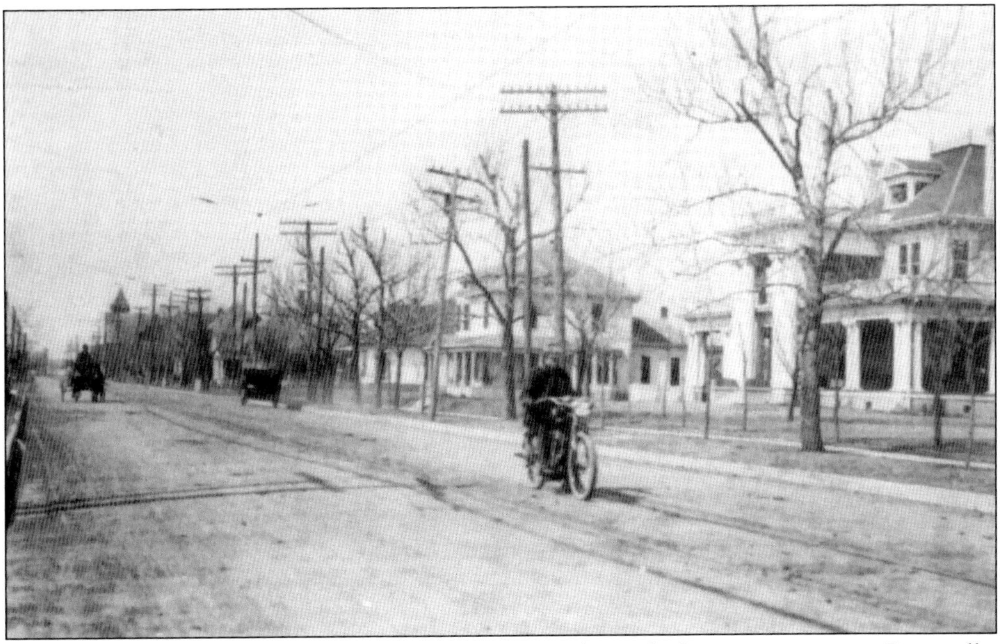

Shortly after the beginning of the 20th century, motorcycles made their appearances in Greenville. First shown at the North Texas Fair in Greenville, motorcycles became a means of exciting transportation. This unidentified gentleman was dressed for the ride, complete with goggles, helmet, and high boots. Note the streetcar tracks on the street. (Courtesy of Hunt County Historical Commission.)

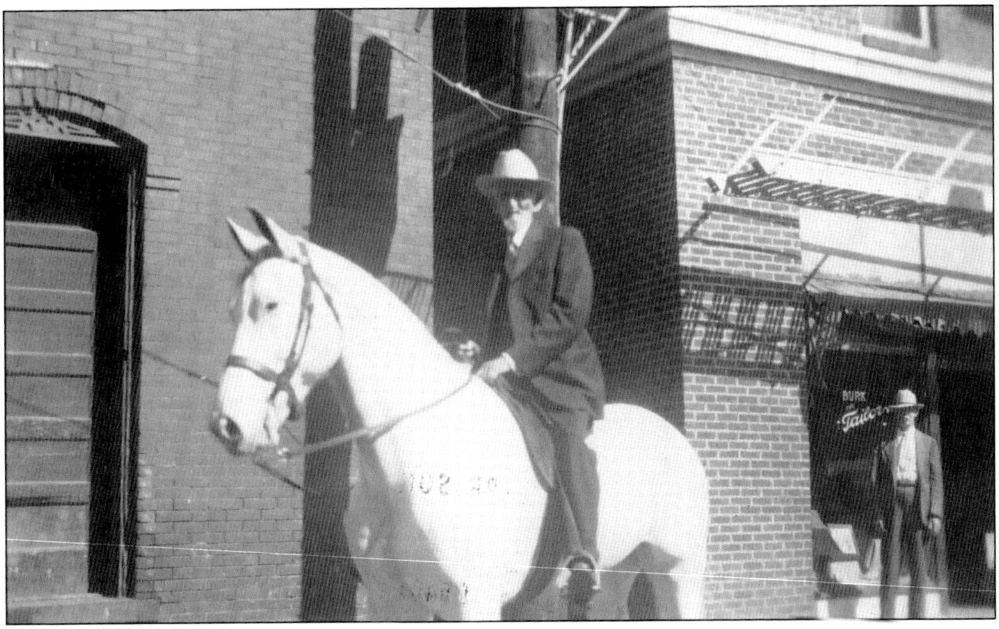

While the rest of Greenville was enthralled with automobiles, streetcars, and motorcycles, one old-timer preferred his horse. In his 80s at the time, Capt. W. M. Arnold, Confederate veteran and civic leader, was known to ride his faithful white horse to town from his home across Town Branch almost daily in the early 1930s. (Courtesy of the author.)

Six

Academics and Athletics

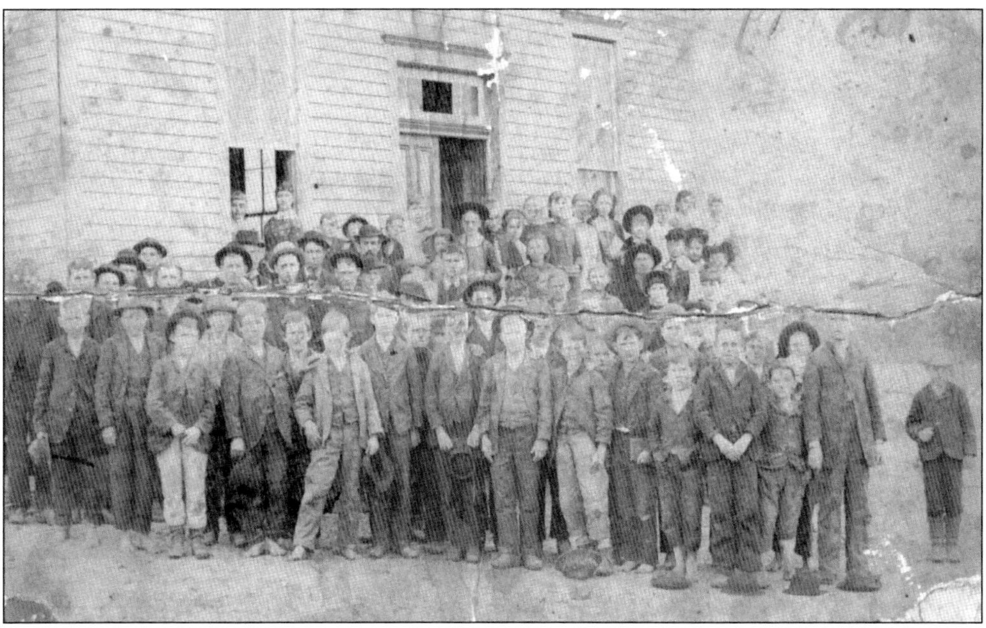

J. E. Edmonds opened a school for children of Greenville parents in 1881. The school was not the first but probably the most successful. The free school pupils ranged between the ages of eight and 14. The town paid teachers $1.50 tuition per student, largely from state appropriation. This photograph taken in 1883 indicated the emphasis that many parents placed on education for boys, rather than girls. (Courtesy of Hunt County Historical Commission.)

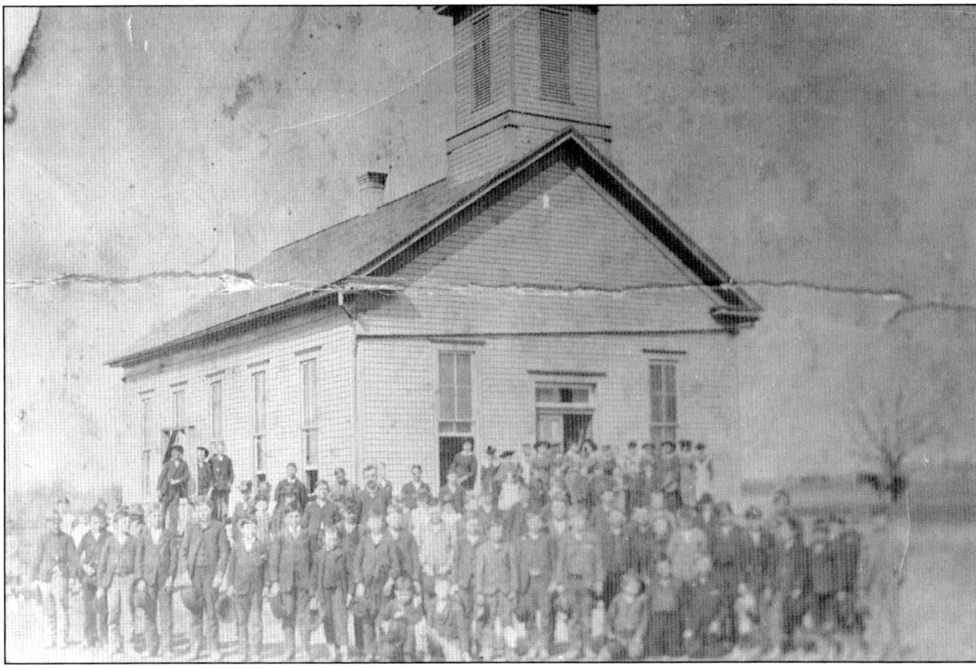

In 1884, the City of Greenville began operation of the schools, levied a tax, appointed trustees, employed teachers with monthly salaries of $75, and paid the rent for the public buildings. The following year the city purchased the Jim Edmonds School, shown here in 1885, for $2,300. At that time there were two more schools, one at the Baptist Church and the other operated by the Misses Whitmore. (Courtesy of the author.)

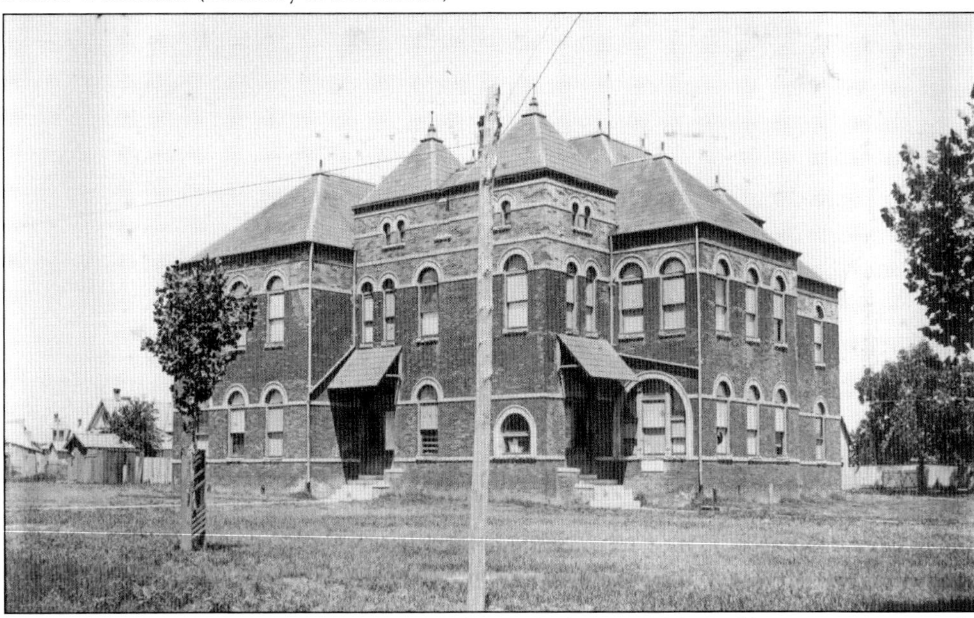

The first Greenville High School was located five blocks west of the public square. In 1898, the first graduating class consisted of nine girls. While parents encouraged younger boys to attend school, most young men dropped out and went to work after age 14. Gradually, boys' names began to appear among the graduates. (Courtesy of W. Walworth Harrison Public Library.)

In this photograph, several members of the 1909 graduating class climbed on part of the roof of the high school building to have their picture taken. From the number of photographs available of this group of students, it seems evident that someone had a new camera and used it frequently. (Courtesy of W. Walworth Harrison Public Library.)

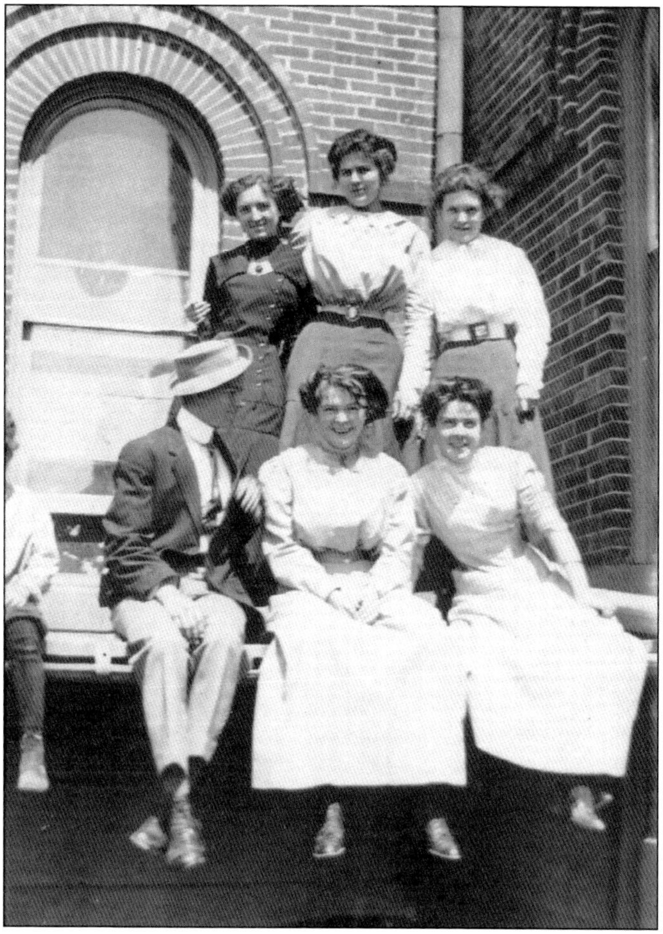

Members of the Greenville High School faculty for the 1909–1910 school year gathered in the library to pose for a formal portrait. The furnishings indicate a refined decorum that prevailed at the school. Students were encouraged to excel in literature and debate. A close camaraderie existed between faculty and the small classes. (Courtesy of W. Walworth Harrison Public Library.)

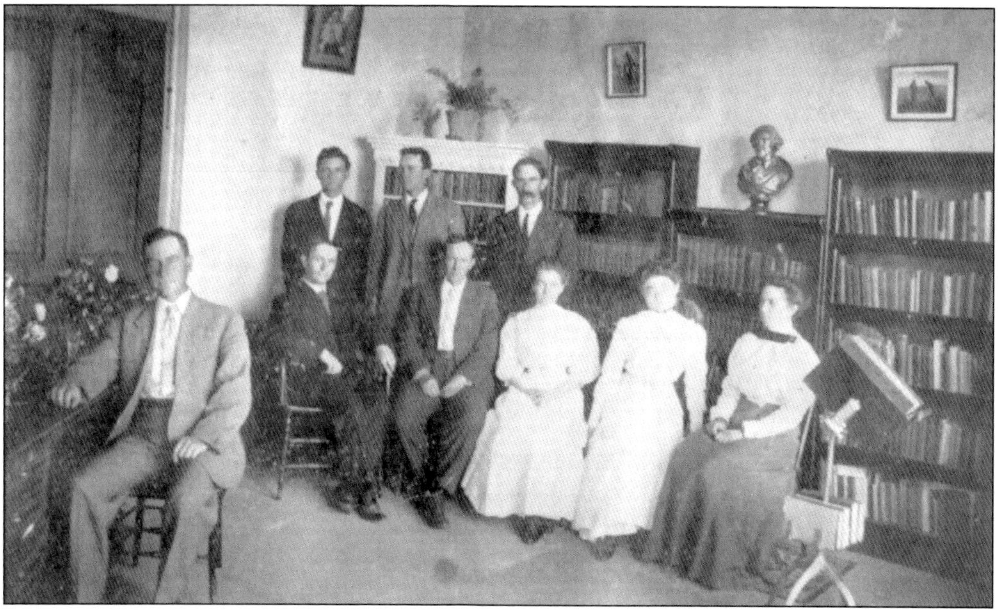

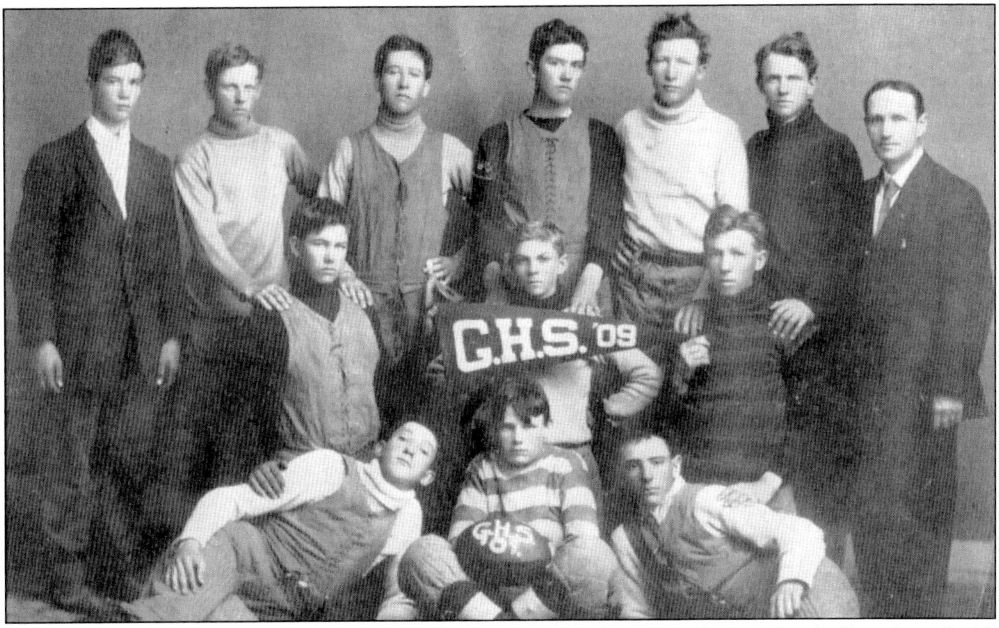

In 1909, Greenville High School won the school's first championship in football with only 12 players. School colors were dark hunter green and white. During World War I, green dye was used for U.S. Army uniforms and not available for public use. It would be several years before the school colors became red and white. (Courtesy of W. Walworth Harrison Public Library.)

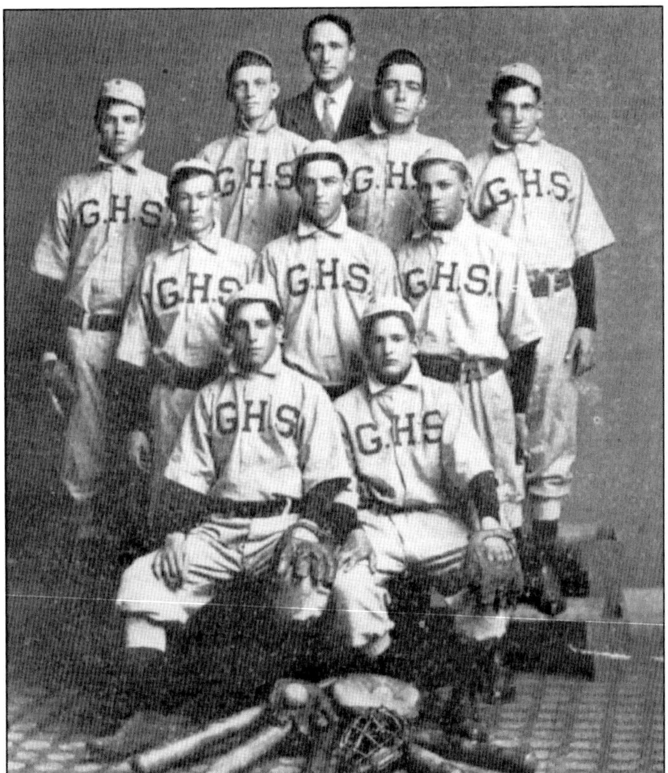

In 1911, nine young men played on the Greenville High School baseball team that won the North Texas Championship. Baseball was an extremely popular sport in both rural areas and towns. Throughout the first half of the 20th century, Greenville fielded semiprofessional and amateur teams every summer. (Courtesy of the author.)

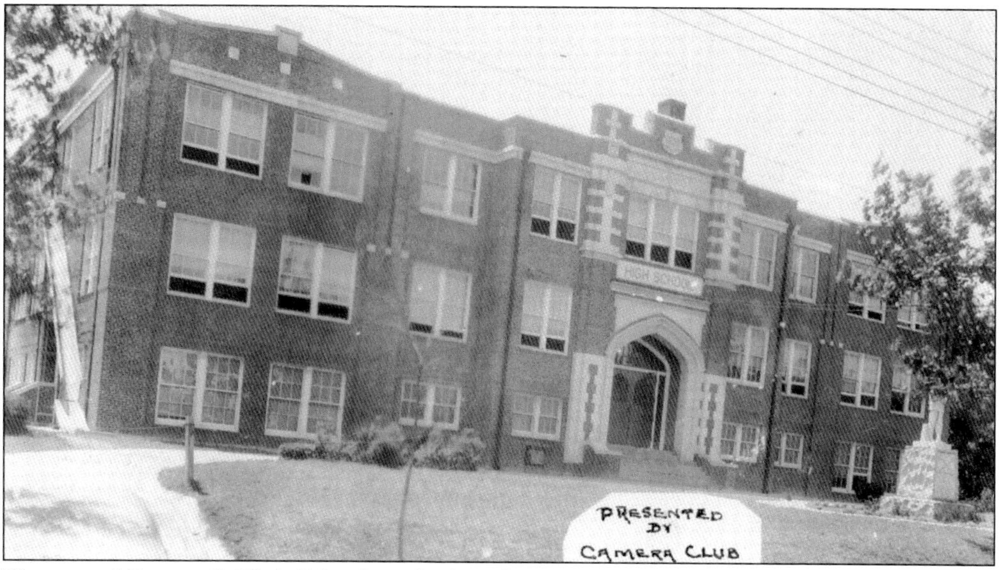

The second Greenville High School was built in the 1920s. On the left appears a gigantic slide that was actually the fire escape. To the far right was the base of a Confederate statue erected by the United Daughters of the Confederacy in June 1926. It was the only such statue to have stood on the grounds of a public school in Texas. (Courtesy of W. Walworth Harrison Public Library.)

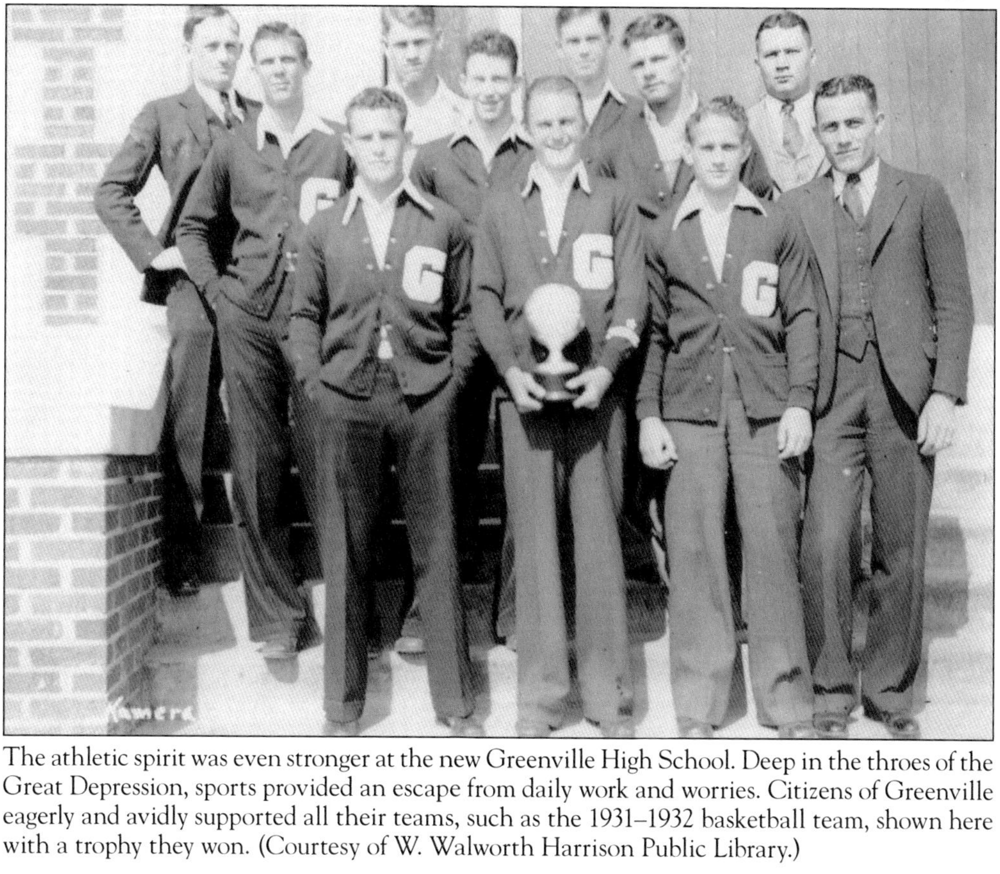

The athletic spirit was even stronger at the new Greenville High School. Deep in the throes of the Great Depression, sports provided an escape from daily work and worries. Citizens of Greenville eagerly and avidly supported all their teams, such as the 1931–1932 basketball team, shown here with a trophy they won. (Courtesy of W. Walworth Harrison Public Library.)

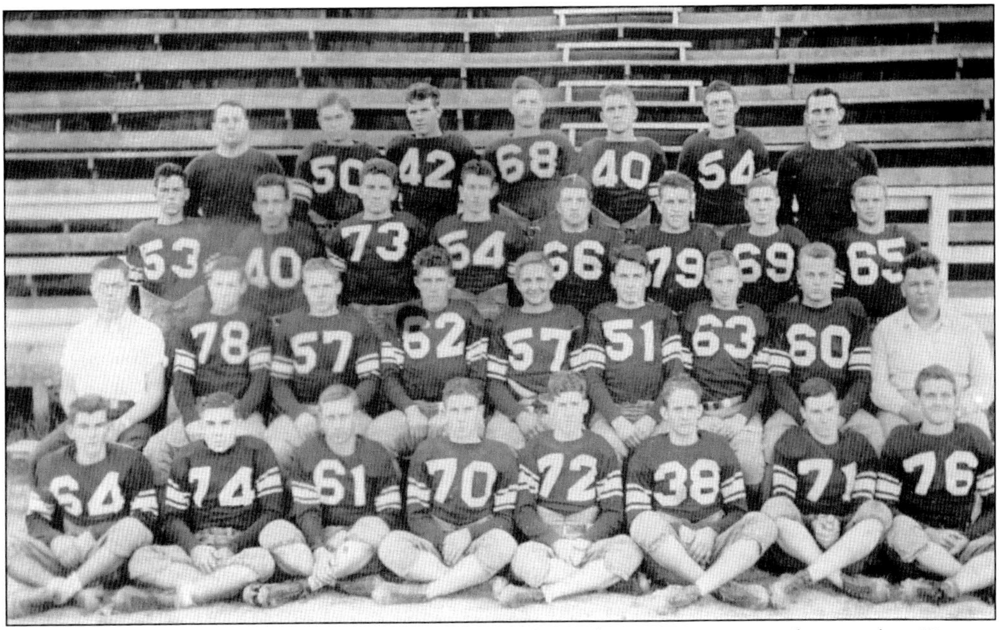

The 1931 Greenville High School football team showed great promise under coaches Dennis Vinzant (left) and Henry Frnka (right). Two years later many of the same young men played on the Greenville High School team that won the state championship. Later these young men valiantly served their country in World War II. (Courtesy of W. Walworth Harrison Public Library.)

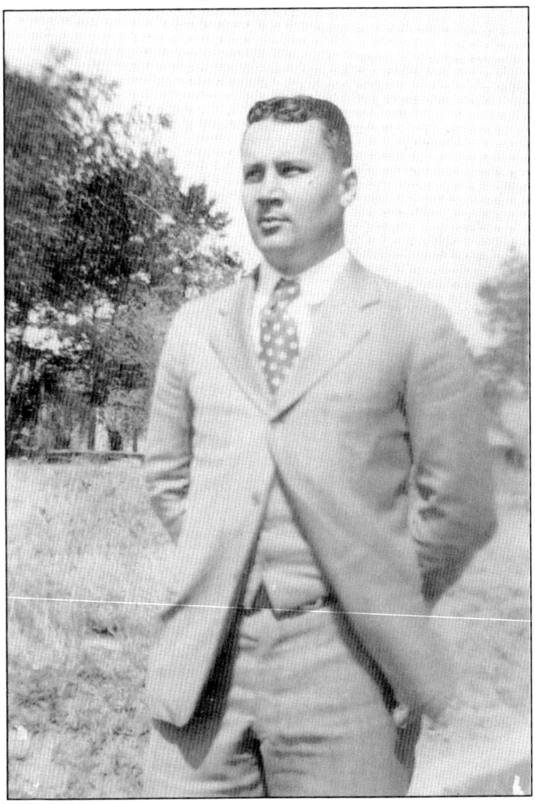

Henry Frnka led the Greenville High School Lions football team to a state championship win in 1933 and semifinal trophies in the two previous seasons. The Frnka era was one of the greatest highlights in Greenville sports. Frnka went on to coach at the University of Tulsa and Tulane University. (Courtesy of W. Walworth Harrison Public Library.)

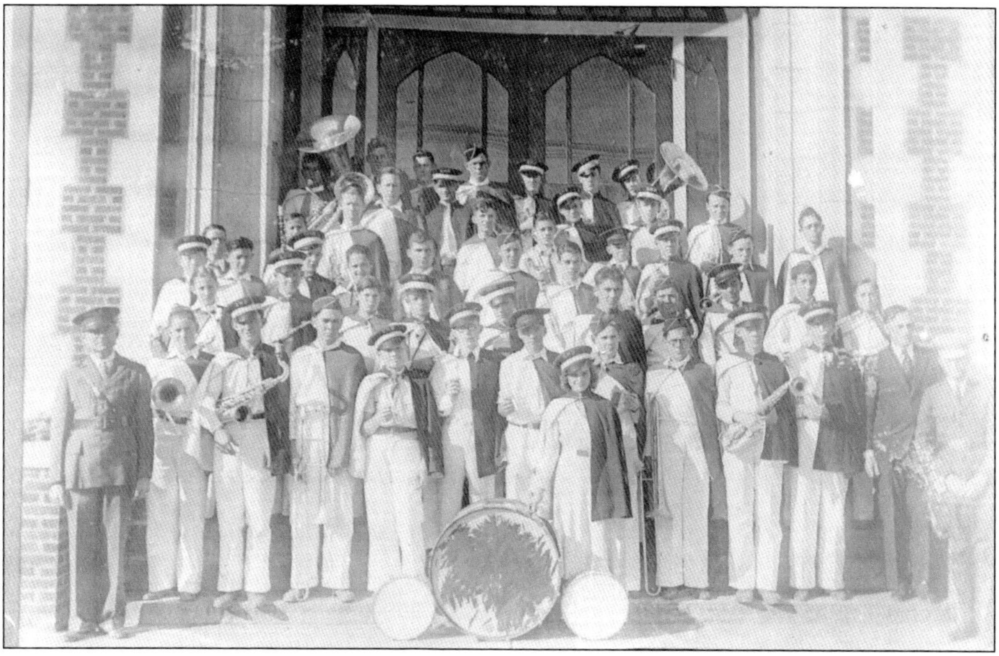

The Greenville Senior High School Band was organized in 1931 under the directorship of Marvin Bush, who also served as the director of the Greenville Municipal Band. Practicing only three days per week, the band performed at all Greenville High School football games, other school events, and in the many parades held in the city. (Courtesy of W. Walworth Harrison Public Library.)

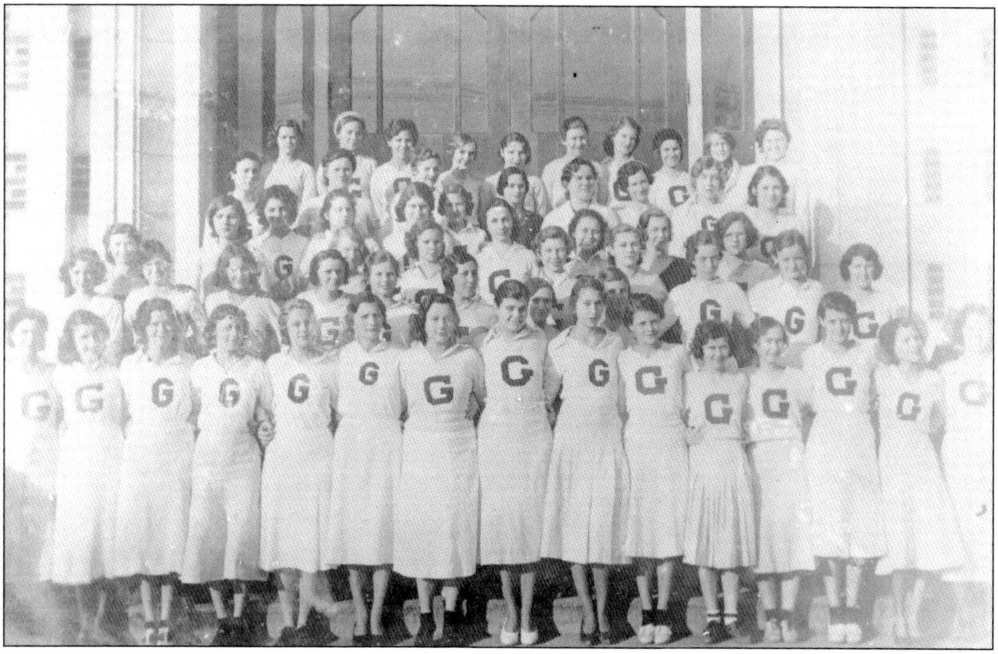

Greenville High School faculty member Gussie Nell Davis organized the Senior High Pep Squad in 1931, the same year the Senior High Band was formed. Like the band, the pep squad performed at all football games, other school events, and local parades. Both the band and pep squad practiced after school. (Courtesy of W. Walworth Harrison Public Library.)

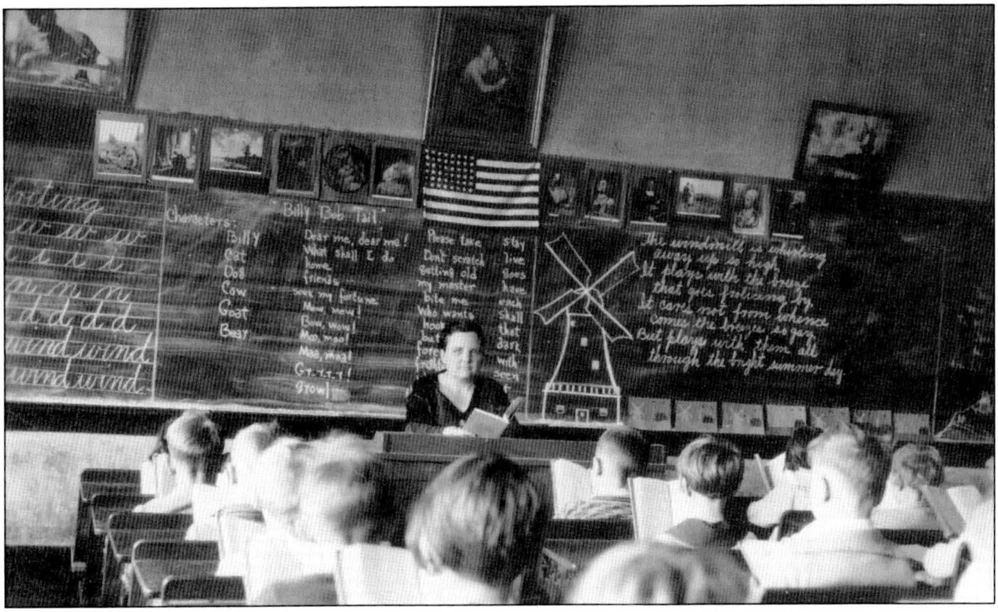

Students were expected to master literature, poetry, and penmanship. The Women's Review Club, instrumental in the founding of the Carnegie Library, purchased patriotic art prints for each classroom. The club also contributed to the school libraries and classroom libraries. Many former students remember spending afternoons and summer vacation at the Carnegie Library. (Courtesy of the author.)

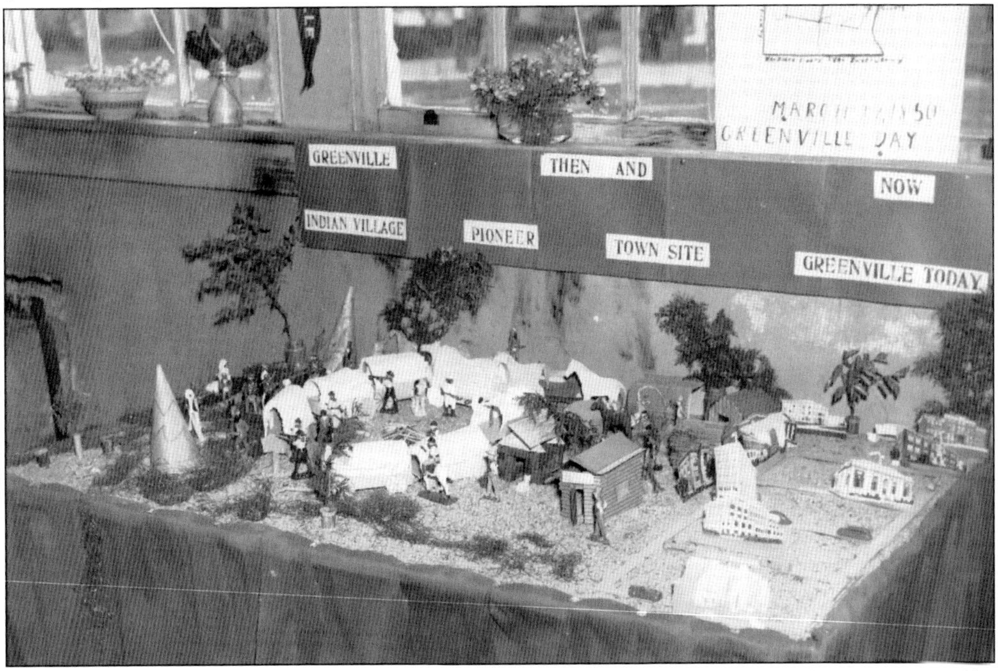

Mae Moulton Harrison (1863–1949), local historian and primary school teacher in Greenville, began her teaching career in 1881. It was through her efforts that citizens became aware of the rich history of the city. In her classroom every year, she crafted a diorama of early Greenville with the addition of more recent major buildings. (Courtesy of the author.)

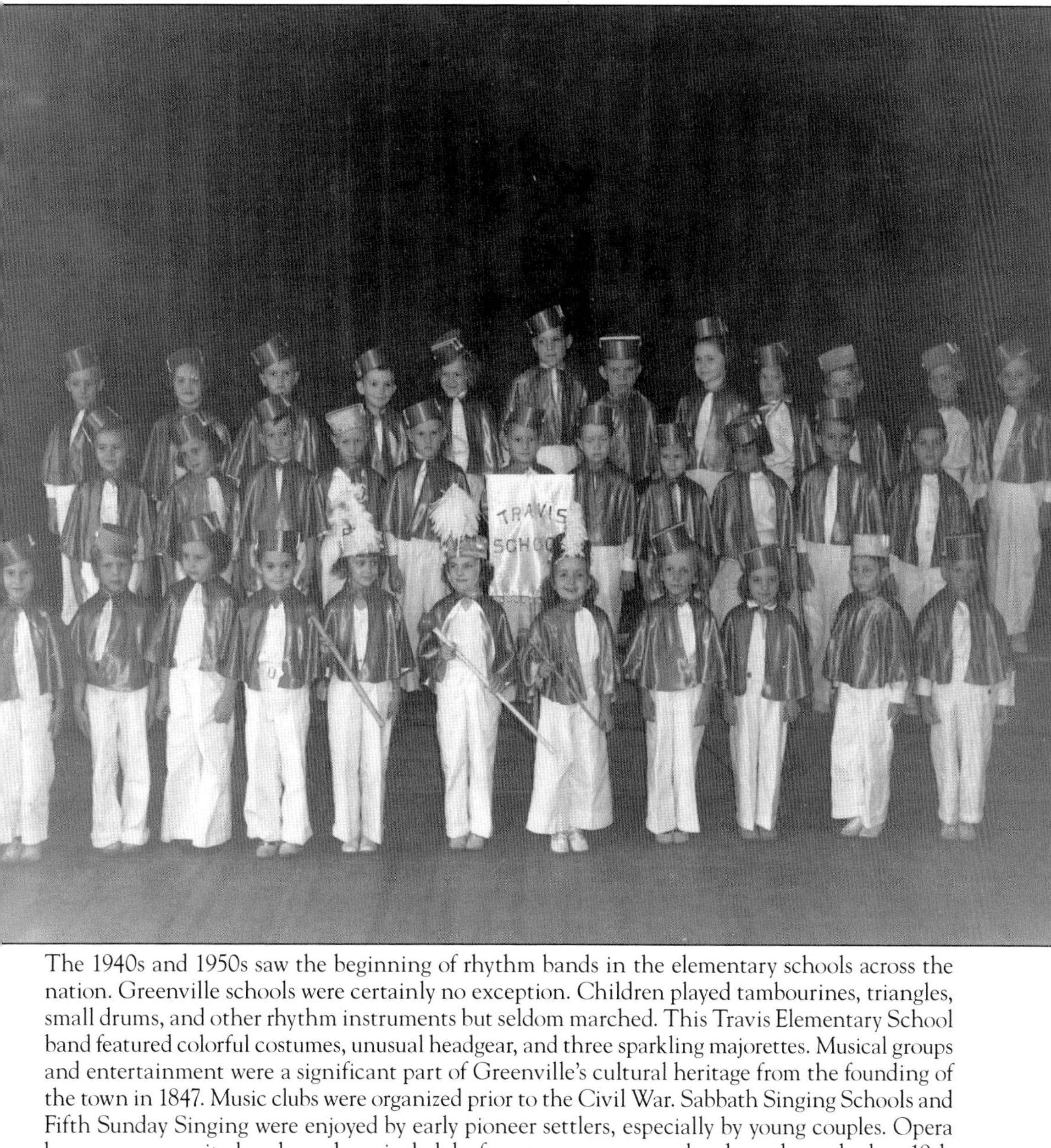

The 1940s and 1950s saw the beginning of rhythm bands in the elementary schools across the nation. Greenville schools were certainly no exception. Children played tambourines, triangles, small drums, and other rhythm instruments but seldom marched. This Travis Elementary School band featured colorful costumes, unusual headgear, and three sparkling majorettes. Musical groups and entertainment were a significant part of Greenville's cultural heritage from the founding of the town in 1847. Music clubs were organized prior to the Civil War. Sabbath Singing Schools and Fifth Sunday Singing were enjoyed by early pioneer settlers, especially by young couples. Opera houses, community bands, and musical clubs for women were popular throughout the late 19th and early 20th centuries. Dallas Symphony in Greenville, Greenville Entertainment Series, and the Kenneth Threadgill Series are venues that continue to provide musical enjoyment to the citizens in the 21st century. (Courtesy of the author.)

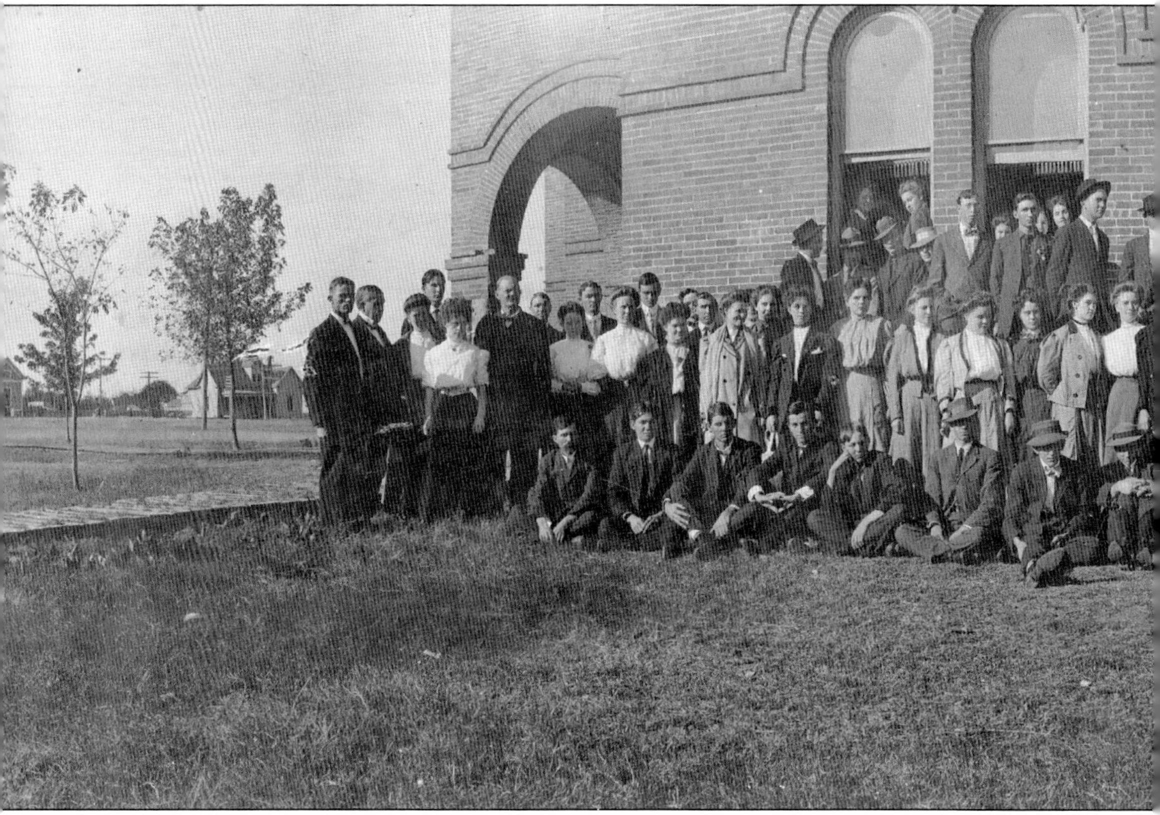

At the Hunt County Baptist Association meeting in 1894 in the neighboring community of Celeste, the idea of a college was formed. The following year a charter was obtained for 50 years. The school began with capital stock of $50,000 and 13 trustees, seven of whom were to be from Greenville. By 1898, all trustees were members of the Baptist Church. Land for the college was donated by nearby residents, including developer Dr. Robert Sayle.

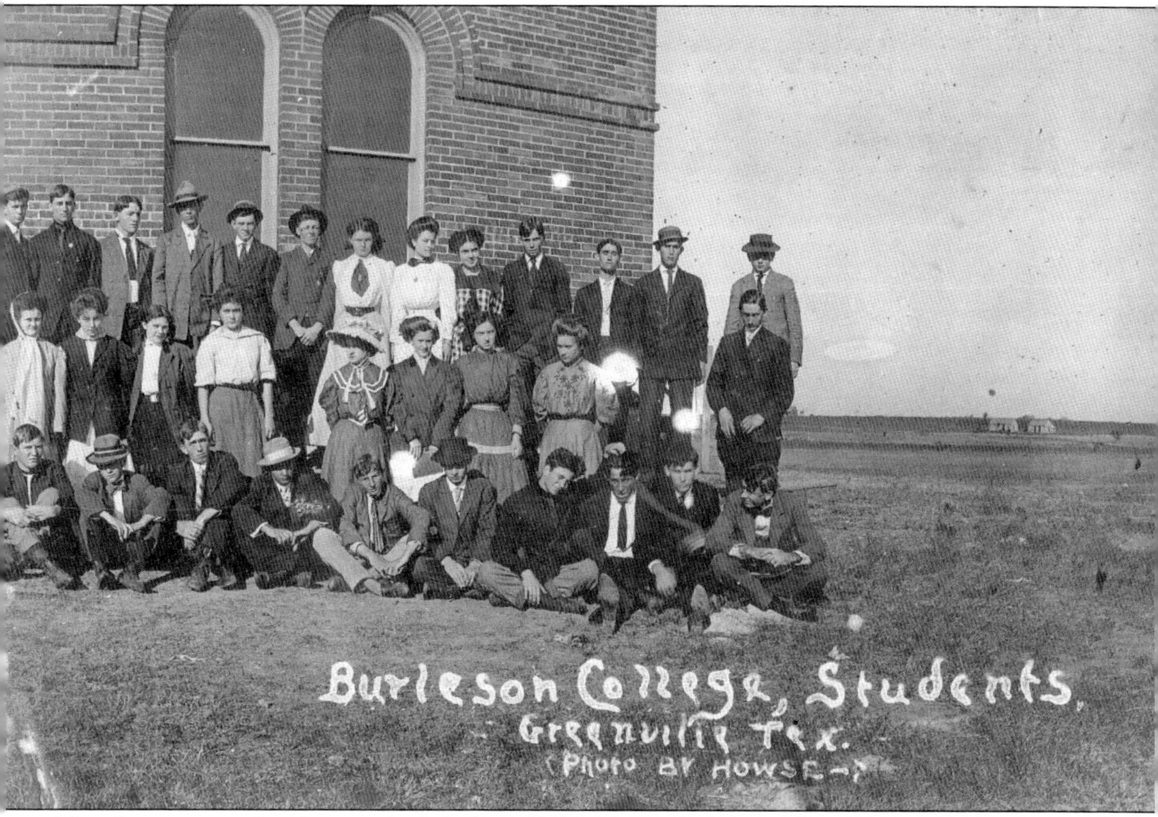

The administration building was built for $14,175. Students at Burleson College gathered for a group photograph in front of the administration building in this undated picture. One former student of the college told how he would stand at one side of a group picture while the photographer snapped his camera and then he would run behind the group and stand on the opposite side of the group. Another trick students liked to play was to sit in windows. (Courtesy of the author.)

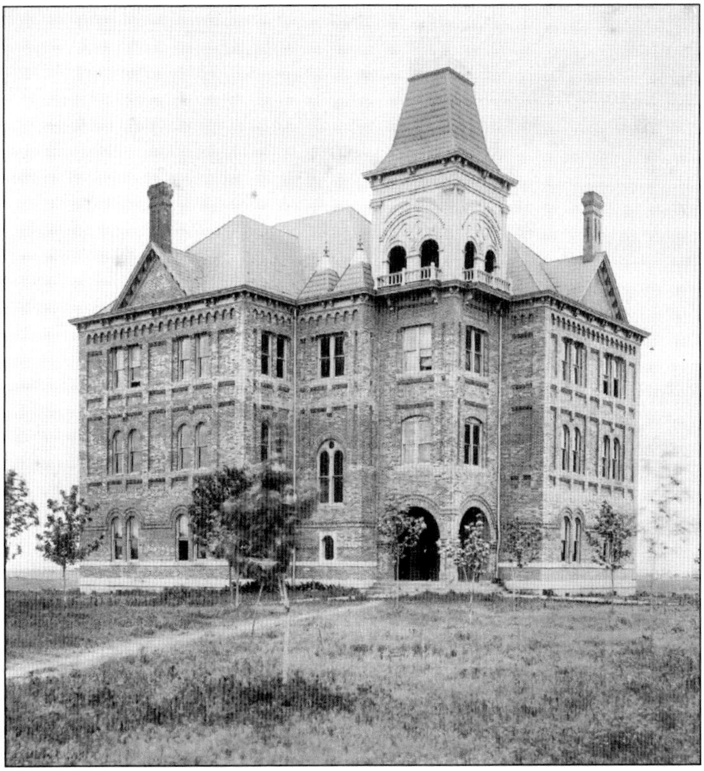

Greenville was home to three colleges; all located outside of walking distance to the downtown saloons. The oldest was Burleson College, founded by the Hunt County Baptist Association in 1895. Shown here, the administration building was located on one of the highest hills in Greenville and could be seen for miles around. (Courtesy of Hunt County Historical Commission.)

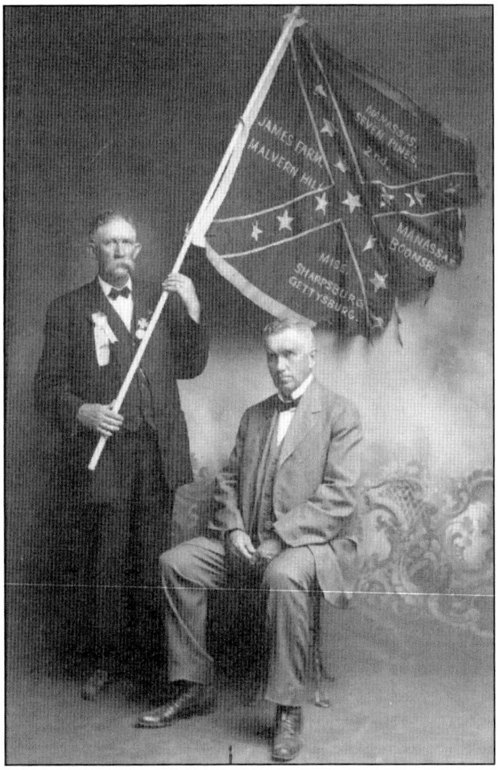

Prof. William Irvin Gibson (seated) served Burleson College first as president for seven years and later as head of the Language Department. An outstanding Greek and Latin scholar, Gibson was a veteran of the 2nd Regiment, Mississippi Infantry, and Confederate army before arriving in Texas. He graduated with honors from the University of Virginia. (Courtesy of Hunt County Historical Commission.)

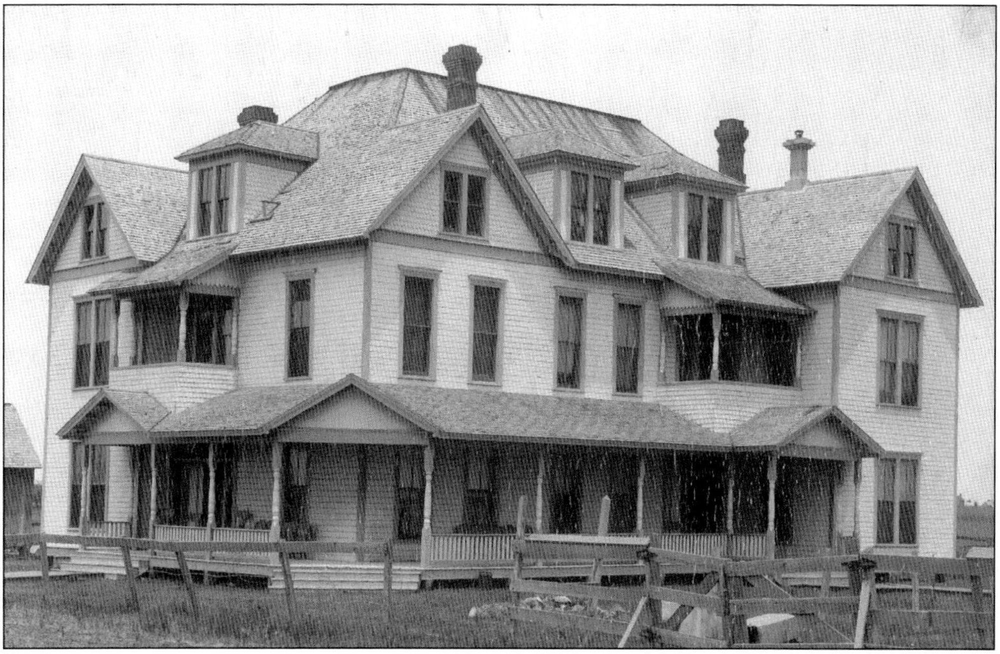

The College Dormitory for Young Ladies at Burleson College was described as a very comfortable building situated on the campus. Each boarding student was required to bring two sheets, two pillow cases, covers, towels, and toilet articles. Gentlemen were able to board with private families near the college. (Courtesy of Hunt County Historical Commission.)

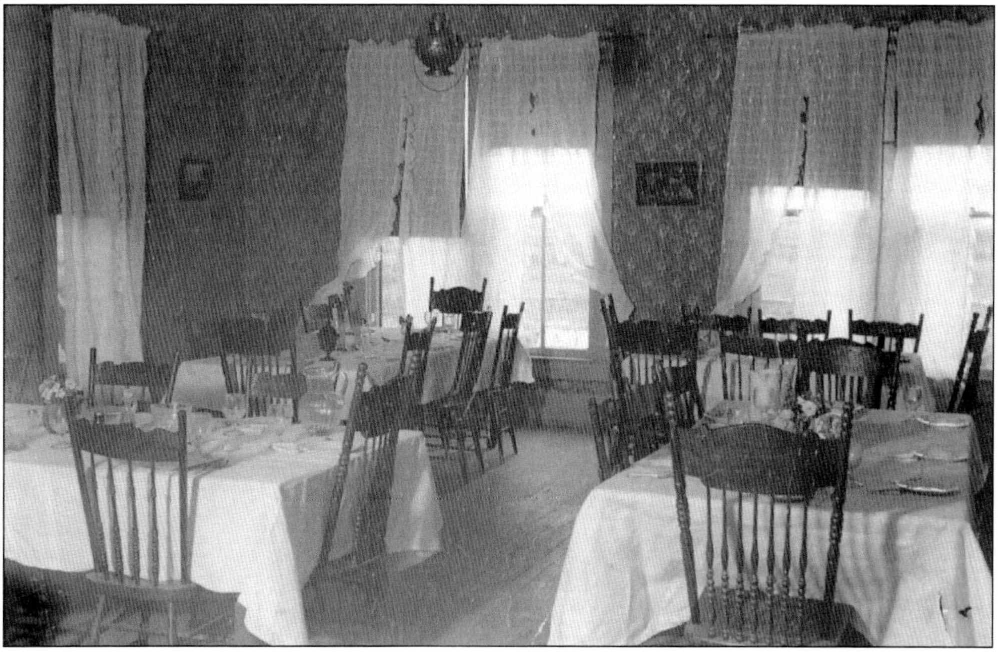

The dining room of the College Dormitory for Young Ladies was furnished in typical decor of the time. Freshly starched table linens, crisp white curtains, china, and silver were the order of the day. Young ladies were expected to be gracious hostesses and guests. Meals were served three times each day. (Courtesy of Hunt County Historical Commission.)

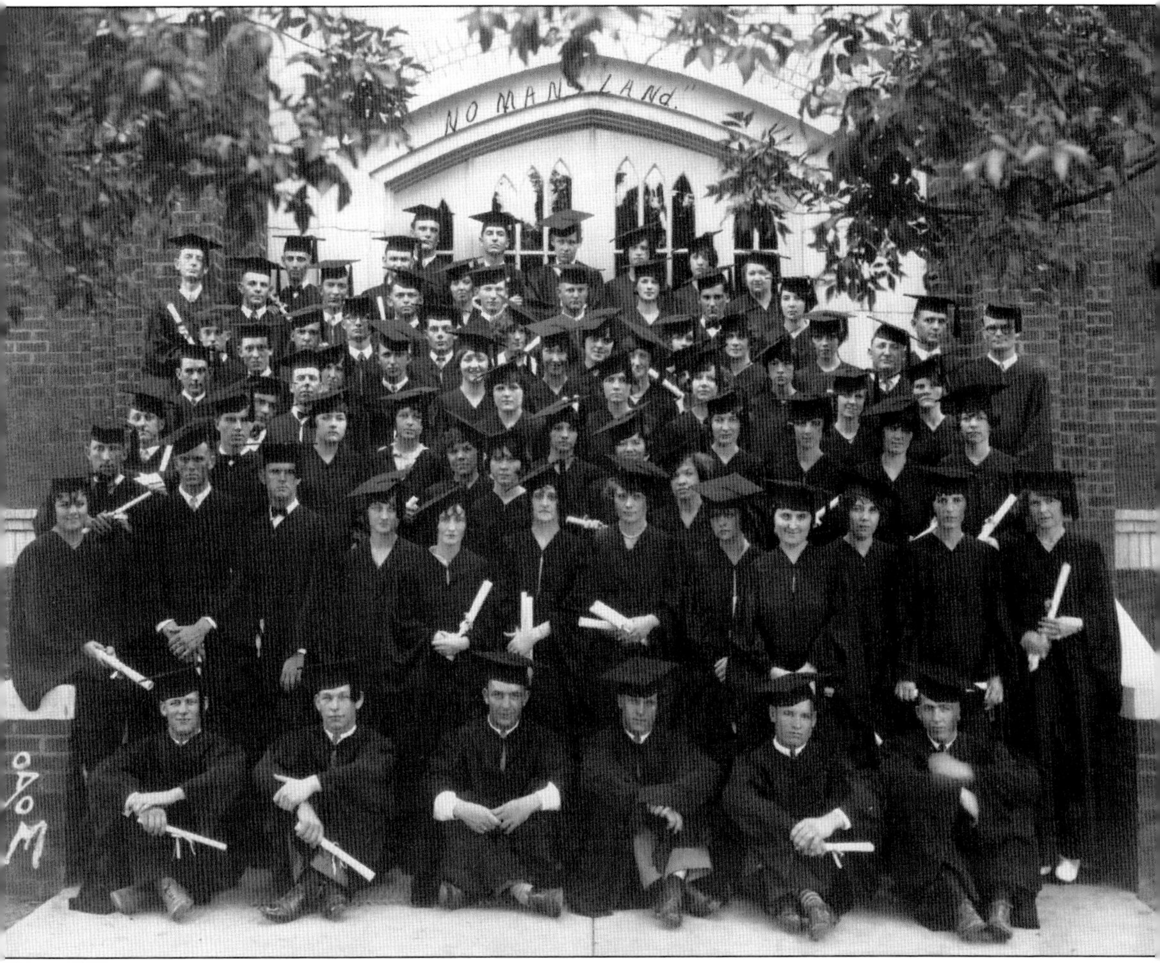

The original frame dormitory on the Burleson College campus was built for $3,000 in 1898. Young ladies occupied the first floor with some young men living on the second floor. The building was well chaperoned. Many of the young men chose to room in private homes near the campus. When the dormitory burned in the 1920s, a new brick dormitory for females was built on the Burleson College campus and ready for the fall term in 1925. The graduating class of 1926 posed for a class picture in front of the new dormitory. Some unidentified young man chose to write the inscription "No Man's Land" over the archway on this copy. The class of 1926 was one of the largest to graduate from Burleson. Constantly plagued by financial woes, the Baptist Junior College was forced to close its doors during the Thanksgiving holiday in 1931. The Great Depression and the proximity of East Texas Normal College, now Texas A&M University-Commerce, contributed to its demise. (Courtesy of the author.)

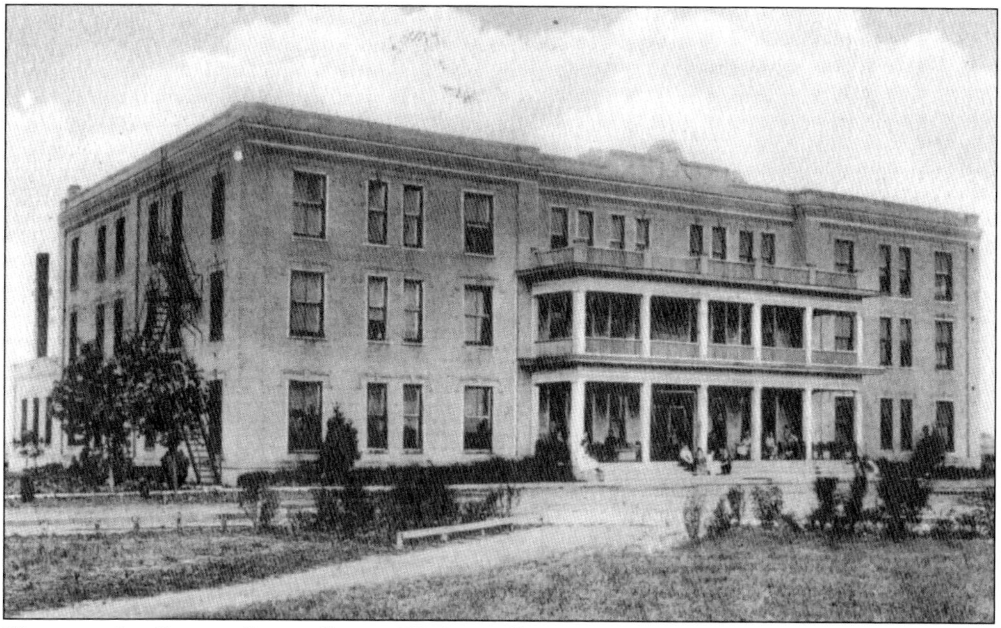

The second college in Greenville was Wesley College, a Methodist junior college located in the south part of Greenville. The school was originally in Terrell, Texas, but moved to Greenville in 1912. Two dormitories flanked the administration building. Wesley Hall was occupied by young ladies at the college. Young men were limited to visits on the front porch. (Courtesy of W. Walworth Harrison Public Library.)

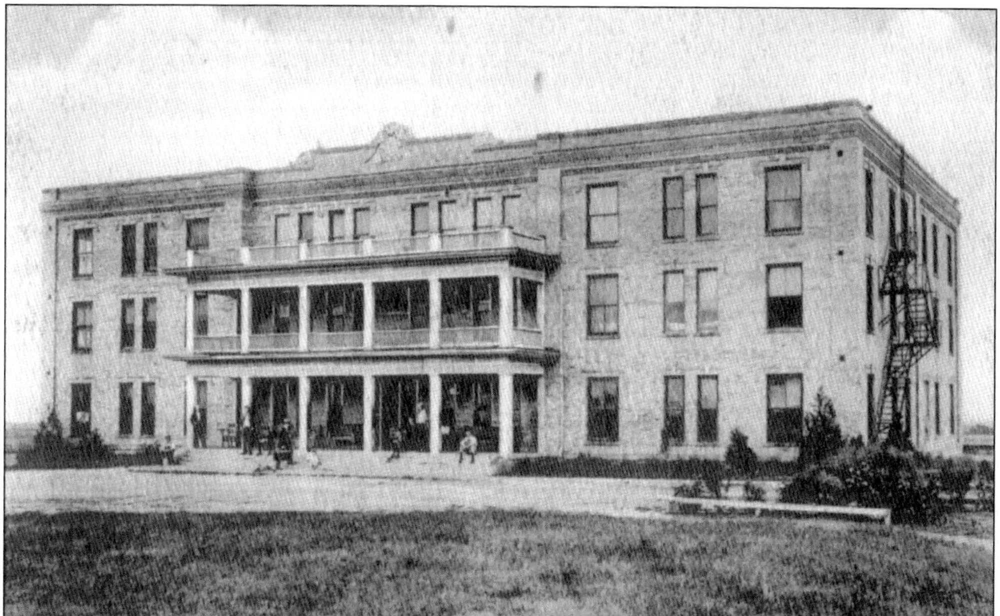

Delany Hall where young male students boarded was to the south of the Wesley College administration building. When the college opened in Greenville, it already had a reputation as a high-grade literary school aimed at preparing students for entrance into the state's universities. The opening enrollment in 1912 was 60 students. (Courtesy of W. Walworth Harrison Public Library.)

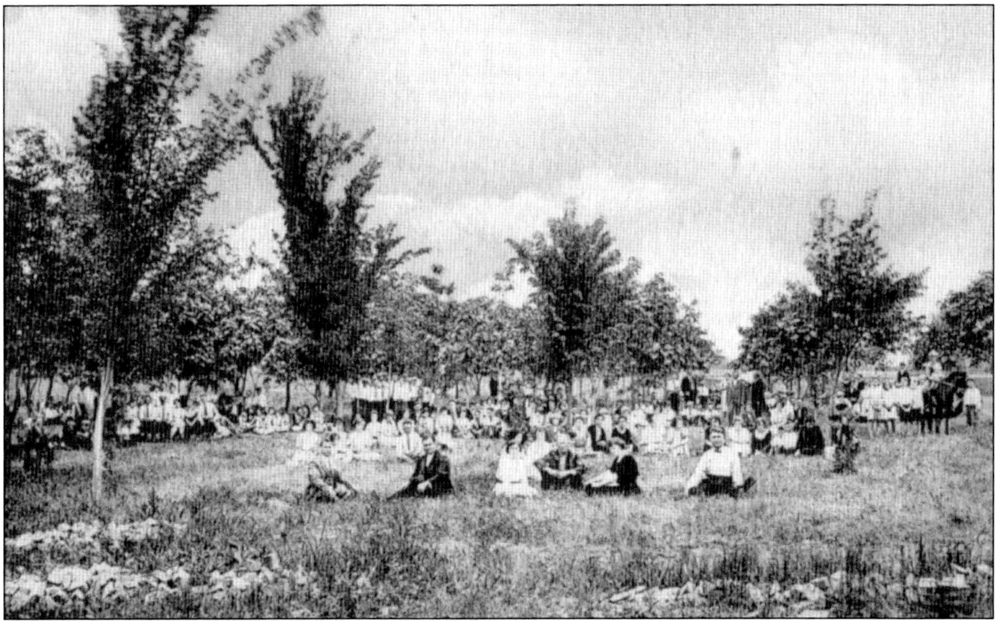

By 1926, Wesley College owned a 75-acre demonstration farm and elegant gardens. Shown here, the S. E. Greene Campus Park was the scene of many picnics, open-air classes, and an occasional camp meeting. Not only did the students and faculty of Wesley College use the park, but also townspeople were more than welcome to visit and enjoy the park. (Courtesy of W. Walworth Harrison Public Library.)

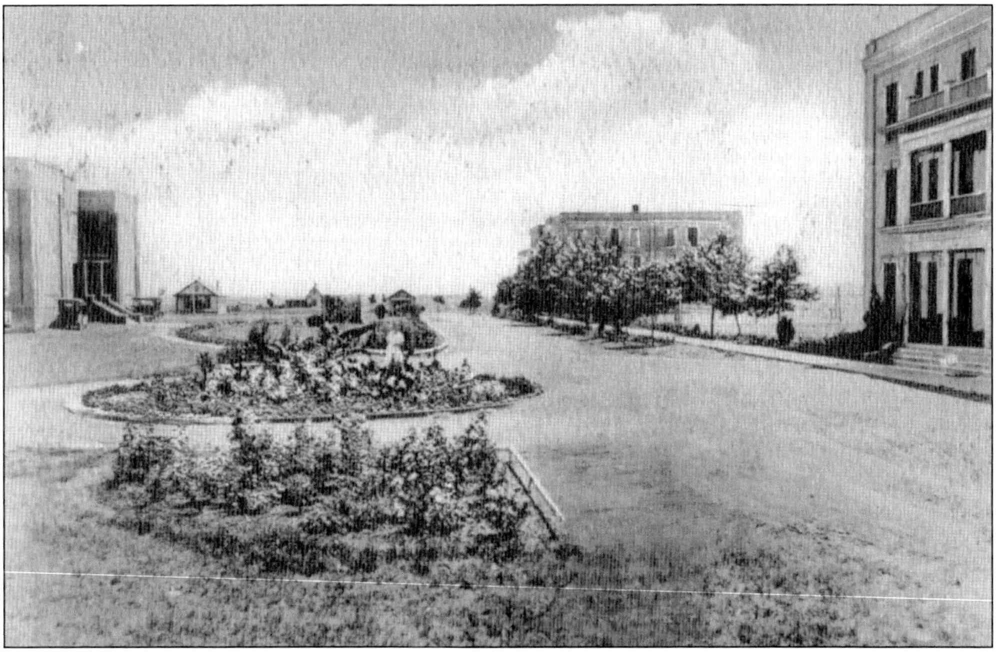

The campus at Wesley College was large with open space not confined by close neighbors; therefore, the campus was laid out with wide avenues and colorful beds of flowers. The area caught the interest of several real estate developers in Greenville who believed that having a college in the area would be an outstanding marketing tool. (Courtesy of W. Walworth Harrison Public Library.)

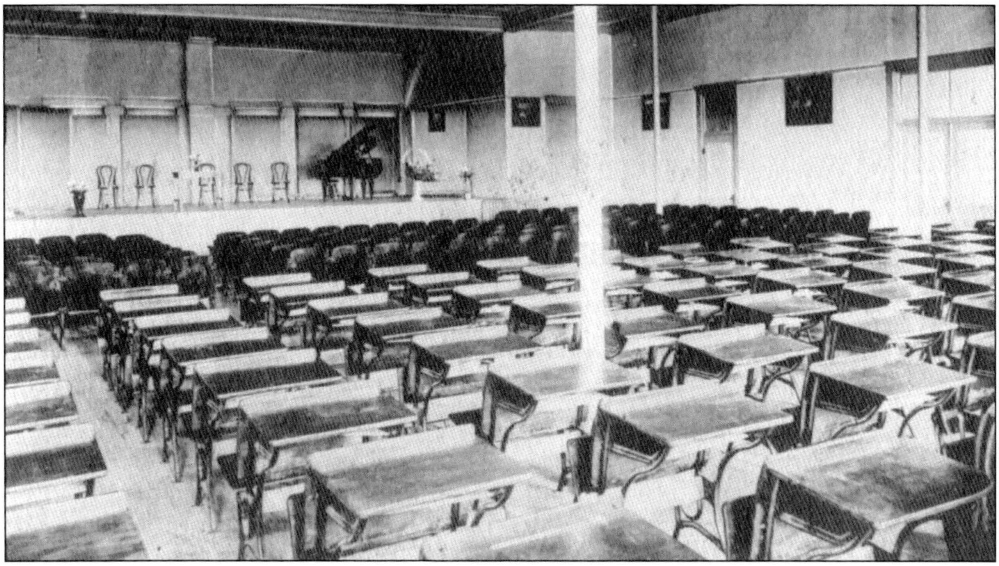

During its 26 years of existence in Greenville, Wesley College maintained an enrollment of approximately 500 students and employed about 15 instructors. Music was one of its specialties, offering lessons in voice, piano, and stringed instruments. The auditorium was often the site of professional quality recitals. At other times, rousing speakers motivated students. (Courtesy of W. Walworth Harrison Public Library.)

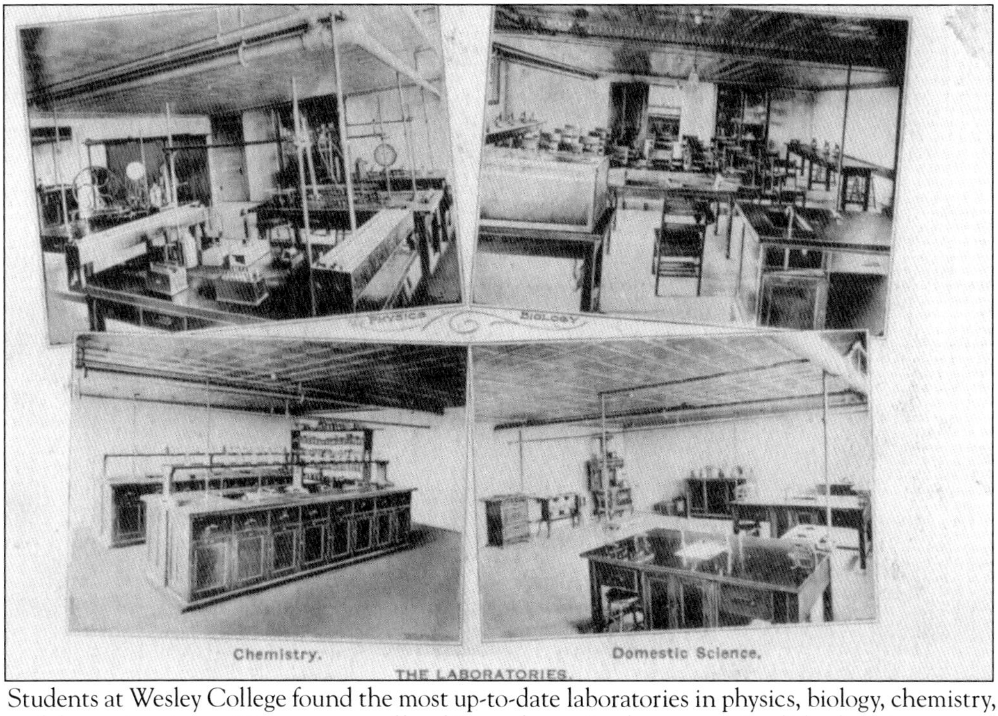

Students at Wesley College found the most up-to-date laboratories in physics, biology, chemistry, and domestic science. Courses were offered in mathematics, languages, English, the sciences, art, music, and business. Although associated with and partially supported by the Methodist Episcopal Church, South, Wesley was not a training school for ministers and missionaries. (Courtesy of W. Walworth Harrison Public Library.)

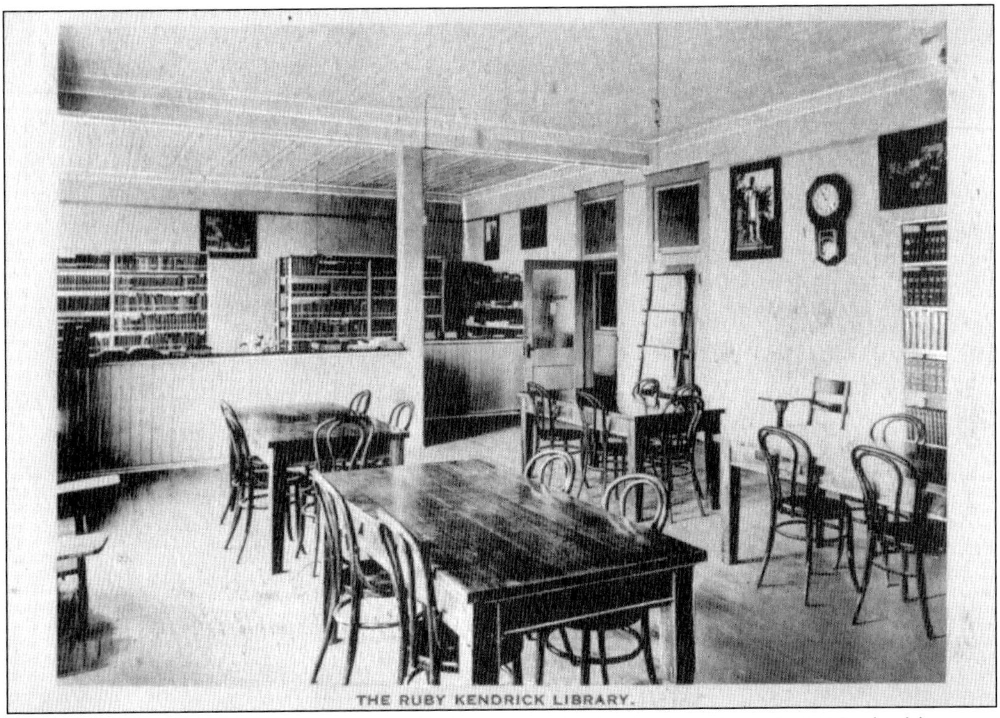

Named for young Methodist missionary Ruby Kendrick who died in Korea in 1907, the library at Wesley College was filled with more than 3,000 volumes. The dedication to Kendrick was fitting for Wesley students, most of whom were members of the Epworth League. Members of this group were devoted to missionaries such as Kendrick. (Courtesy of W. Walworth Harrison Public Library.)

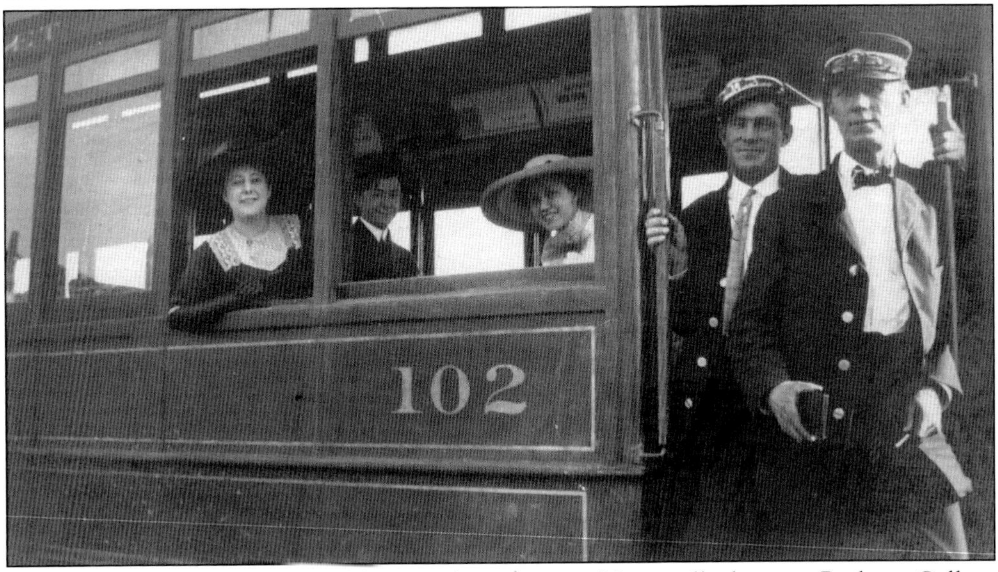

Wesley College was more removed from residential areas of Greenville than was Burleson College when it first opened in 1912. Fortunately, the Greenville Electric Street Railway laid tracks to the campus and an adjacent mineral well. Passengers rode the streetcars to obtain the healing waters of the well, and students made use of the inexpensive transportation to class. W. T. "Skipper" Wright, right, was the trolley man who befriended many Wesley students. (Courtesy of the author.)

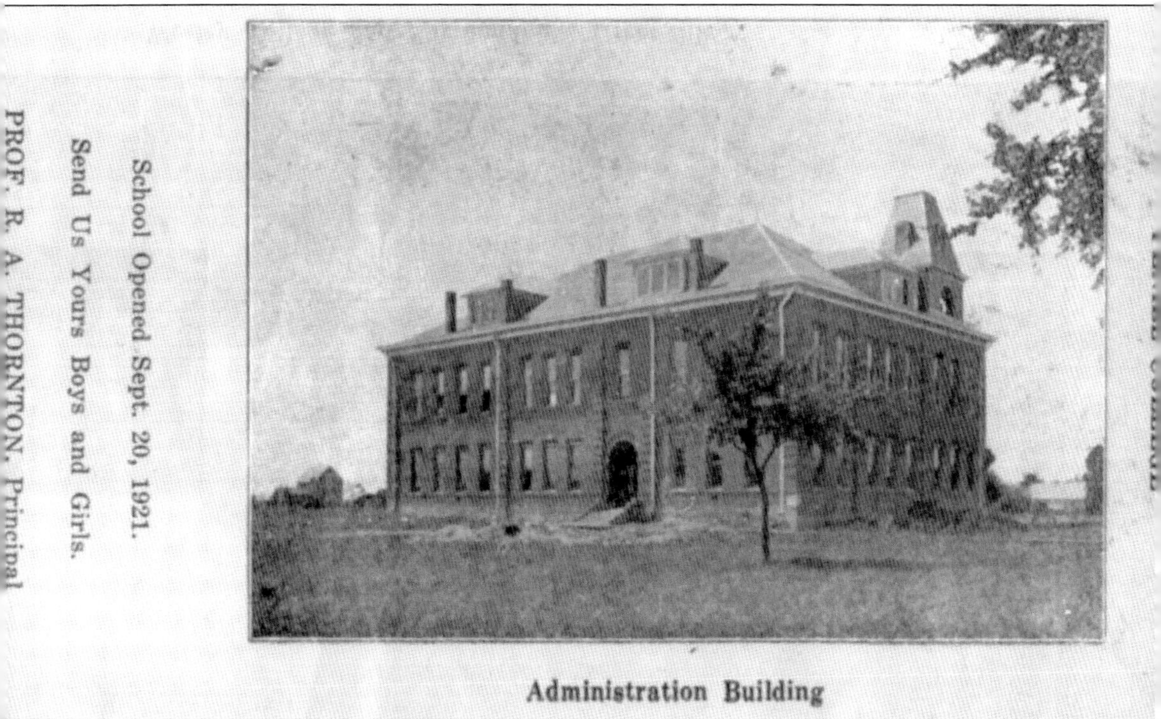

In 1894, Rev. E. C. DeJernette conceived the idea of providing a Holiness campground for the residents of Greenville and the surrounding area. He acquired a beautiful spot on the banks of the Sabine River northwest of Greenville. Later the 20 acres were devoted to a college campus, first known as Peniel College and later changed to Texas Holiness University in 1911. Founded in 1898, Peniel College opened in September 1899 with 77 students. By the end of the term, 108 students were enrolled. The Greenville Electric Streetcar Company ran a line to the college with the stipulation that no objectionable advertising, such as liquor, tobacco, theaters, or Sunday ball games, be displayed. It was claimed that no profanity was heard on the campus or in the community of Peniel. In 1920, the college merged with Southern Nazarene University in Bethany, Oklahoma. (Courtesy of the author.)

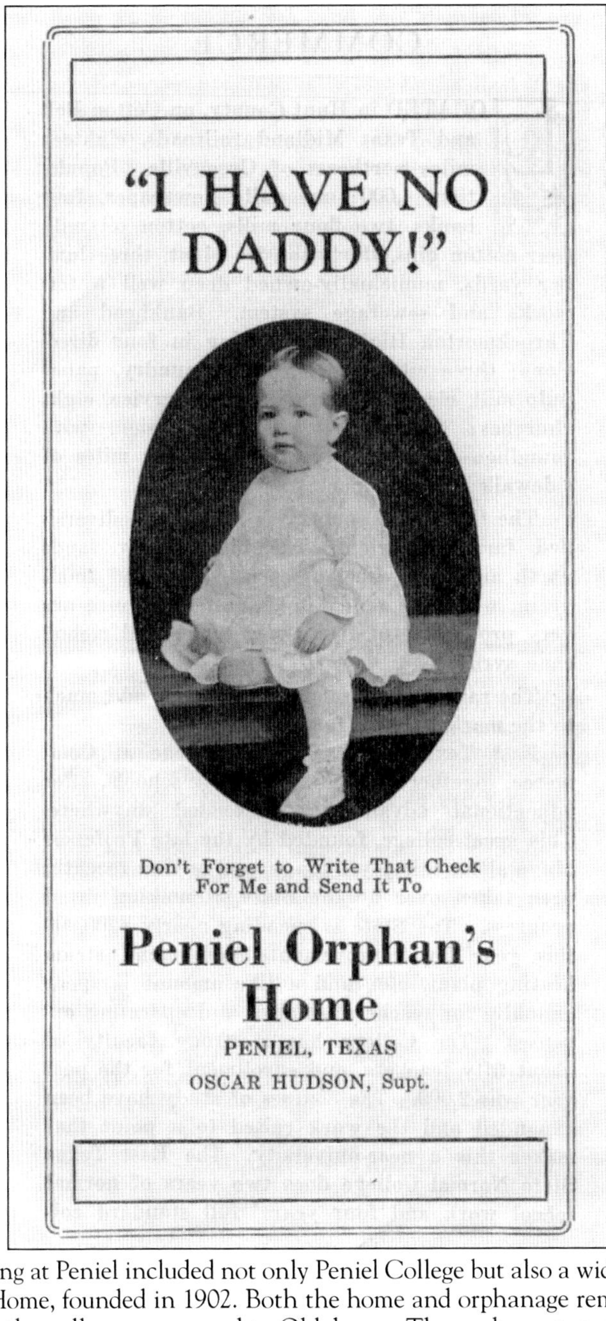

The parklike setting at Peniel included not only Peniel College but also a widow's home and the Peniel Orphan's Home, founded in 1902. Both the home and orphanage remained in the small community when the college was moved to Oklahoma. The orphanage consisted of one large building that housed the 30 plus children and a 40-acre farm. With little work and no means to support large families, many parents made the painful decision to ask for and receive help at Peniel Orphan's Home. Children from around the state of Texas found a new home here. Kindly, old Rev. E. C. DeJernette served as father figure for the orphanage. Churches in Greenville regularly brought clothing, toys, and food for the children. Local citizens regularly contributed to the needs of both the widows' home and children's home until the facilities closed in 1929. (Courtesy of the author.)

Seven

FUN TIMES

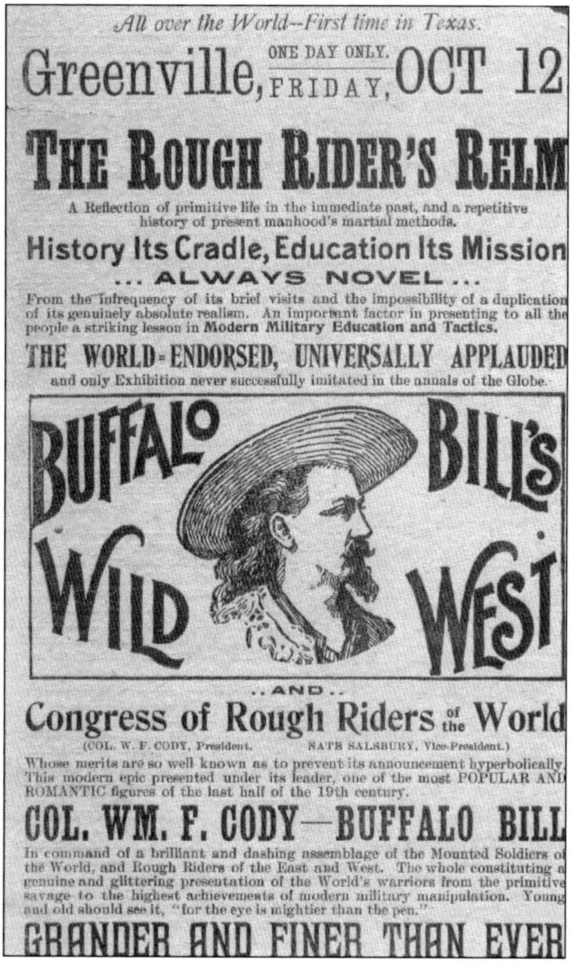

Residents of Hunt County enjoyed special entertainment on Friday, October 12, 1900, when Buffalo Bill's Wild West Show arrived to perform at the fairgrounds. Admission was 50¢ for adults and 25¢ for children under nine years old. The timing was perfect; farmers and tenants had recently sold their cotton crop and had spending money for entertaining the family. (Courtesy of the author.)

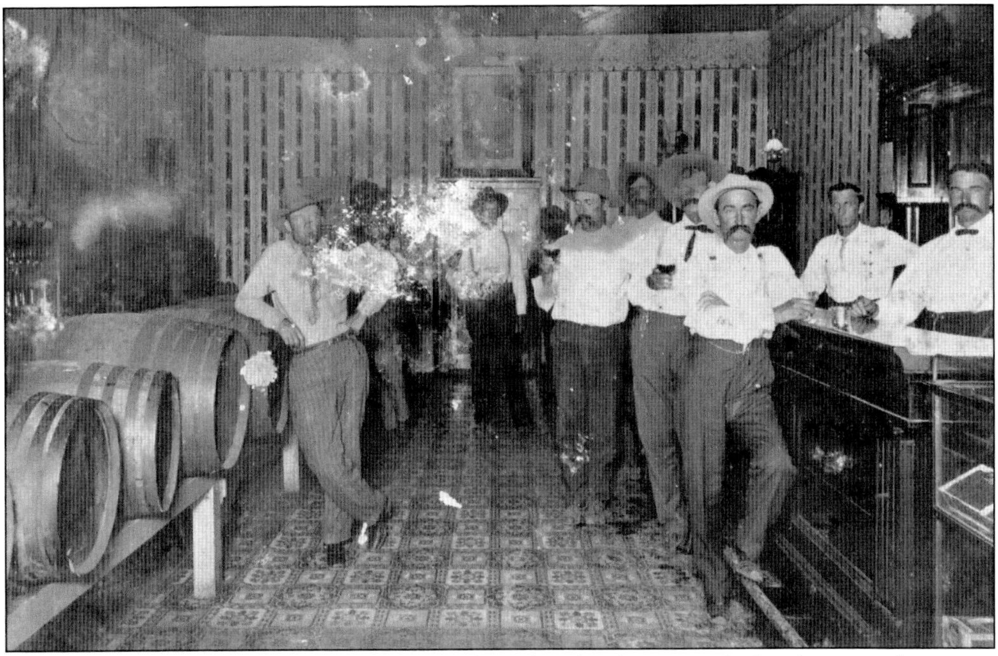

The buildings around the public square were dotted with saloons until a local option election in 1902 closed them down. Here locals and rural farmers were able to enjoy beer or whisky, a good cigar, and gossip with others. With no women present, hats were not removed inside the saloon. (Courtesy of the author.)

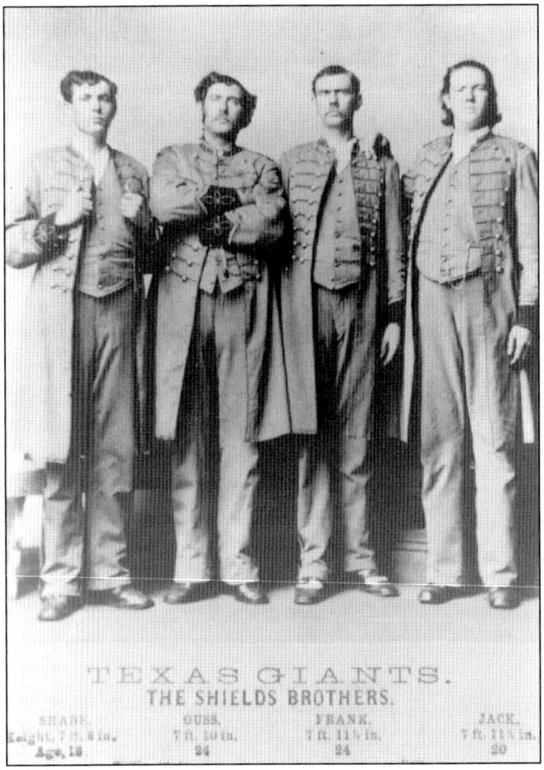

Shown at the far left, Shade Shields owned at least two saloons in Greenville; both faced the public square. Prior to entering the beverage business, Shade and his three brothers, known as the Texas Giants, toured with P. T. Barnum, Barnum and Bailey, and Buffalo Bill's Wild West Show. The brothers began touring in 1877. (Courtesy of the author.)

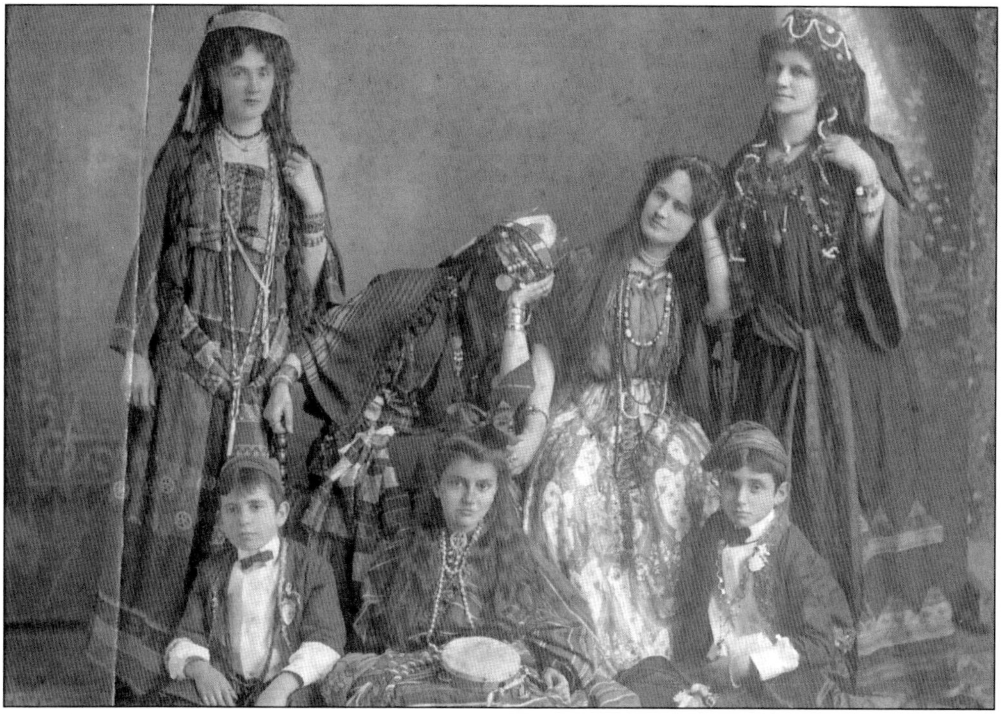

Not all amusements in Greenville were of the earthy sort. The Women's Review Club met twice weekly for intellectually enlightening programs. This photograph was taken at the Ben Hur Reception in 1903, held in the home of Franciska Rosenberg. The costumed cast performed an ever popular tableau. For this particular performance, the children of members were included. (Courtesy of the author.)

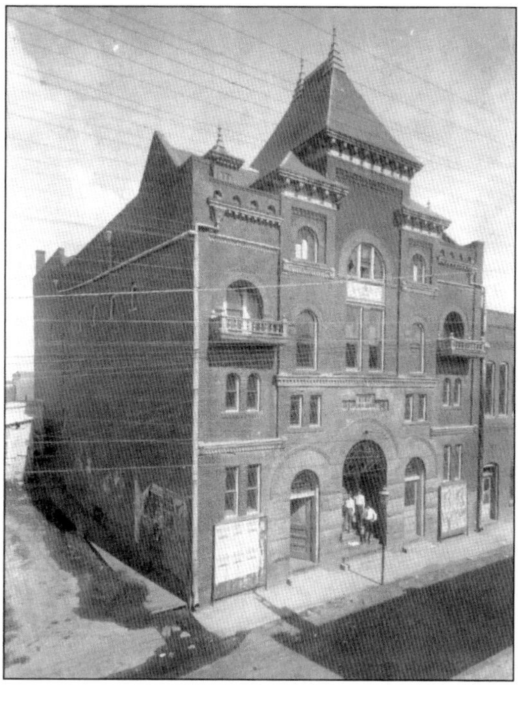

The King Opera House was chartered in 1890 by a group of stockholders led by Tom H. King. The following year King paid $30,000 for total ownership, the most ever paid thus far in Greenville for a piece of property. The building burned in 1894 and again in 1898. This photograph shows the King Opera House after it was rebuilt in 1901. (Courtesy of Hunt County Historical Commission.)

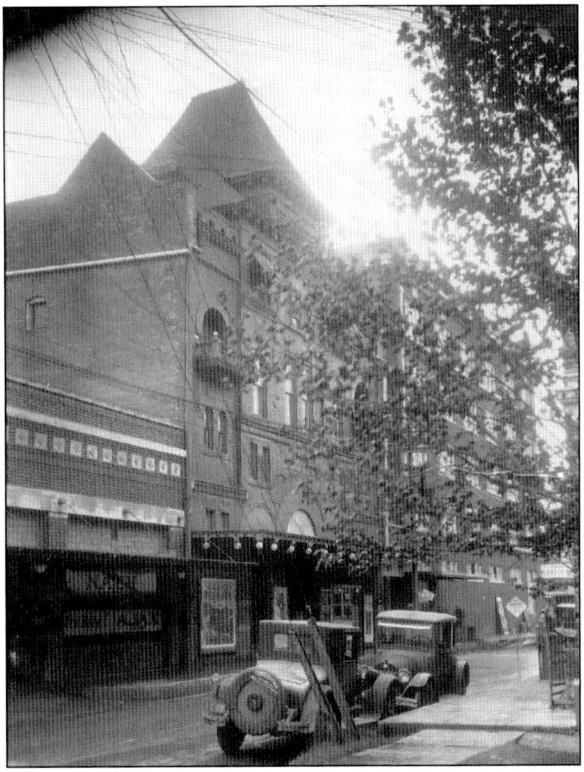

The first moving picture shown in the King Opera House was Edison's *Vitascope* during the 1896–1897 season. Throughout the life of the opera house, moving pictures, minstrel shows, and vaudeville performances entertained Greenville audiences. High school graduation lasted six evenings each spring with most of the events held at the King Opera House. (Courtesy of Hunt County Historical Commission.)

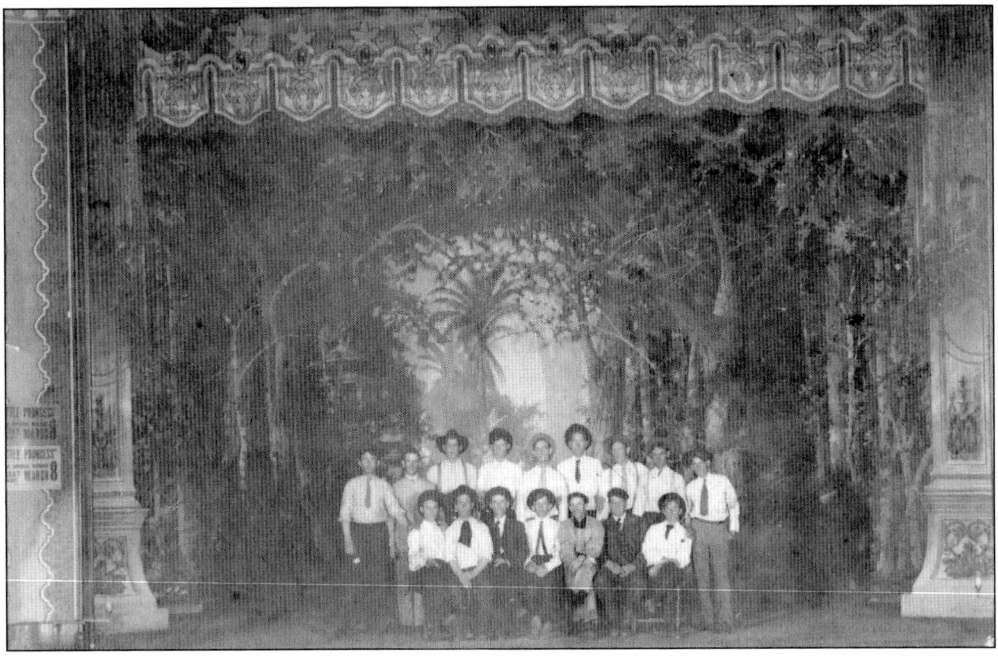

The permanent staff of the King Opera House posed on stage for this undated photograph. While working for manager Tom King in 1895, employee Joe Teagarden bought scenery and seating from Sosman and Landas of Chicago. The King Opera House was considered as fine as any theater in the South during its day. (Courtesy of Hunt County Historical Commission.)

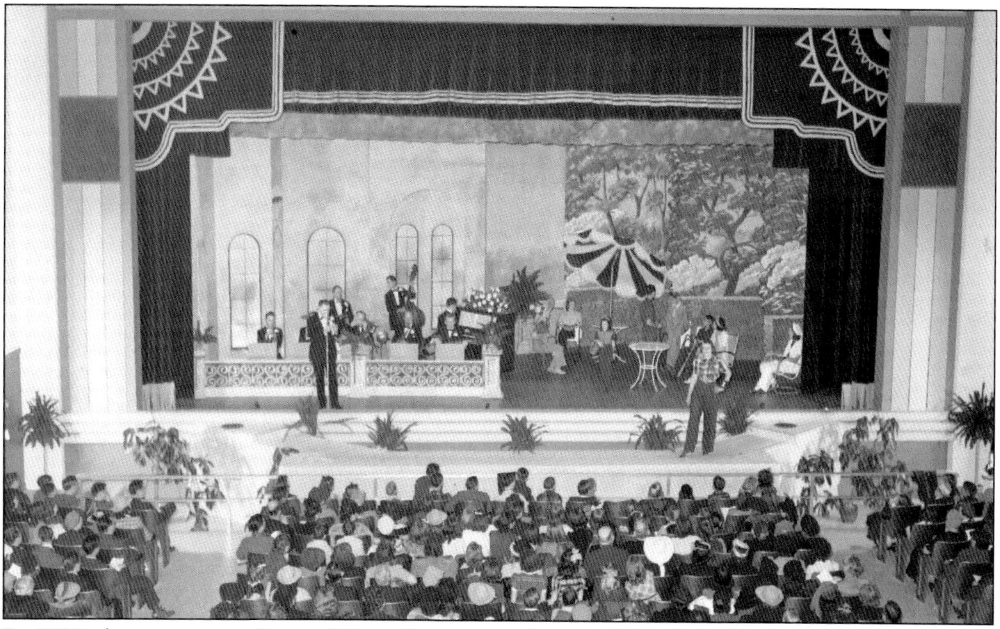

By 1920, there was a cry for a public auditorium in Greenville. When the King Opera House was razed in 1934, the need became more imperative. Finally, in 1939, the long awaited auditorium opened as part of the WPA–built Municipal Building. Since then, it has been home to the Greenville Entertainment Series, the Dallas Symphony Orchestra in Greenville, and numerous other musical venues. (Courtesy of City of Greenville.)

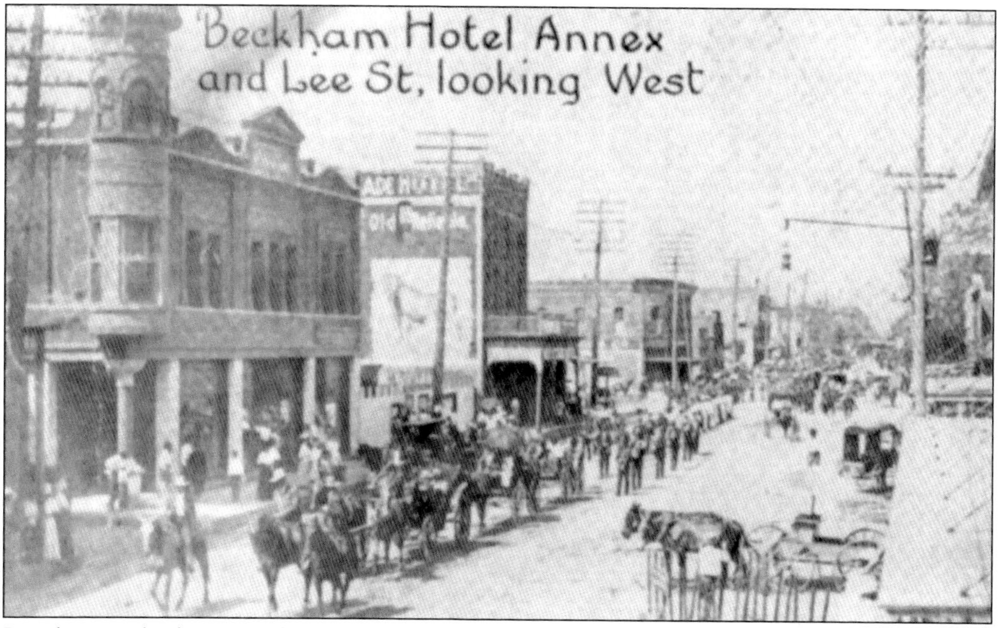

Parades were by far enjoyed by more people in Greenville and the surrounding areas than other forms of entertainment. Marching bands, dignitaries in fancy carriages, and handcrafted floats paraded from the Missouri, Kansas, and Texas depot to the public square at least once a year from the 1880s forward. This particular parade occurred after 1891 when electric streetlights were installed. (Courtesy of W. Walworth Harrison Public Library.)

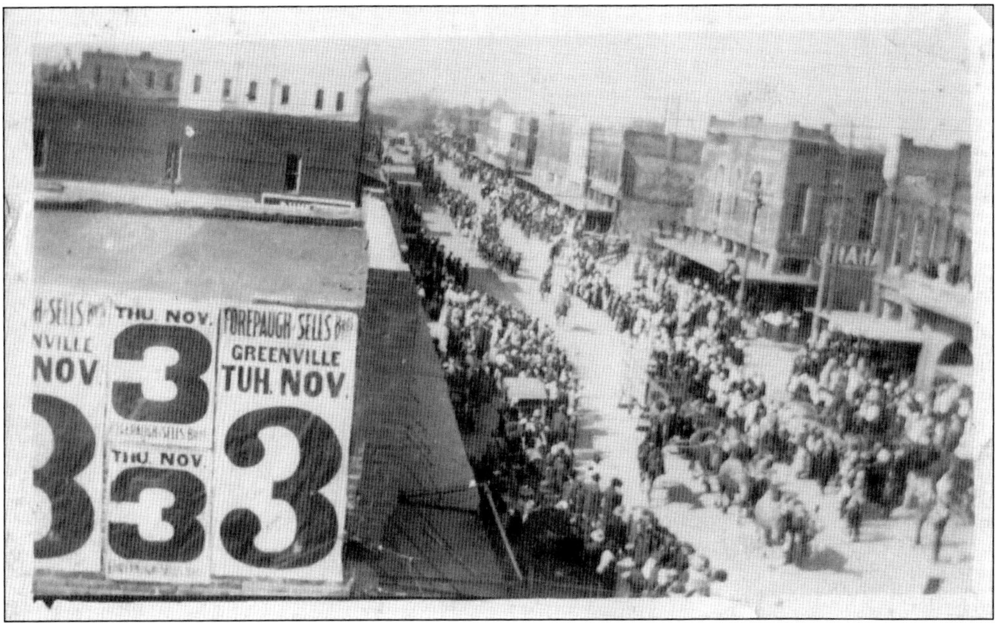

The Forepaugh and Sells Circus arrived in Greenville for a show sometime after 1902. Again the timing was perfect for cotton farmers to have cash for family fun. The large parade led by a bevy of elephants passed the public square on the way to the Exhibition Grounds on East Lee Street. (Courtesy of the author.)

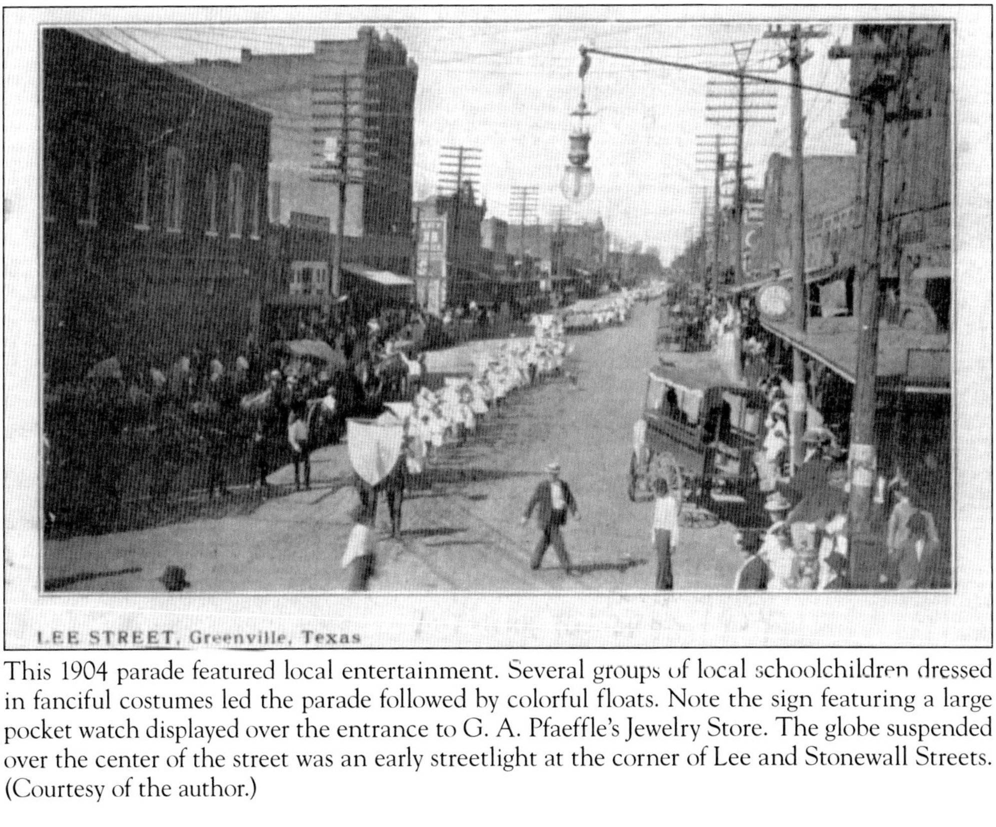

This 1904 parade featured local entertainment. Several groups of local schoolchildren dressed in fanciful costumes led the parade followed by colorful floats. Note the sign featuring a large pocket watch displayed over the entrance to G. A. Pfaeffle's Jewelry Store. The globe suspended over the center of the street was an early streetlight at the corner of Lee and Stonewall Streets. (Courtesy of the author.)

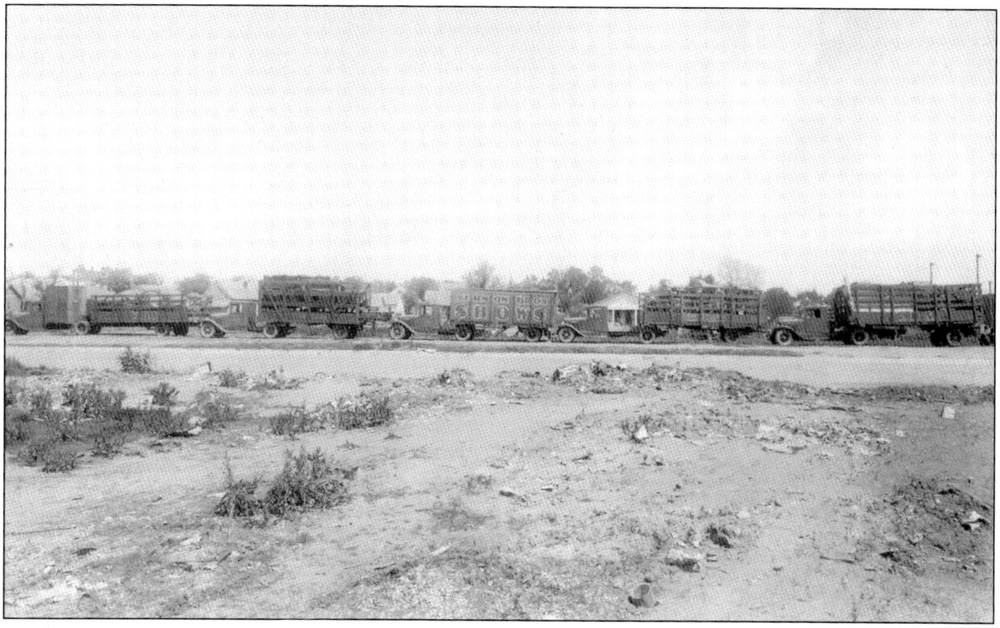

By the 1930s, circuses and carnivals arrived in Greenville in their own trucks. Vernon Brothers Show set up on a large lot in the east part of town reserved for circuses, patent medicine shows, carnivals, and other traveling amusements that crossed the nation during the Great Depression. At one time, soapbox orators espoused such controversial topics as socialism there. (Courtesy of Hunt County Historical Commission.)

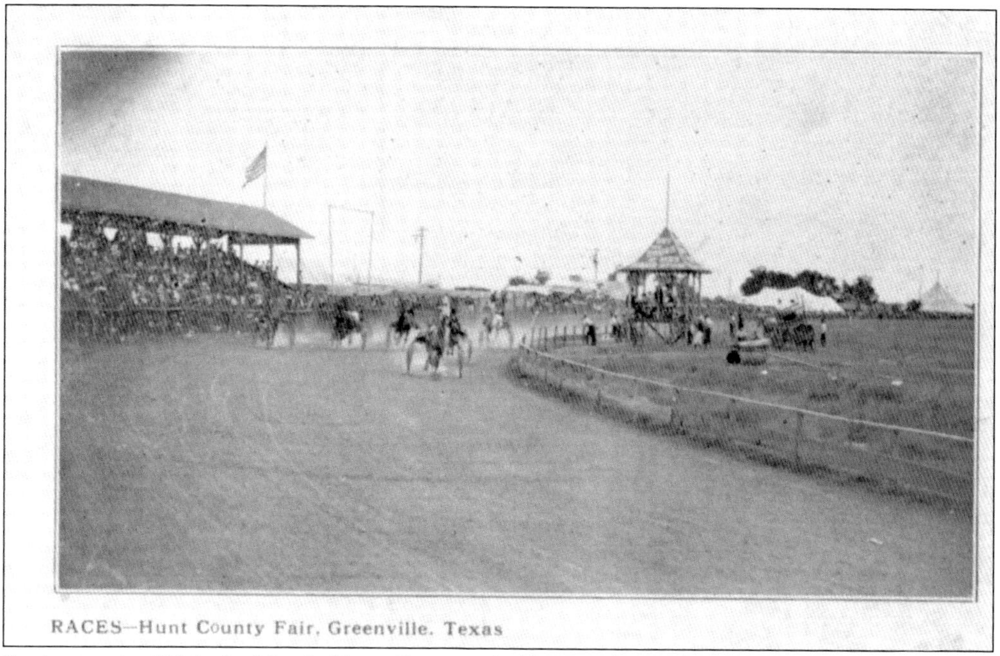

Beginning in 1904, the North Texas Fair was held annually in the fall. One of the highlights was horse racing of every sort. At a time when betting was legal in Texas, the fast half-mile track attracted race fans with horses from throughout the South. The first ice cream cones served in Greenville were at the North Texas Fair. (Courtesy of the author.)

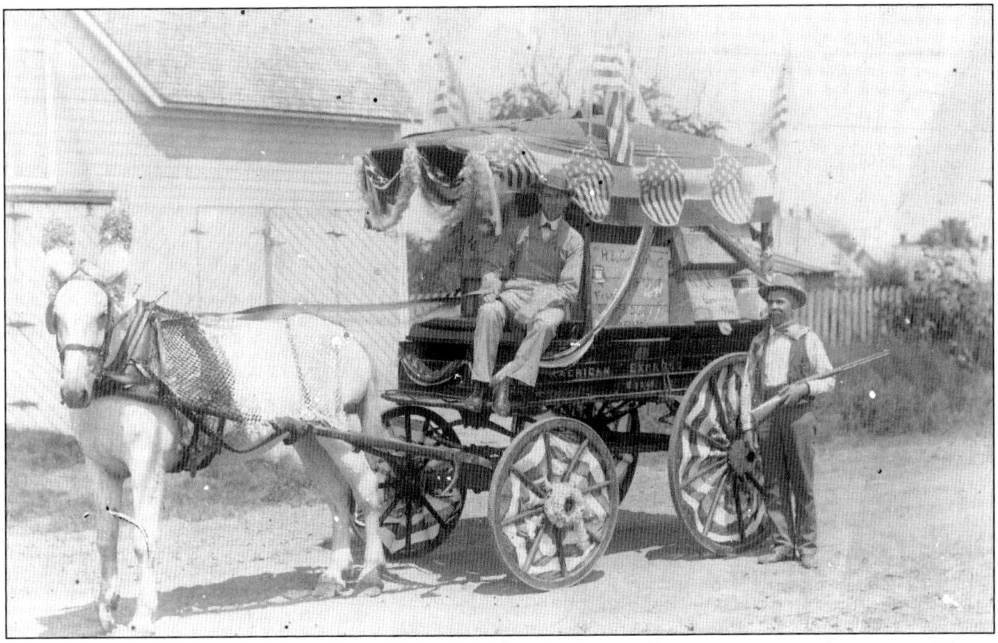

Whenever there was a local parade in Greenville, American Express was on the scene. These two photographs were taken on the same day at different locations in town. Brightly decorated in patriotic red, white, and blue, the dray was drawn by a white horse. Even the horse had a special hat to cover its ears. Careful examination of the boxes loaded on the dray reveal names of local businesses to whom American Express delivered on a regular basis. Amazingly, the names of senders were also included. Note that the dray had much larger rear wheels to enable it to travel through the rainy season and thick black mud. (Both courtesy of Jack Horton.)

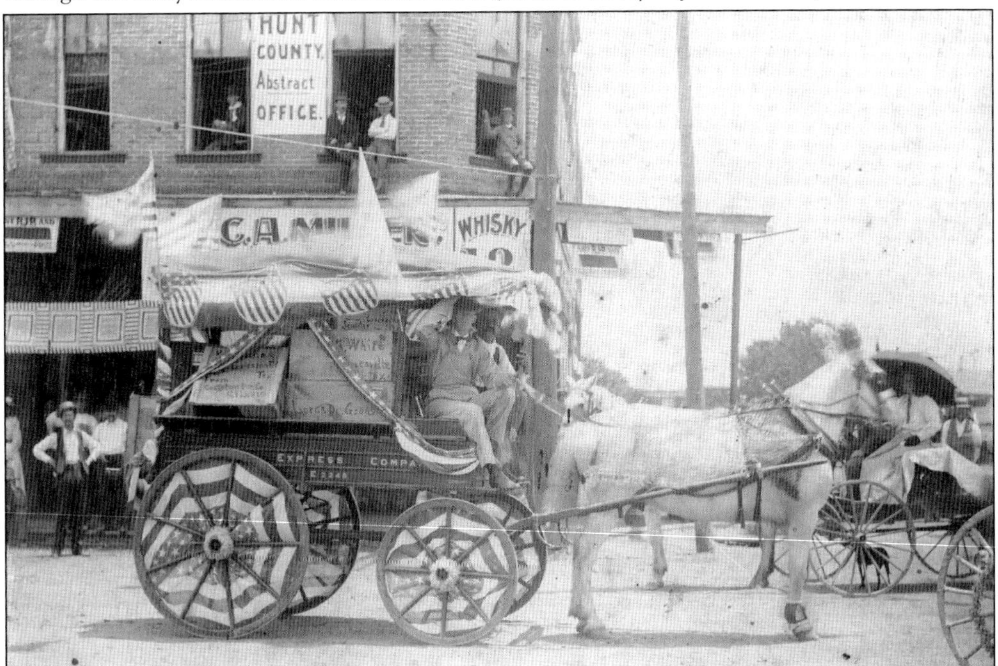

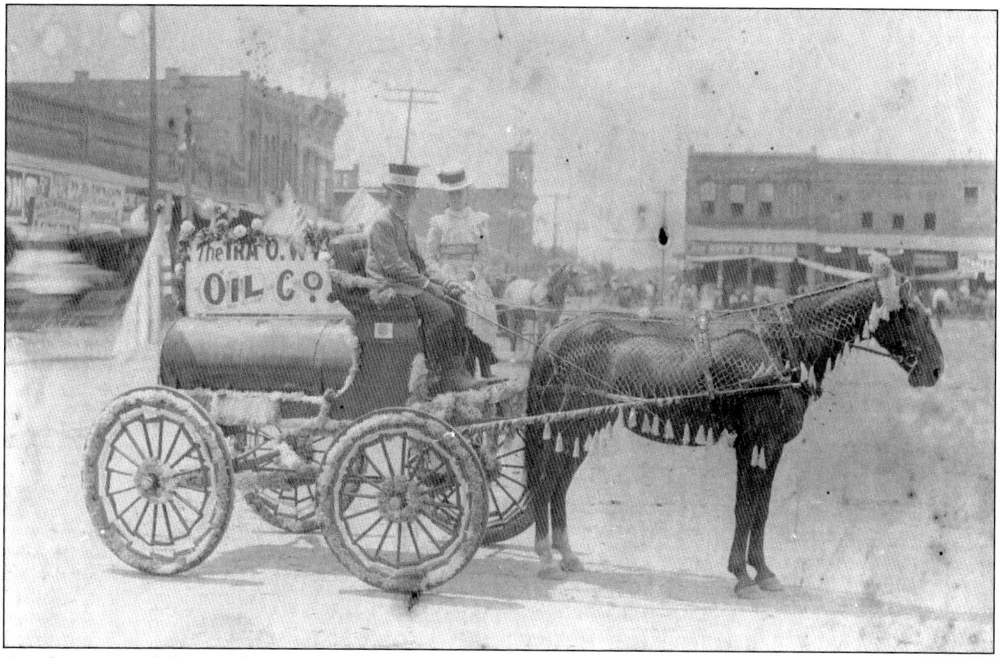

At the turn of the 20th century, Greenville merchants organized Midsummer Carnivals, two- and three-day events in July that began with elaborate parades. In July 1901, the Ira O. Wyse Oil Company entered this decorative float with one of its oil barrels. The buggy, the riders, and even the mule were festively decked out. (Courtesy of Jack Horton.)

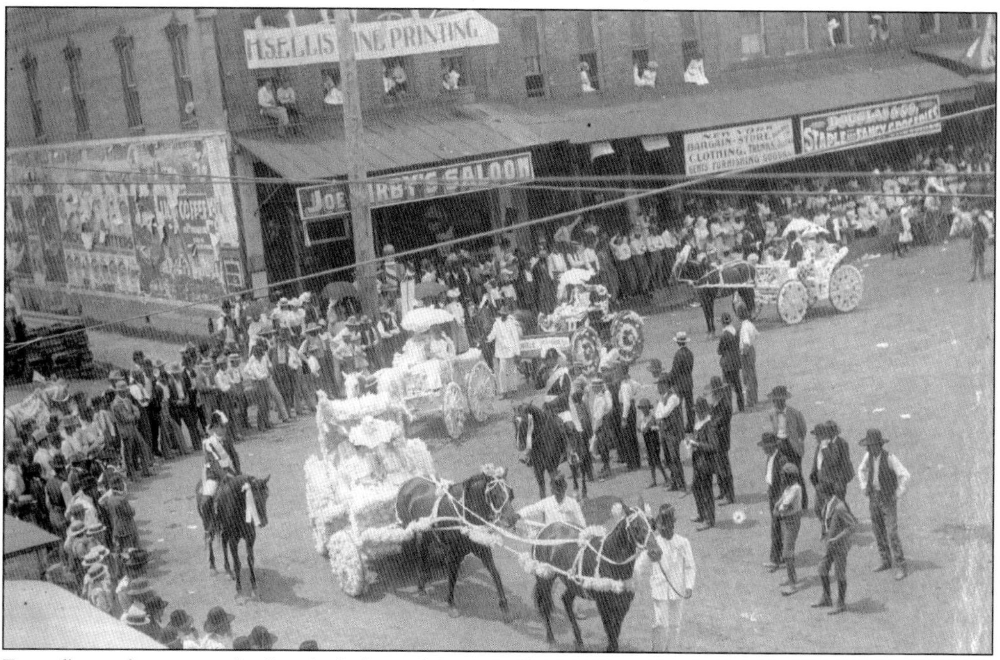

Four floats featuring the lovely ladies of Greenville made the turn on the southeast corner of the public square. Note the crowds enjoying the parade from the second-floor windows of Joe Kirby's Saloon. Few if any women drove their carriages; either a man rode with them or African Americans dressed as footmen led the horses. (Courtesy of Jack Horton.)

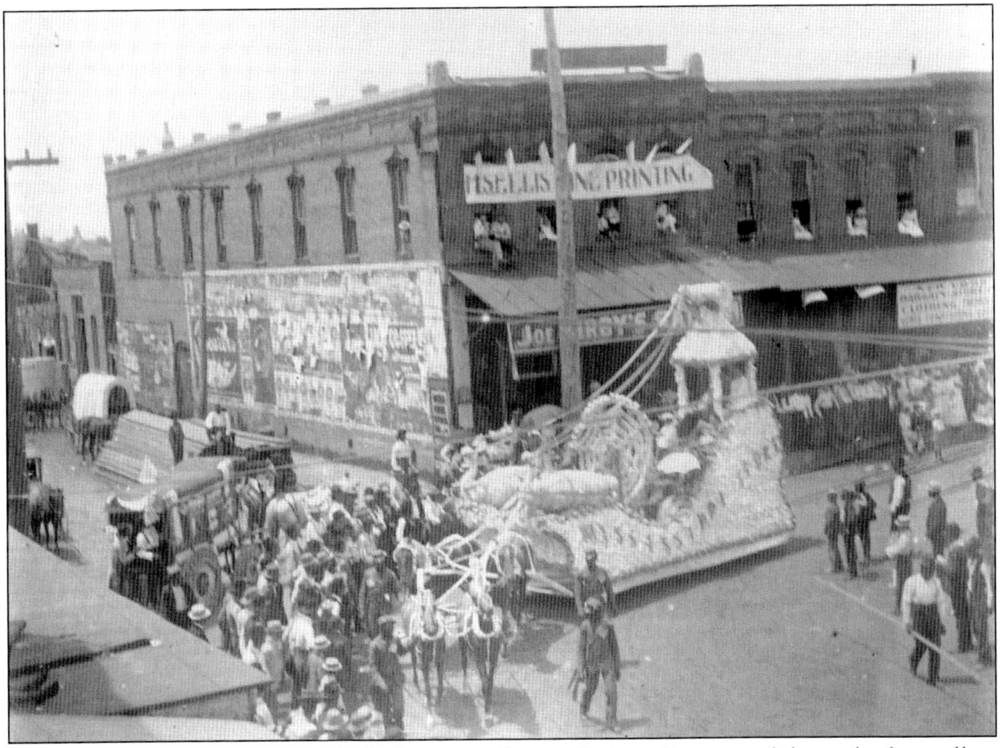

The Mississippi Store float was decked out in yellow and white flowers and drawn by four yellow horses. Stores in Greenville at that time had unusual names such as the Tennessee Store, the Misfit, Staple and Fancy Groceries, and the Racket Shop. Merchants ran large advertisements in the local newspapers during the Midsummer Carnival. (Courtesy of Jack Horton.)

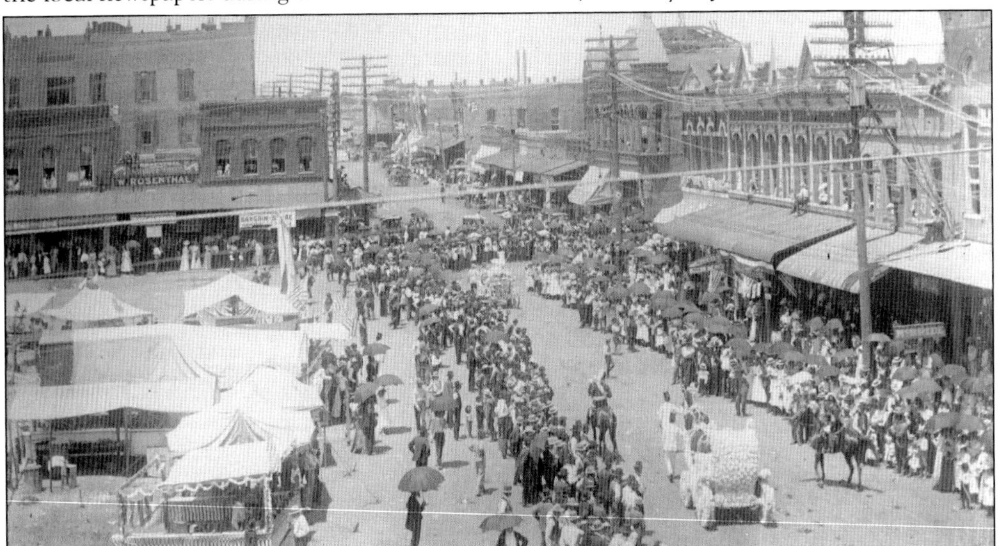

The 1901 Midsummer Carnival parade was described as a "Monster Parade." Festivities began with a concert by the Woodmen of the World band in the courthouse square gazebo. The parade began at 11:00 a.m. with throngs of people crowding the streets in town. The crowds began arriving before daylight by wagon, buggy, and train. (Courtesy of Jack Horton.)

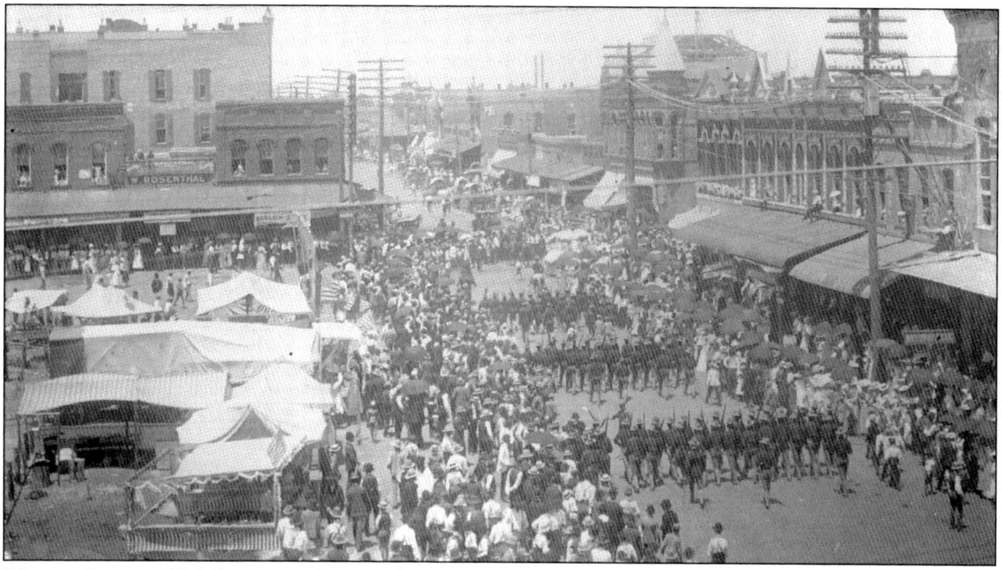

The tradition of Midsummer Carnival occurred shortly after the Spanish-American War. That war served to cement loyalty between former Confederate veterans and the United States. The young men who volunteered for service in the Spanish-American War were local heroes. As such, they marched in formation in parades. Other benevolent and fraternal organizations also participated as marching groups. (Courtesy of Jack Horton.)

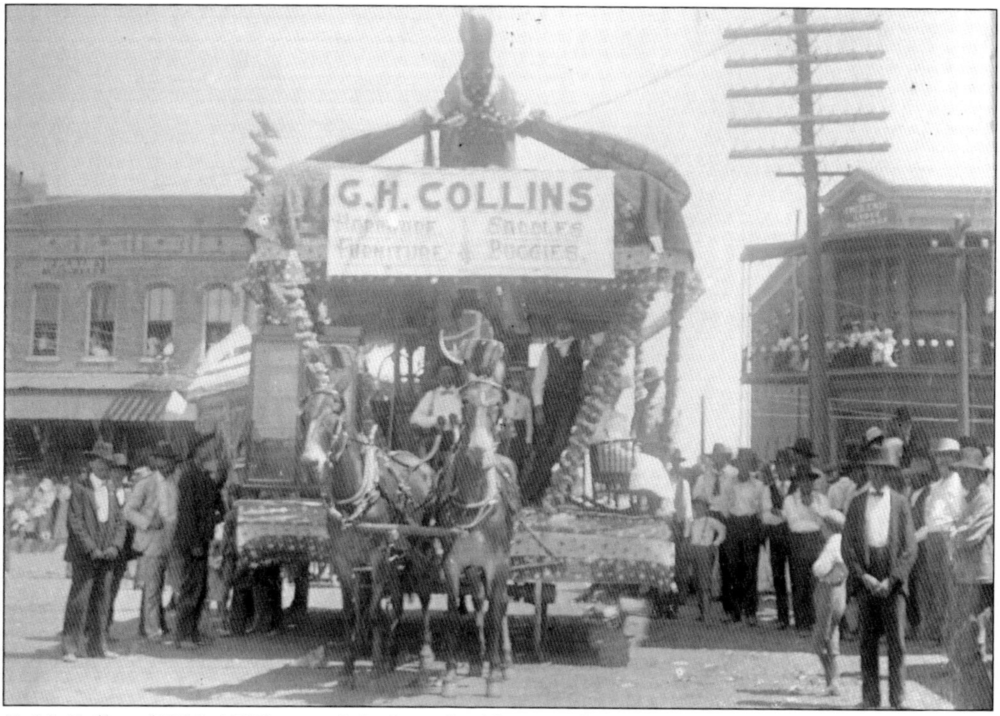

G. H. Collins (1864–1915) owned the large building on the northeast corner of the public square. His float represented his business showing furniture, hardware, and harness departments. In the early 1890s, Collins sold handcrafted coffins at his store. Later he hired the first undertaker in town. He was also one of the most successful purveyors of buggies. (Courtesy of Jack Horton.)

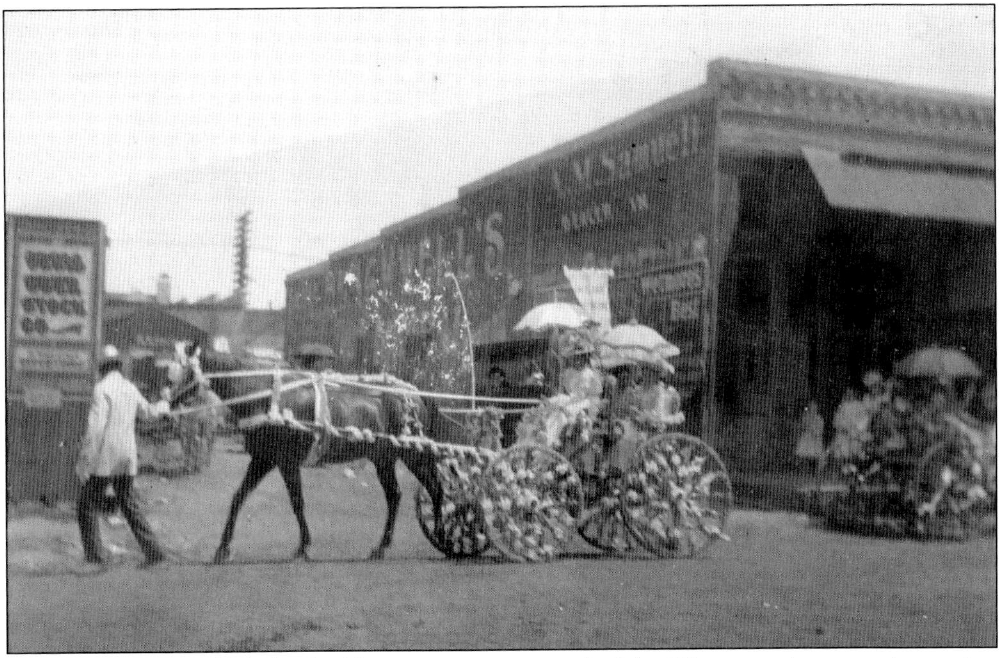

Since 1891, Greenville ladies had been active in women's clubs. They were intent on improving their minds as well as having weekly social sessions. Many of the women's clubs entered elaborately decorated buggies. In addition, certain merchants decorated buggies or surreys and asked the lovely ladies to grace them with their presence. (Courtesy of Jack Horton.)

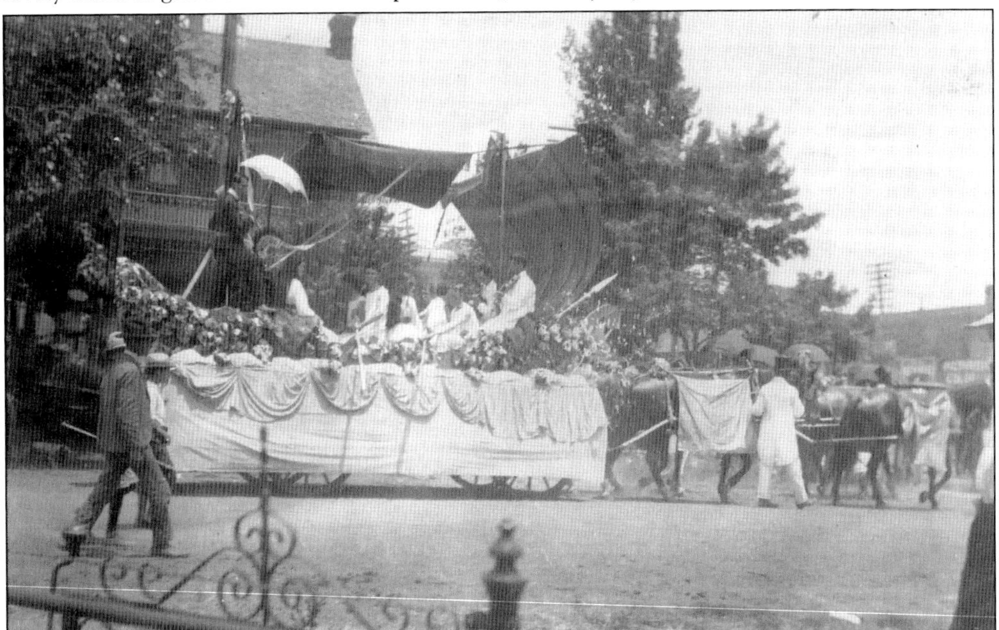

W. T. Graham Department Store created this elaborate float depicting Cleopatra's Barge on the River Tarsus. Cleopatra is facing the front of the float with her adoring subjects gazing upon her with awe. Note the footmen tending the horses. Part of the parade route ran through residential neighborhoods a few blocks from the public square. (Courtesy of Jack Horton.)

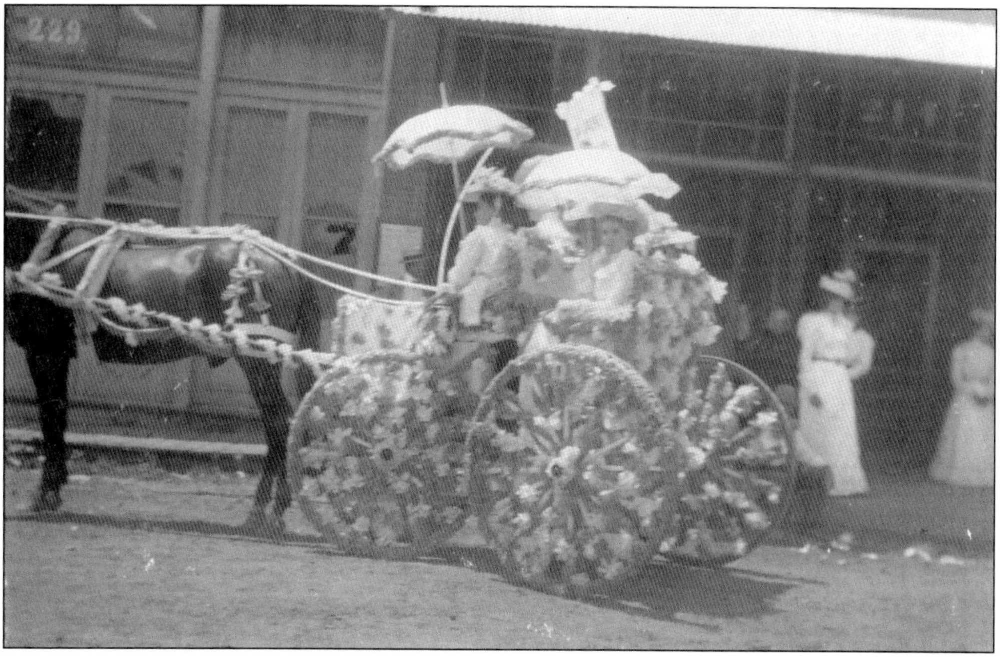

Another of the women's club floats turns the corner of Stonewall and Washington Streets. The July heat determined the attire of the day. Many women wore white dresses and carried white or lightly colored parasols. By noon, the summer sun was ferocious. Merchants provided barrels of free ice water for participants and observers. (Courtesy of Jack Horton.)

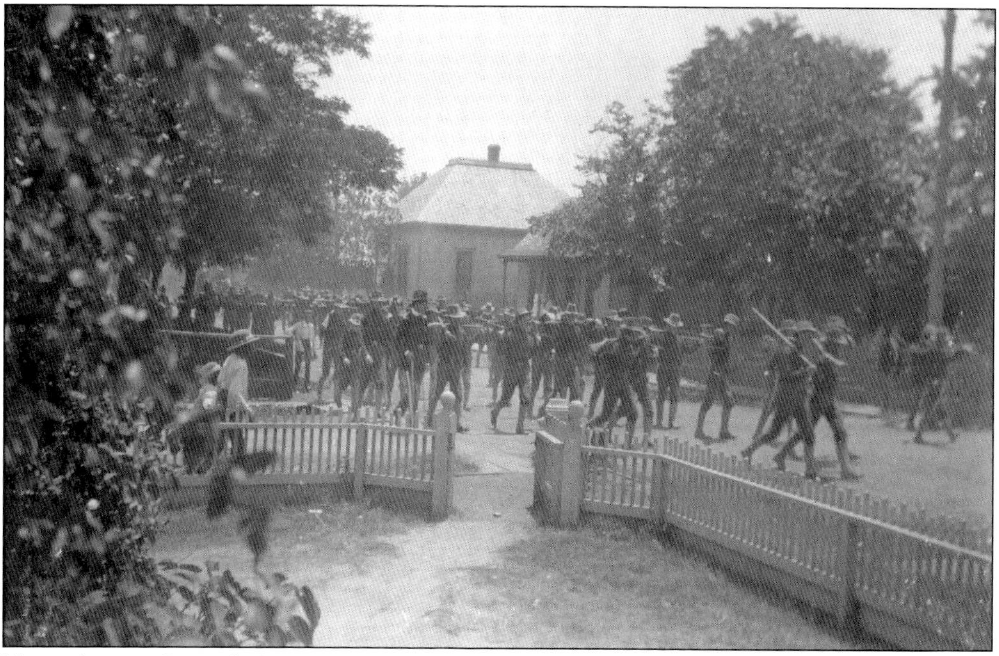

Not only were Spanish-American War veterans honored in the Midsummer Carnival Parades but also groups such as the Greenville Rifles, Denison Rifles, and Lloyd Rifles. After the parades concluded, sham battles were conducted by Confederate veterans using blank ammunition. A stock show was held at the fairgrounds along with horse races. (Courtesy of Jack Horton.)

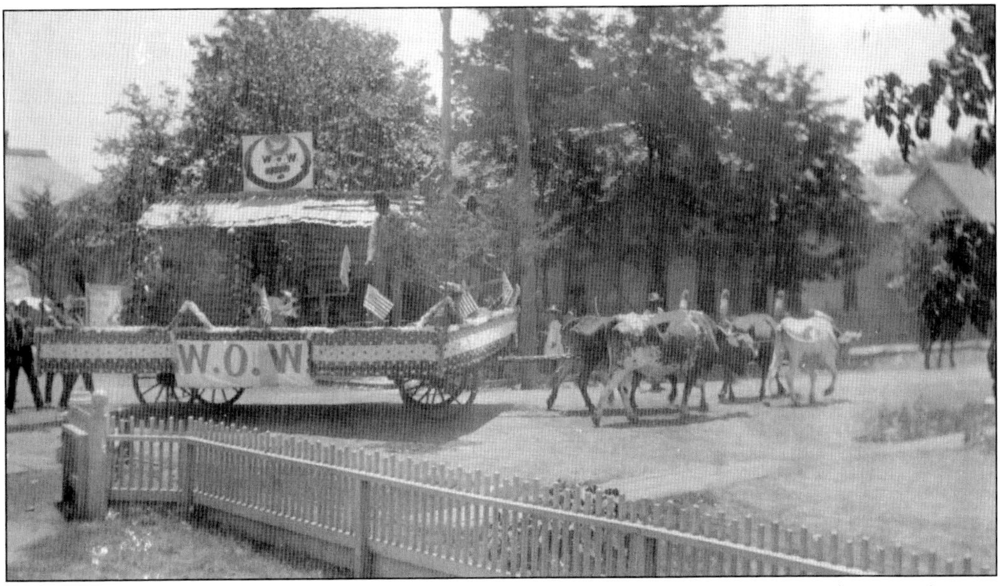

The Woodmen of the World float had two log cabins showing the different styles prevalent in frontier days. To keep with the frontier spirit of the float, the Woodmen obtained two yoke of oxen to pull the float. By the turn of the 20th century, oxen were almost a thing of the past; however, they were widely used 50 years earlier when Greenville was first settled. (Courtesy of Jack Horton.)

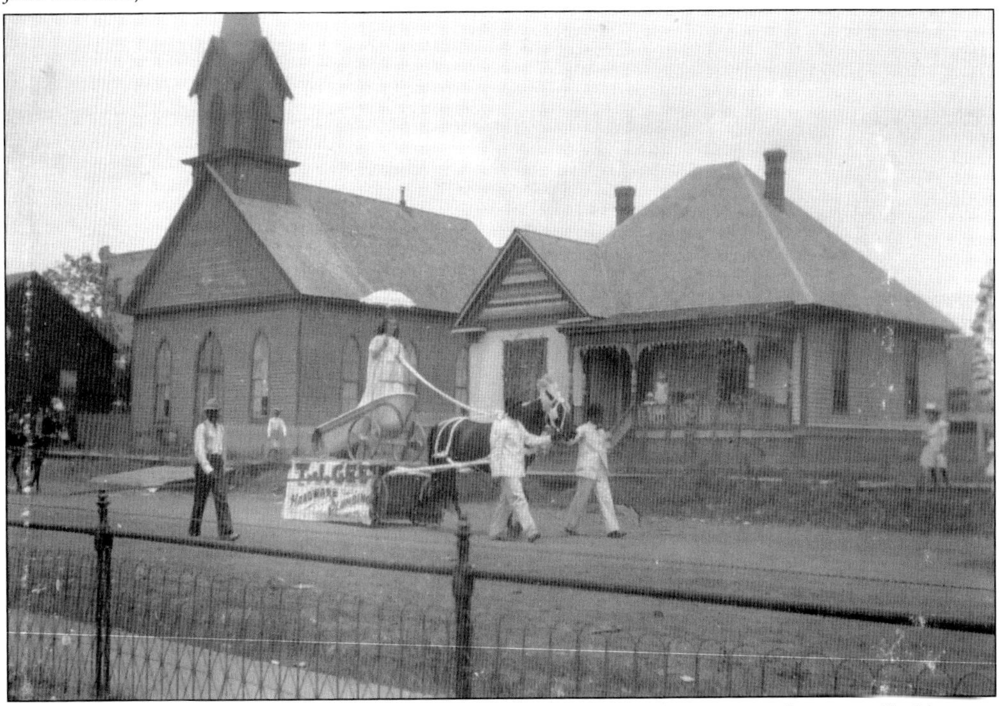

Merchant Thomas Jefferson Gee's award-winning float featured a Roman chariot pulled by one black horse. Vera Gee appears to be driving the chariot, but upon closer examination, two footmen are actually leading the horse. Notice that the chariot is actually a cast iron bathtub with claw feet, a deceptive but very imaginative float. (Courtesy of Jack Horton.)

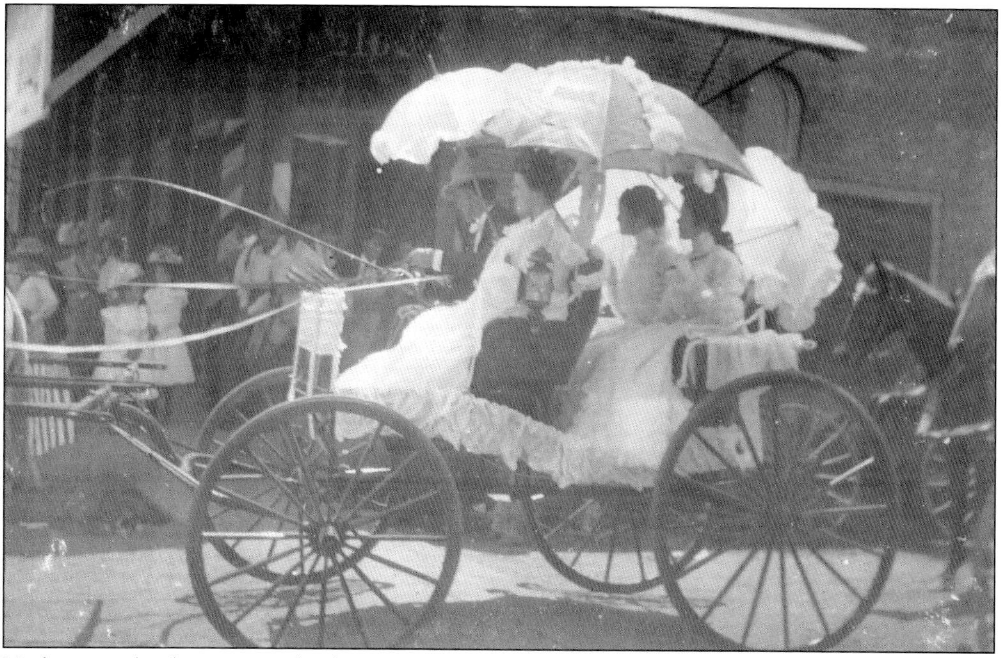

Unfortunately, the sign on this buggy is not visible to determine what businessman participated in the parade with these beautiful ladies. It is interesting that even the two small girls in the background are wearing white dresses. A contemporary newspaper article described many of the floats and buggies as decorated with the patriotic colors. (Courtesy of Jack Horton.)

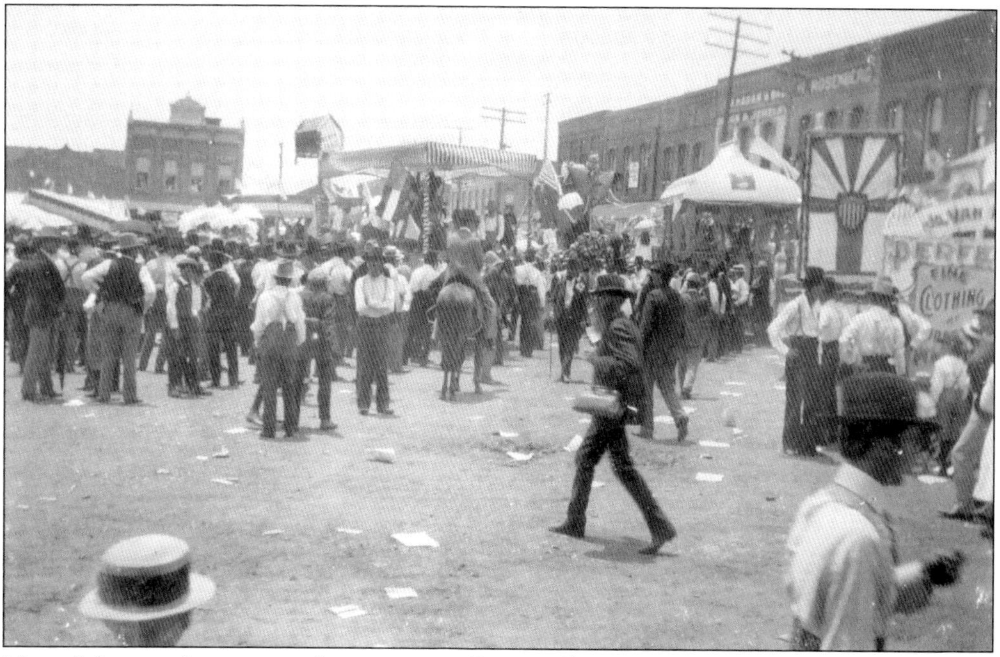

Most of the crowds were out-of-town visitors. Reportedly, 300 people arrived by train from Paris, Texas, some 50 miles away. The Texas Midland Railroad claimed that 1,200 people came from as far away as Hillsboro to enjoy the celebration. Of course, the crowds were a huge financial boost to merchants in Greenville. (Courtesy of Jack Horton.)

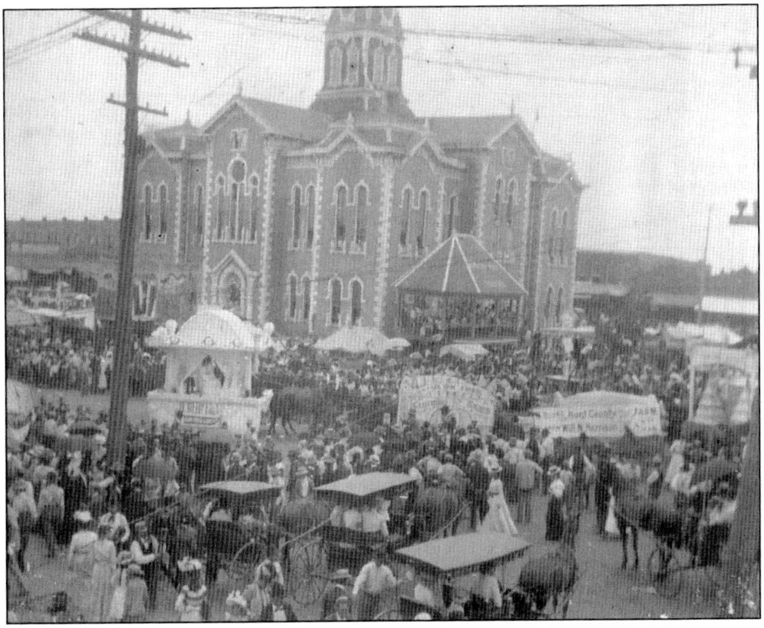

At the corner of Stonewall and Lee Streets, crowds gathered to watch the floats, bands, and decorated buggies and surreys. It is interesting to note how near the crowds drew to the parade participants. Also noteworthy is the fact that people remained in their vehicles to watch the parade. The newspapers mentioned the calm crowds. (Courtesy of Jack Horton.)

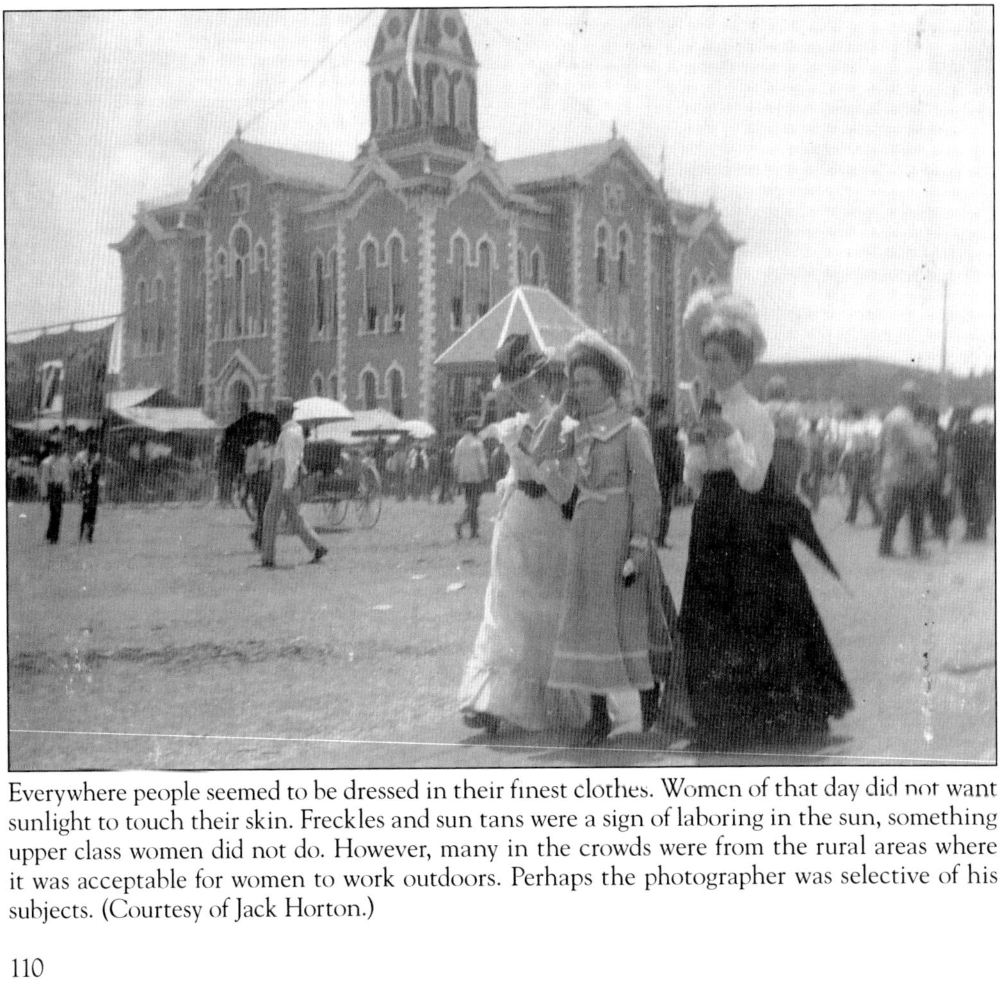

Everywhere people seemed to be dressed in their finest clothes. Women of that day did not want sunlight to touch their skin. Freckles and sun tans were a sign of laboring in the sun, something upper class women did not do. However, many in the crowds were from the rural areas where it was acceptable for women to work outdoors. Perhaps the photographer was selective of his subjects. (Courtesy of Jack Horton.)

This crowd scene was taken at the corner of Stonewall and Lee Streets in front of the Greenville National Exchange Bank. Over the years, Greenville experienced devastating fires that destroyed property and lives. Notice the fire hydrant in the lower right corner; it was a sign of progress and a vital necessity. (Courtesy of Jack Horton.)

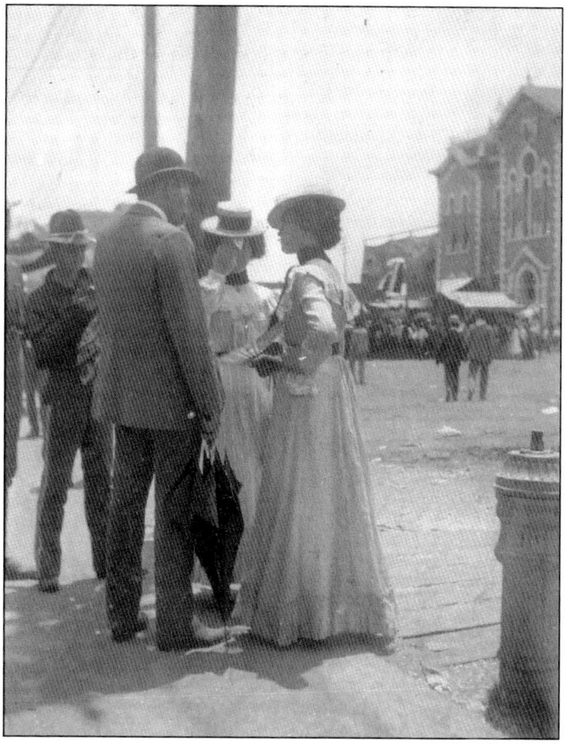

This couple walked the board sidewalks on Lee Street west of the public square. In the background is the dome of the courthouse. All along the street are gaily decorated shop windows, awnings to offer some protection from the hot July sun, and American flags flying. The banner hanging across the street is a novel marketing ploy for that time. (Courtesy of Jack Horton.)

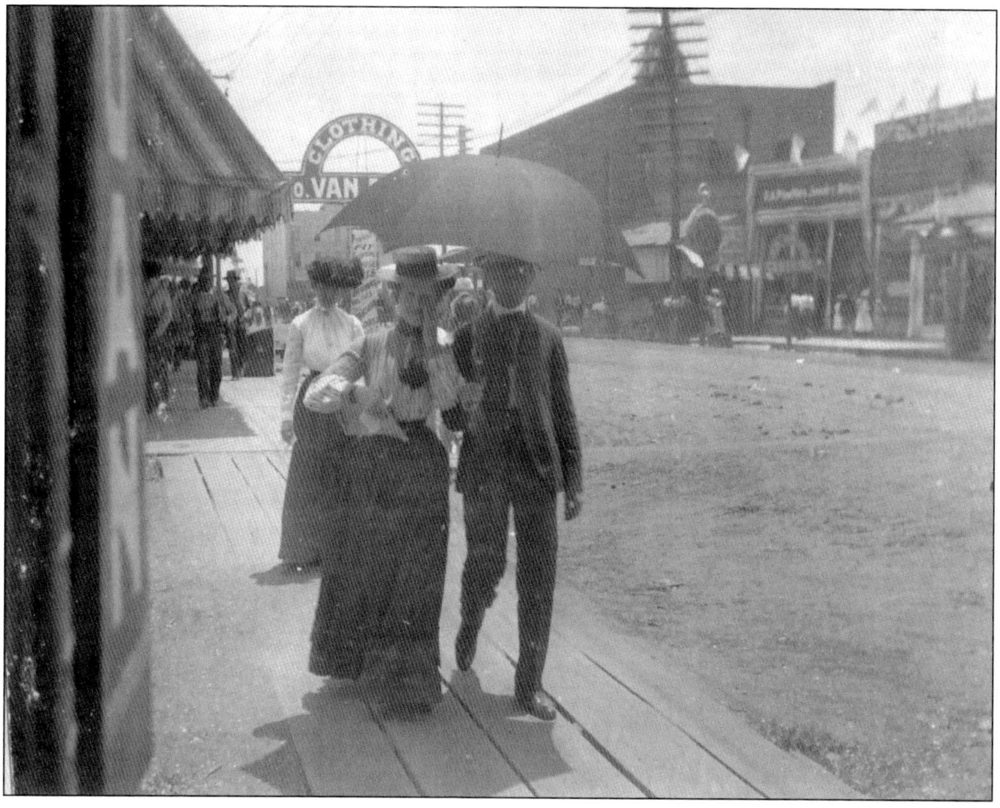

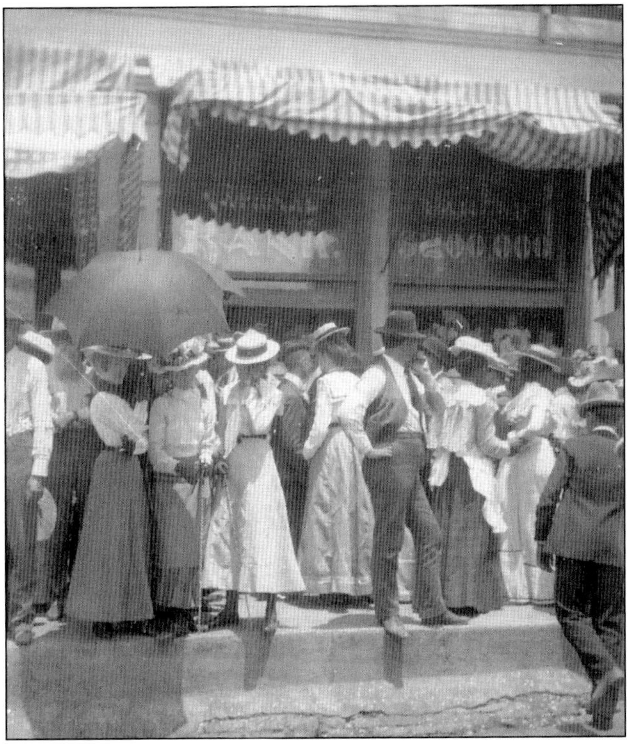

With nine railroad outlets and 22 passenger trains daily, a huge crowd of 10,000 gathered in Greenville in July 1901 for Midsummer Carnival. Railroads offered special rates allowing the crowds to return home in the evening and then come back for more fun the next day. Two special trains were made up at Jefferson, Texas, located on the Louisiana border, and brought visitors both days. (Courtesy of Jack Horton.)

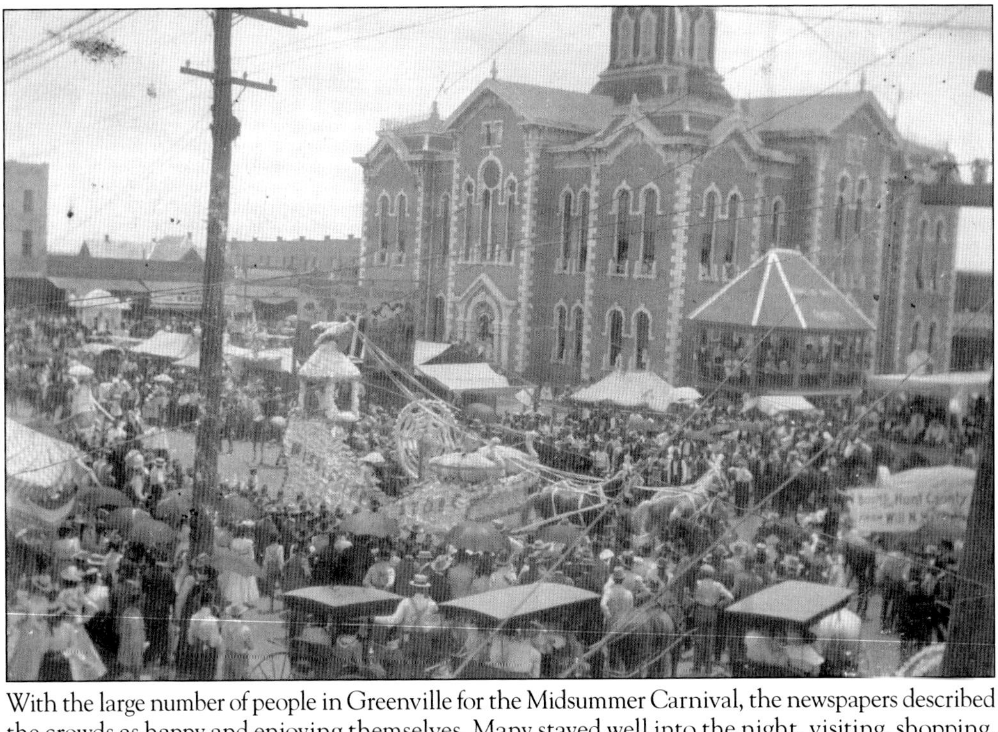

With the large number of people in Greenville for the Midsummer Carnival, the newspapers described the crowds as happy and enjoying themselves. Many stayed well into the night, visiting, shopping, and enjoying the countless displays set up for their pleasure. Even the schoolchildren performed during the afternoon, displaying their work in regular exercises. (Courtesy of Jack Horton.)

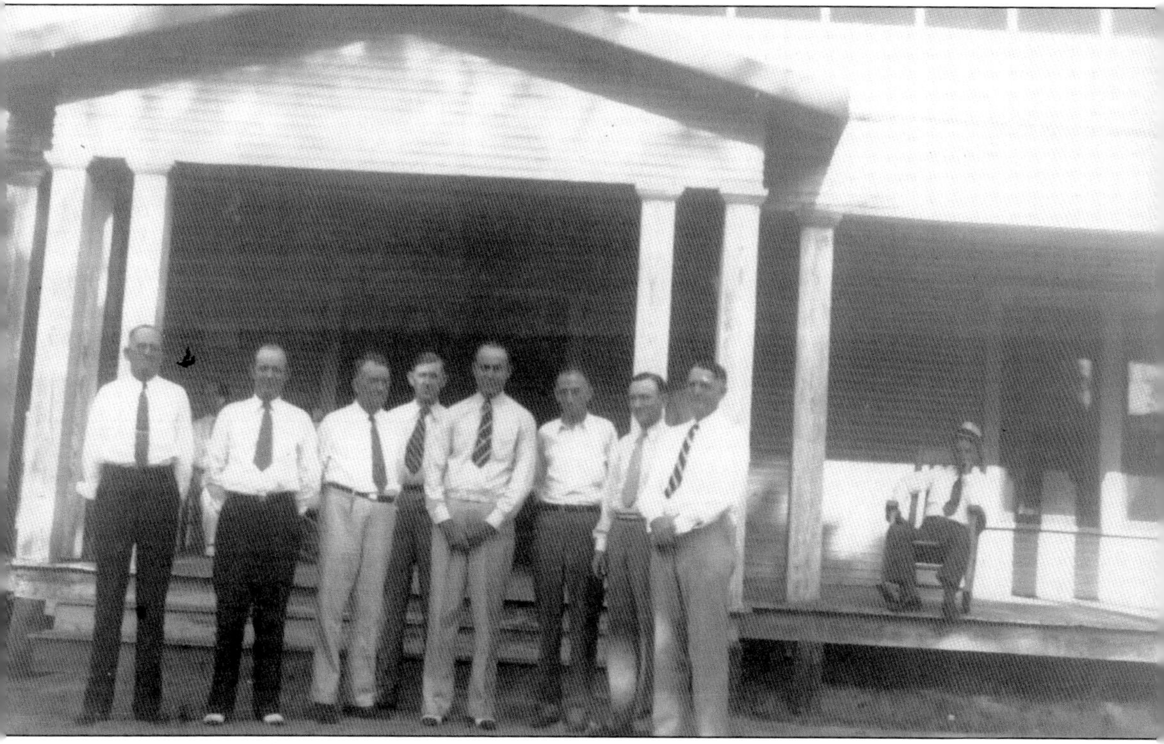

At the beginning of the 20th century, residents of East Texas began to create small private lakes for hunting and fishing. Greenville civic leaders located their 350-acre lake to the south of Greenville just above the confluence of McGrew Creek and Cedar Creek, which are tributaries of the Sabine River. Subscription memberships were sold to pay for the recreational site. Construction began in 1917 with mule-drawn equipment. The dam was completed in 1921, but it was two more years before the lake completely filled with water. The original clubhouse sat on a scenic point overlooking the lake. Its roomy two stories featured wraparound porches and a large dining room. This group of men associated with the Cotton Experimental Station took a break during their meeting for photographs and some rocking chair time. (Courtesy of the author.)

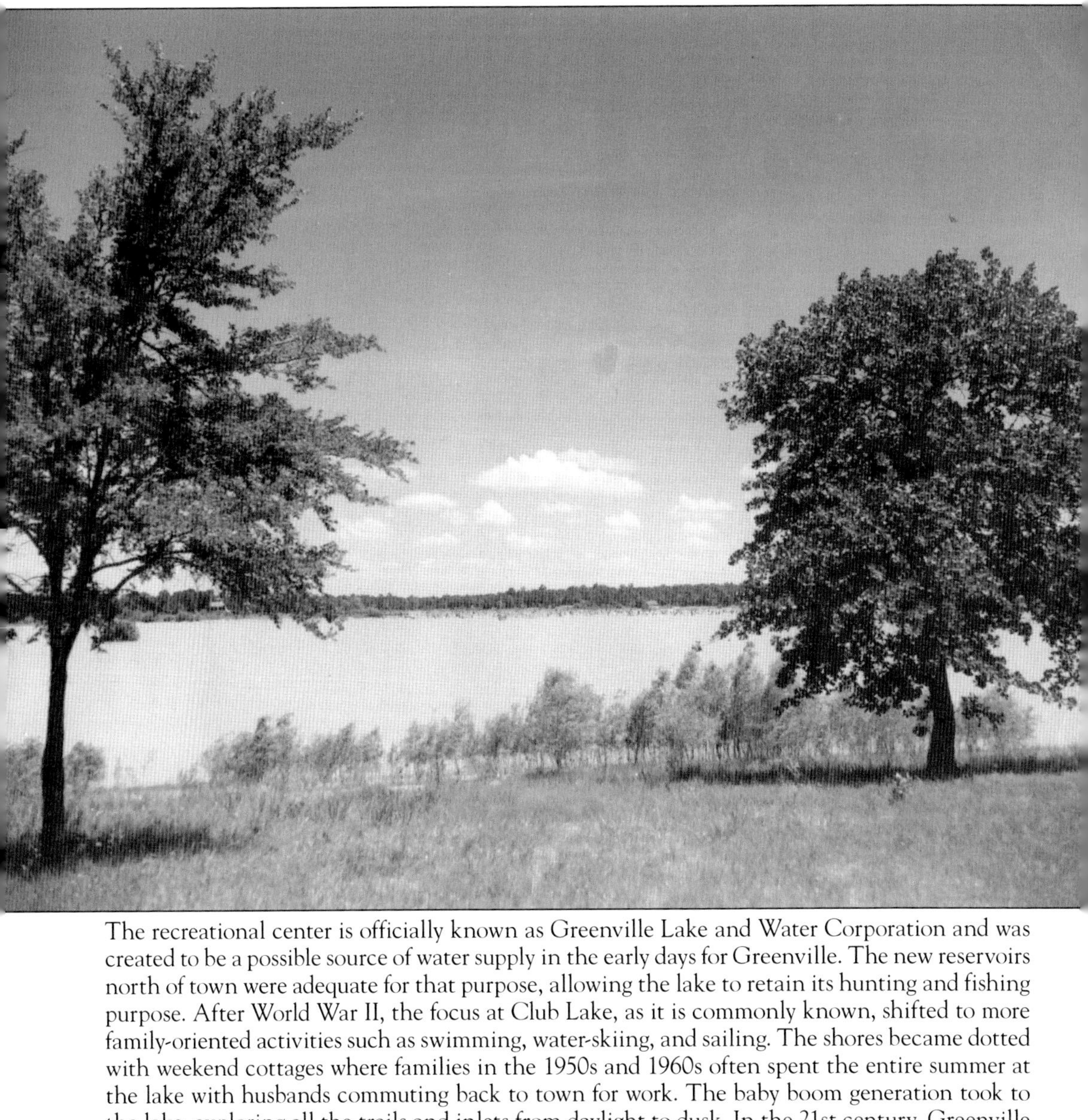

The recreational center is officially known as Greenville Lake and Water Corporation and was created to be a possible source of water supply in the early days for Greenville. The new reservoirs north of town were adequate for that purpose, allowing the lake to retain its hunting and fishing purpose. After World War II, the focus at Club Lake, as it is commonly known, shifted to more family-oriented activities such as swimming, water-skiing, and sailing. The shores became dotted with weekend cottages where families in the 1950s and 1960s often spent the entire summer at the lake with husbands commuting back to town for work. The baby boom generation took to the lake, exploring all the trails and inlets from daylight to dusk. In the 21st century, Greenville parade fever spread to Club Lake, and a flotilla of boats parade at sundown around the lake on the Fourth of July, followed by an elaborate fireworks display. (Courtesy of the author.)

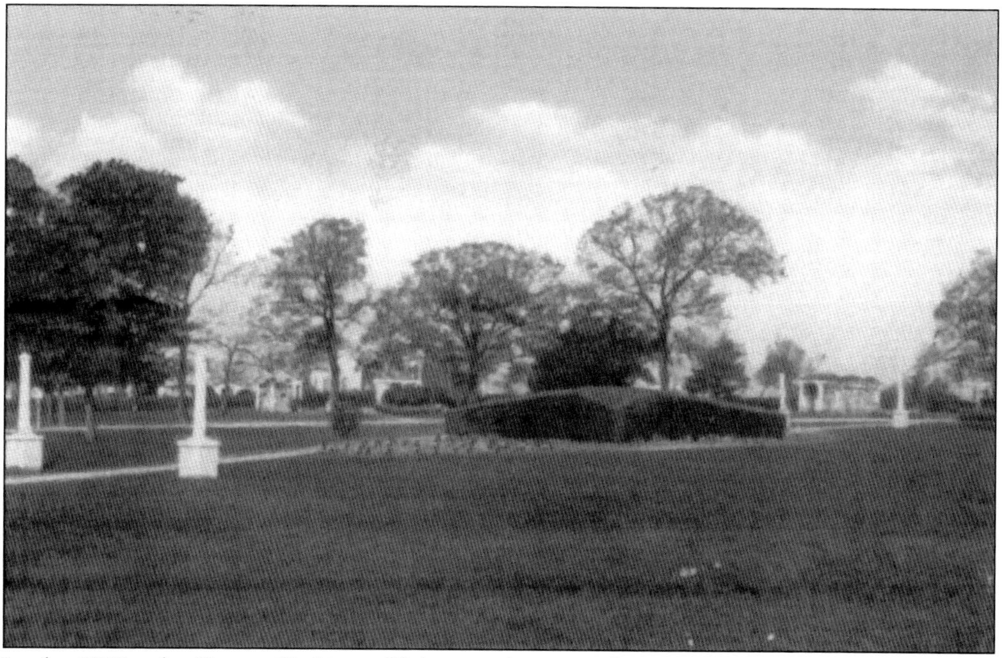

In the 1920s, the Greenville Lions Club agreed to provide maintenance for Graham Park in the north part of town. The club hired Joe Stanford who turned the long neglected area into a showplace. Large shrubs were pruned into fanciful shapes such as this star surrounded by a bed of flowering annuals. (Courtesy of W. Walworth Harrison Public Library.)

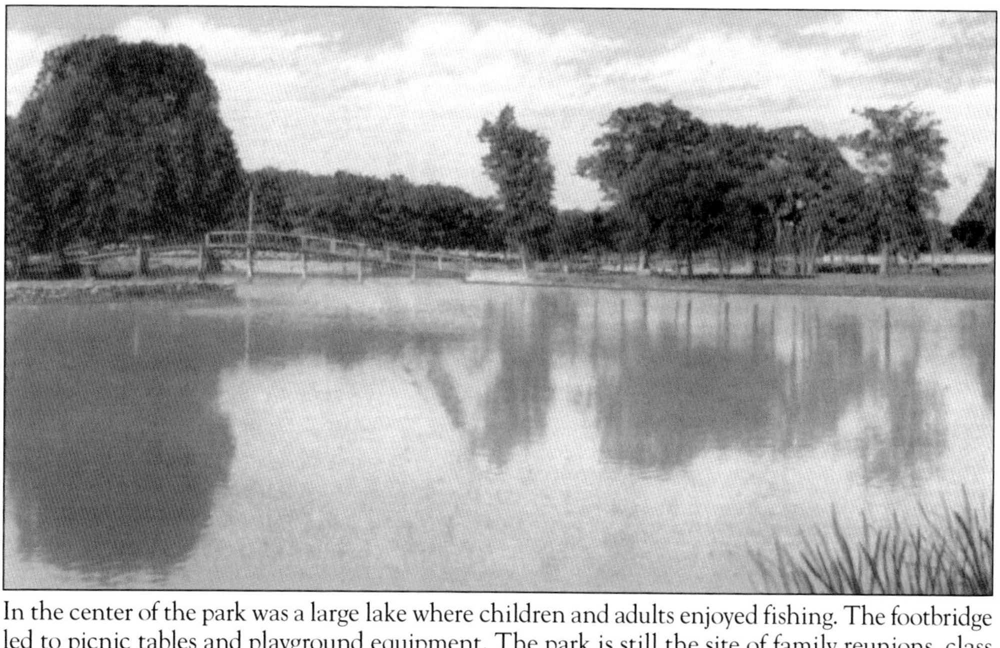

In the center of the park was a large lake where children and adults enjoyed fishing. The footbridge led to picnic tables and playground equipment. The park is still the site of family reunions, class parties, and at one time, the city sponsored Fourth of July celebrations there. Also, a small zoo was maintained at the park for a time. (Courtesy of W. Walworth Harrison Public Library.)

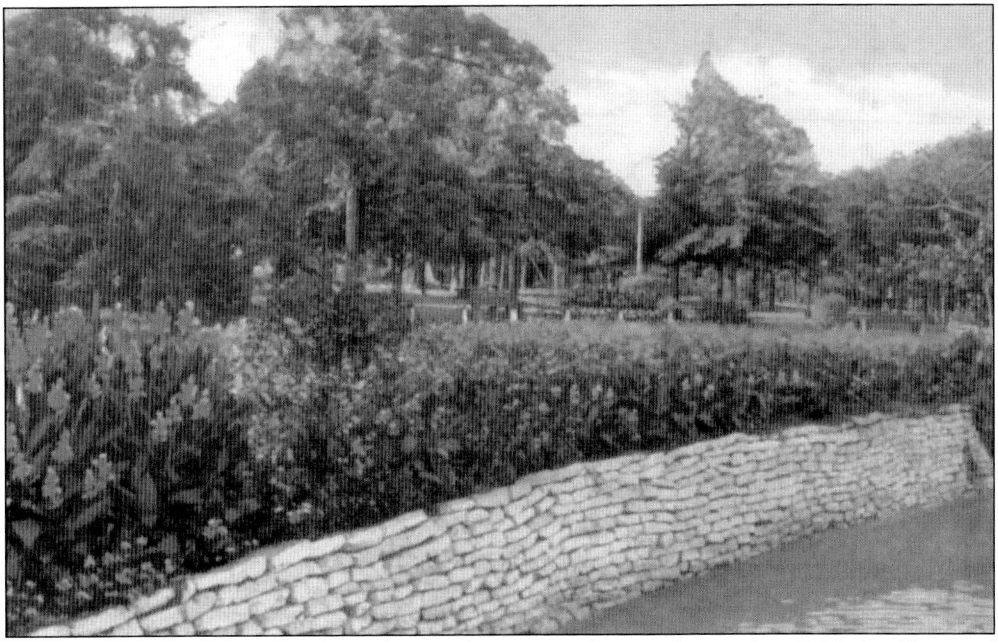

Joe Stanford's handiwork transformed a mundane city park into a horticultural delight. His use of colorful plants, retaining walls, and benches created a tranquil scene among the native oak trees. Sanford worked tirelessly to transform Graham Park into a place of natural beauty. For many years, it was a natural meeting place for the citizens of Greenville. (Courtesy of W. Walworth Harrison Public Library.)

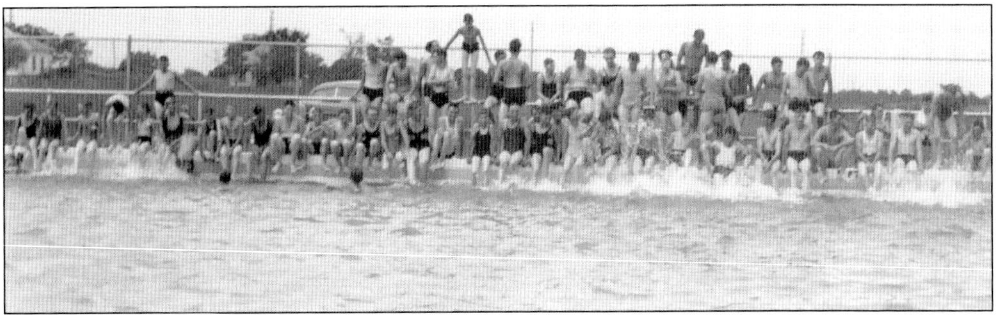

It was 1915 when a long, concrete settling basin at the water works was converted into a swimming pool. A bathhouse was constructed from used lumber, and youngsters flocked to the new summer attraction. Later a modern pool, shown here, was constructed at the east edge of Graham Park. (Courtesy of W. Walworth Harrison Public Library.)

Eight

The Heart of Greenville

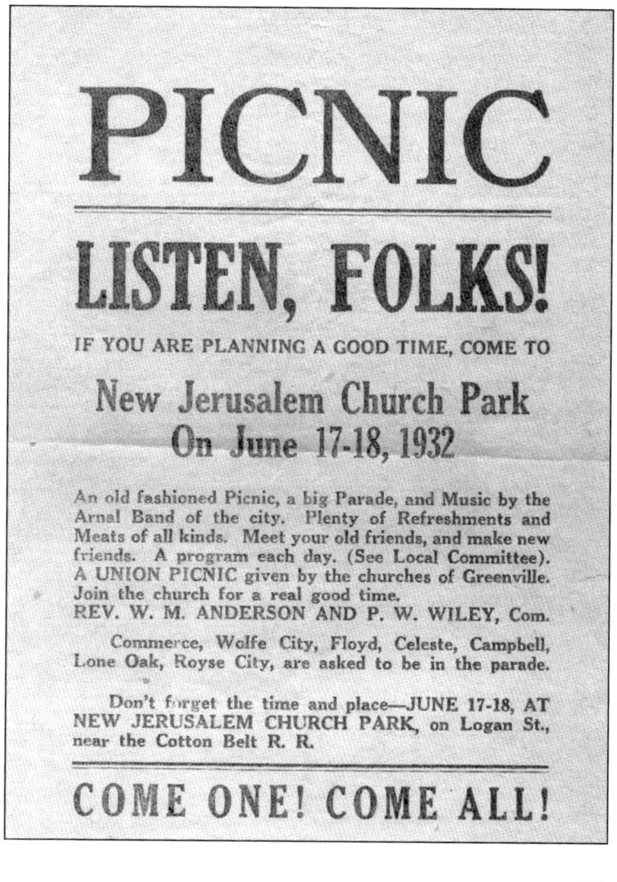

PICNIC

LISTEN, FOLKS!

IF YOU ARE PLANNING A GOOD TIME, COME TO

New Jerusalem Church Park
On June 17-18, 1932

An old fashioned Picnic, a big Parade, and Music by the Arnal Band of the city. Plenty of Refreshments and Meats of all kinds. Meet your old friends, and make new friends. A program each day. (See Local Committee). A UNION PICNIC given by the churches of Greenville. Join the church for a real good time.
REV. W. M. ANDERSON AND P. W. WILEY, Com.

Commerce, Wolfe City, Floyd, Celeste, Campbell, Lone Oak, Royse City, are asked to be in the parade.

Don't forget the time and place—JUNE 17-18, AT NEW JERUSALEM CHURCH PARK, on Logan St., near the Cotton Belt R. R.

COME ONE! COME ALL!

In the depths of the Great Depression, this flyer was passed out in Greenville and the surrounding area inviting everyone to the Juneteenth Celebration at the New Jerusalem Church Park. The African American Church typified the role of churches in the history of Greenville. Churches and homes have been the heart of the city since the founding of the city in 1847. (Courtesy of the author.)

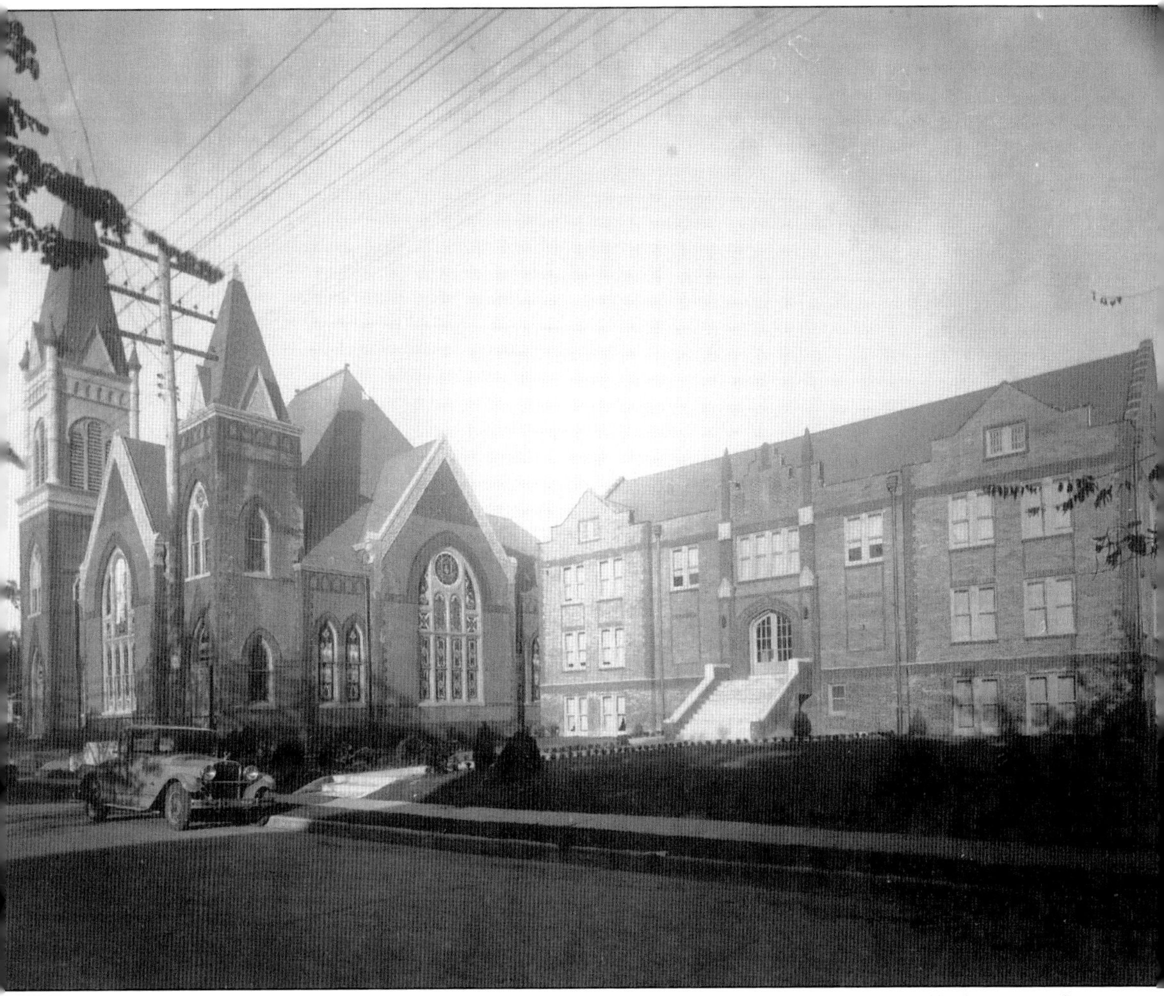

Central Christian Church has been one of the treasures of downtown Greenville for more than a century. The present Gothic Revival structure was designed by local architect W. R. Ragsdale and completed in 1899. The congregation can trace its beginnings to early religious movements in Greenville and the surrounding rural area to 1848. In 1879, the church was officially organized as the First Christian Church of Greenville. A small frame building was constructed a short distance to the south of the present structure. When the current building was erected, the name was changed to Central Christian Church. The most liberal donor was Virginia Oldham King. She gave the elaborate stained-glass window in memory of her mother. The west sun shining through the window creates a stunning sight. King also furnished a Prayer Room in the southwest corner of the church. The large sanctuary was designed to be partitioned into smaller rooms when needed. Overhead carved oak panels can be lowered to the floor by hand cranks. Much of the original furnishings are still in use. (Courtesy of Hunt County Historical Commission.)

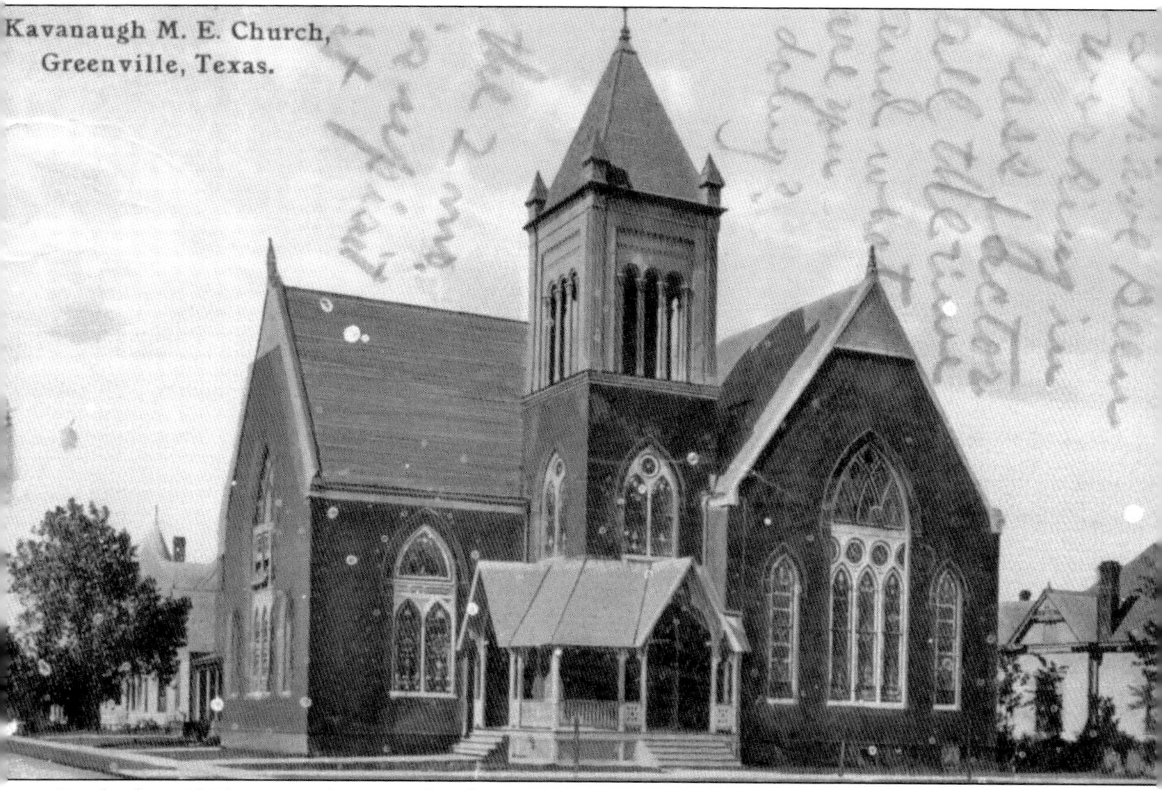

By the late 1880s, a new housing development began south of Town Branch, the traditional southern boundary of Greenville. Along Park Avenue, the most successful merchants and businessmen built splendid new homes. Between Park Avenue and Wesley Methodist Church were railroad tracks and saloons, no place for women and children to walk past. At that time, men only attended church services, leaving Sunday school to women and children. A Methodist Sunday school was started in the South Ward School in 1892. In November 1896, Kavanaugh was organized, and a red brick building was soon erected. The church was well attended and in 25 years, outgrew the facilities. The congregation decided to erect a larger building on the same sight. This church was razed, and the congregation built the tabernacle behind the parsonage. Later this was sold to Park Street Baptist Church. (Courtesy of the author.)

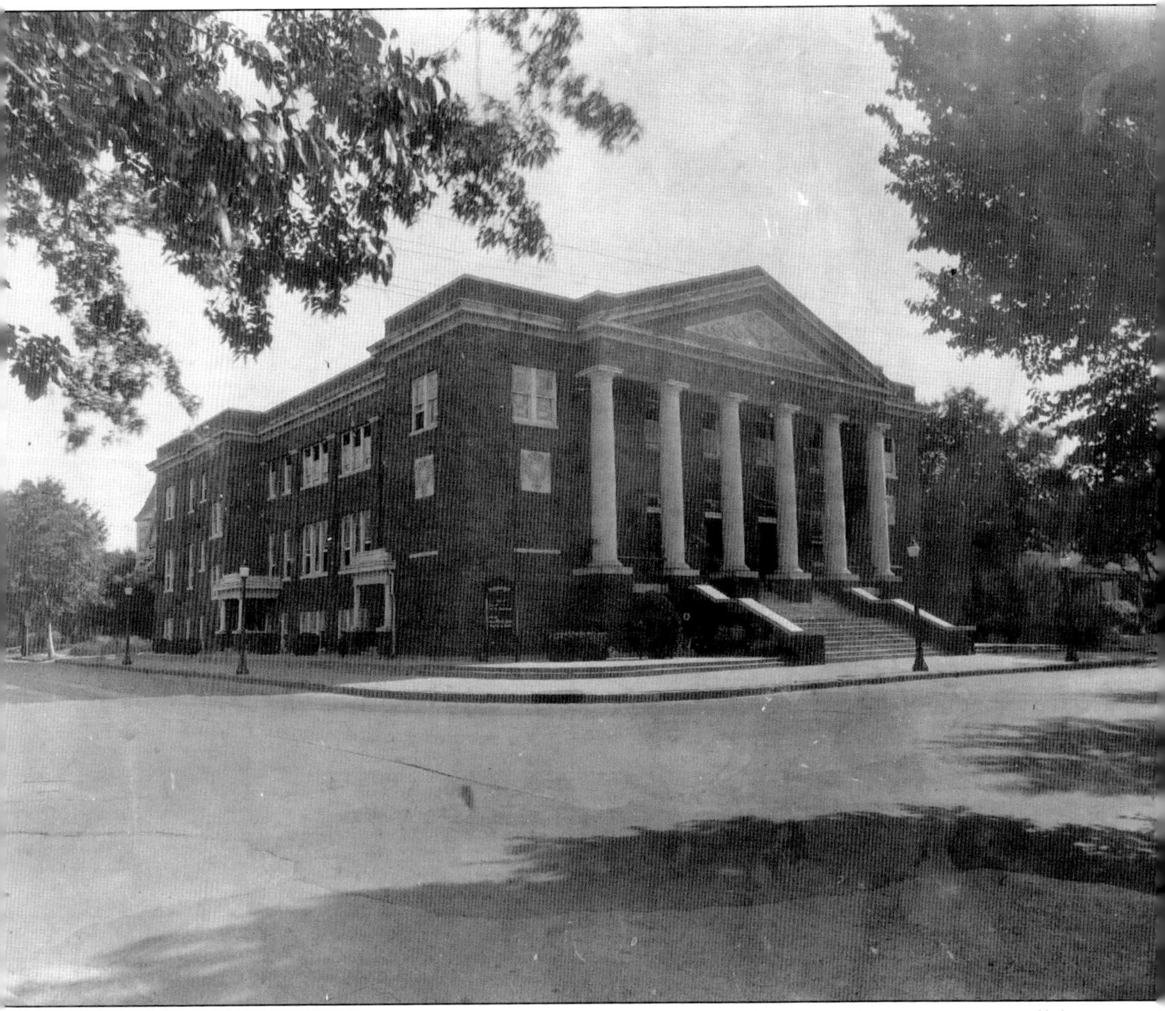

As the south part of Greenville developed, the congregation at Kavanaugh outgrew its small four-room building. In 1921, a revival was held where a new building was proposed. Local architects Lindsey and Kilmer designed the Gothic structure with six large columns and broad gray stone steps leading to the second floor sanctuary. The exterior is constructed of brown vitrified brick with stone trim. Fifty stained-glass windows provided light and ventilation. Three years later, the new church was dedicated. It should be noted that when the building opened the debt of $100,000 was completely retired. The church was named for Bishop Hubbard H. Kavanaugh, originally from Kentucky. In 1854, Kavanaugh was elected Methodist bishop in 1854 at Columbus, Georgia. He was best known for his two-hour sermons that could move people from laughter to tears. In 1961, the church constructed an educational building behind the original structure. The property to the east was deeded to Kavanaugh and is now a lovely Biblical Garden. (Courtesy of the author.)

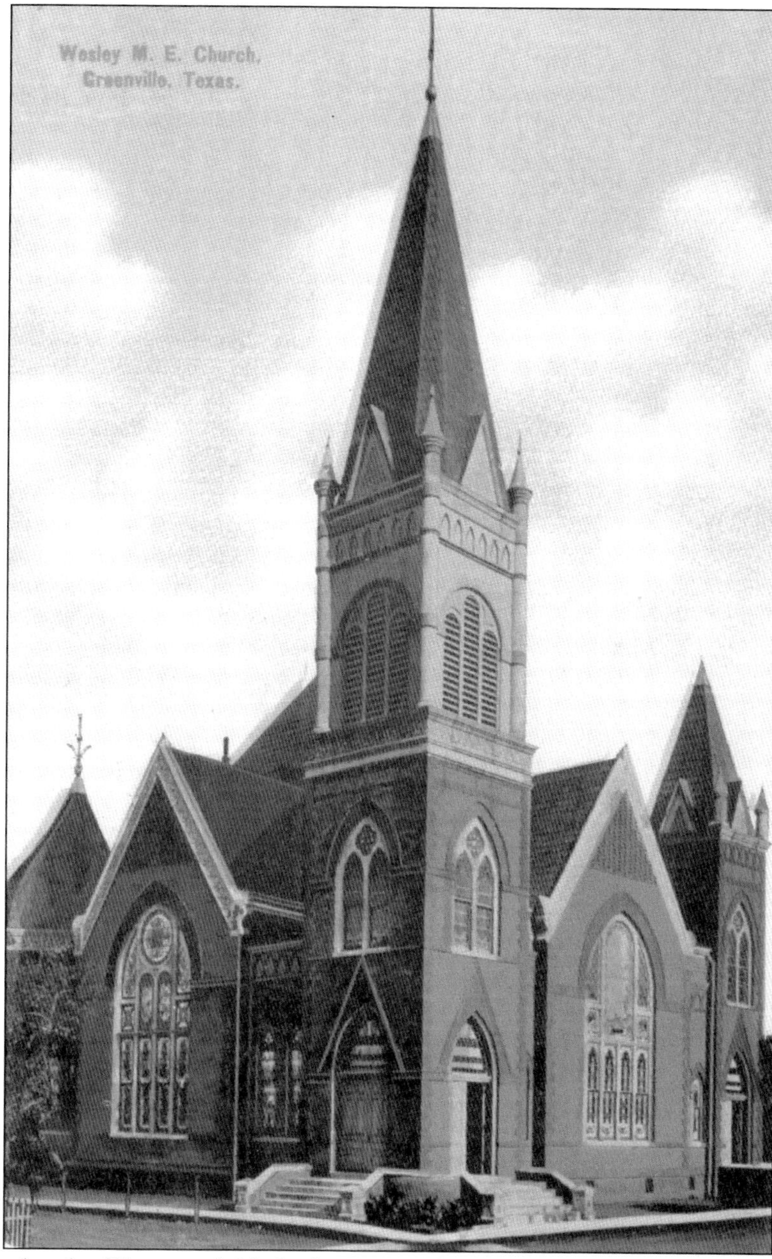

The parent church of Kavanaugh Methodist was Wesley Methodist, the oldest in Greenville. The first mention of the church stated that services were held under trees and led by circuit riders. Later services were held in the Masonic Lodge, the courthouse, and Ende's Store on the public square. A building was in place by 1870 when it was destroyed by a storm that also damaged the courthouse. In 1872, the congregation had moved to a building on Lee Street where the first church Christmas tree was held. In 1874, the congregation purchased a lot at the corner of Wesley Street and Church Street. The church itself was named for John Wesley, founder of Methodism. By 1875, the church had a full-time minister. In 1885, a small frame building was erected. In 1898, the congregation constructed a large brick building. Later in 1929, during the building boom in Greenville, Wesley Methodist Church added an Educational Building. (Courtesy of the author.)

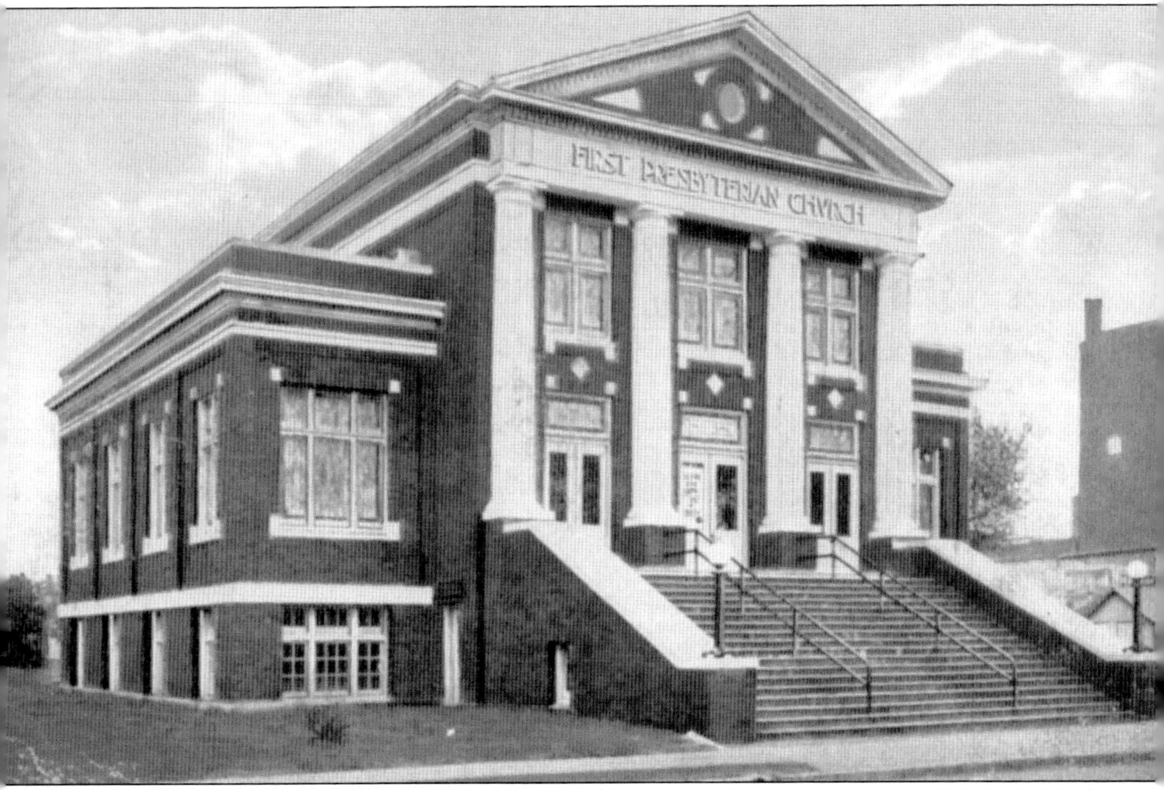

The First Presbyterian Church was organized in October 1880. On February 21, 1887, the Sabbath School was organized with 34 pupils and five teachers. The early years were ones of growth and struggle. Services were held in the courthouse, the back of a store, and on the second floor of an engine house that later burned, resulting in the loss of an organ, hymnals, a small library, and furniture. Later the church met in the old opera house, a store on the public square, and finally shared space with the Cumberland Presbyterian Church. As a result of work and cooperation of the Ladies' Aid Society, the first building was located at the corner of Wesley and Pickett Streets. The first regularly installed pastor was Rev. Charles T. Caldwell, who arrived in 1894. The cornerstone for this building was laid in October 1915 with the first service held in 1916. It became known as the City Temple for many years. It was often the site of the Pure Food Show and other community events. (Courtesy of W. Walworth Harrison Public Library.)

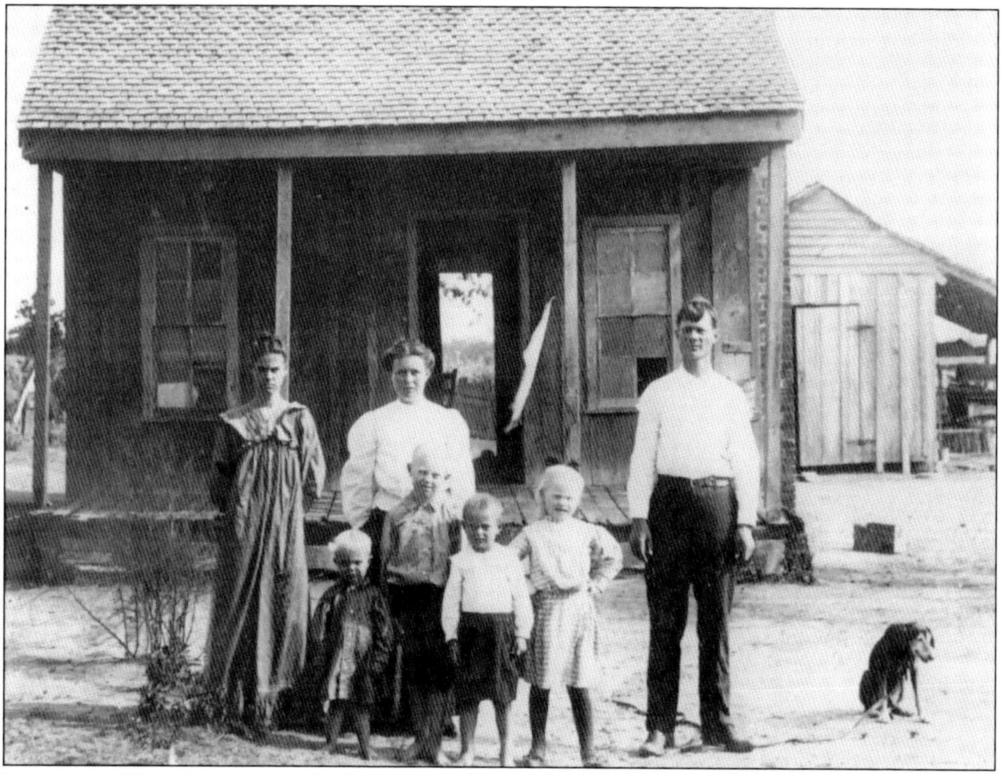

Many early Texas homes were built with a wide open hallway down the middle. While this house is of a later period as shown by the plank siding, it retained the dogtrot style. Early pioneers left the hallway open in order to bring large barrels of water on skids pulled by oxen for the family water supply. (Courtesy of the author.)

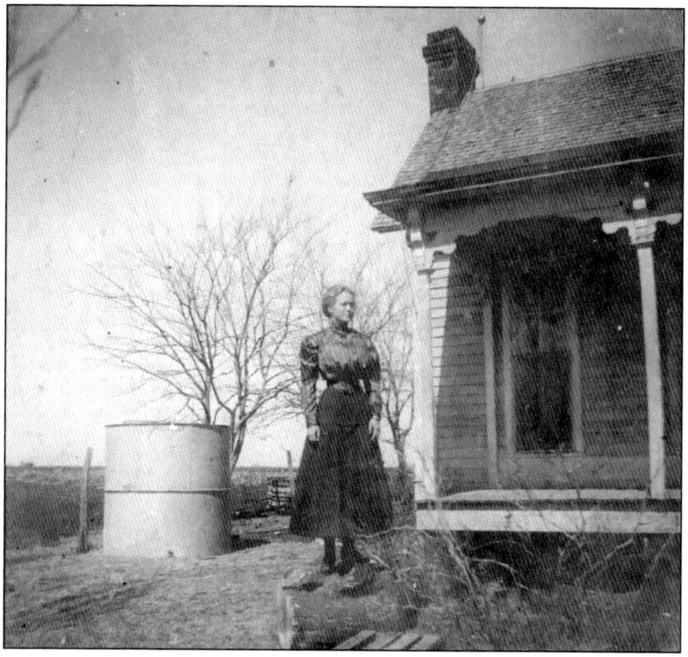

Later homes had large metal tanks, either on the ground or on stilts, to catch rainwater. These cisterns were covered with screen wire to keep out birds. Water was available at all times, even during extremely dry periods. The City of Greenville built cisterns at various locations in the ground to catch rainwater for public use and for fire protection. (Courtesy of the author.)

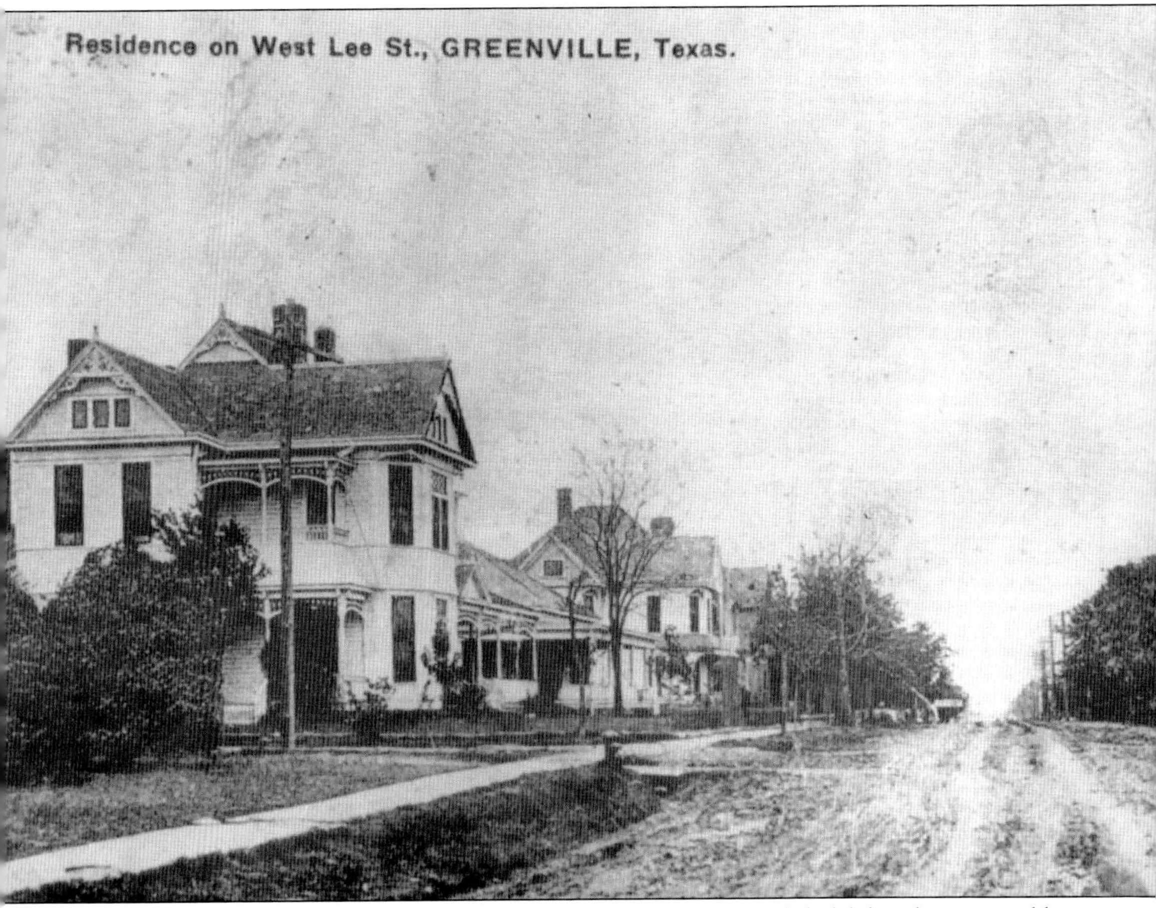

In 1863, when Robert Sayle completed his medical training in Philadelphia, he returned home to Louisville, Kentucky, where he bought a horse and saddle and set out for Texas. Arriving in the vicinity of present-day Commerce two months later, Dr. Sayle set up practice on the prairie near North Sulphur Creek. He married Texana Kimble in 1866. They were the parents of two daughters, Anna who married Dr. Joe Becton Sr. and Eula who married L. N. Byrd. In 1878, Dr. Sayle bought a large tract of land west of what would soon be the Katy depot for $8 per acre. The family built a home at the corner of Sayle and Bourland Streets. Three years later, Dr. Sayle petitioned the City of Greenville to open Lee Street west of the Katy depot with the intent of opening a housing development. These large bungalows and two-story Victorian homes are the results of his efforts. Texana Sayle gave each minister in Greenville a fat turkey at Christmas every year. (Courtesy of Hunt County Historical Commission.)

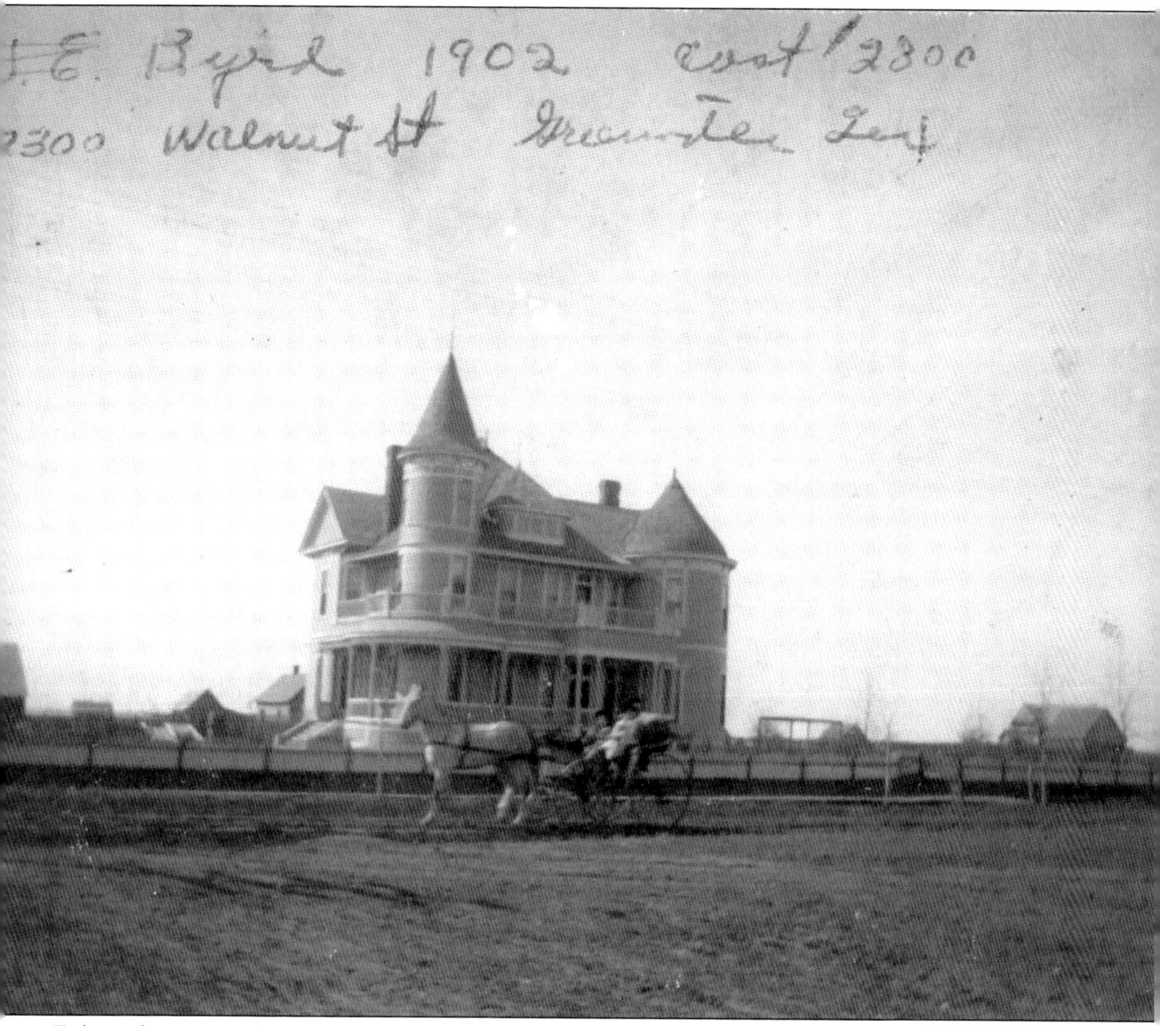

Eula and L. N. Byrd built this home on Walnut Street in 1902 at the cost of $2,300. The Byrds were active in civic affairs in Greenville. They enthusiastically supported sidewalks and paved streets, the streetcar line, good roads, and helped to found Lee Street Methodist Church in their neighborhood. Byrd was raised in the Scatter Branch community between Greenville and Commerce where he taught school. Later he moved to Greenville to become vice president of the First National Bank. Even though the home was within the city limits, it was operated as a farm. The absence of trees is a characteristic of the black land prairie. Early residents planted young saplings each spring. Today the area boasts tree-lined streets. (Courtesy of the author.)

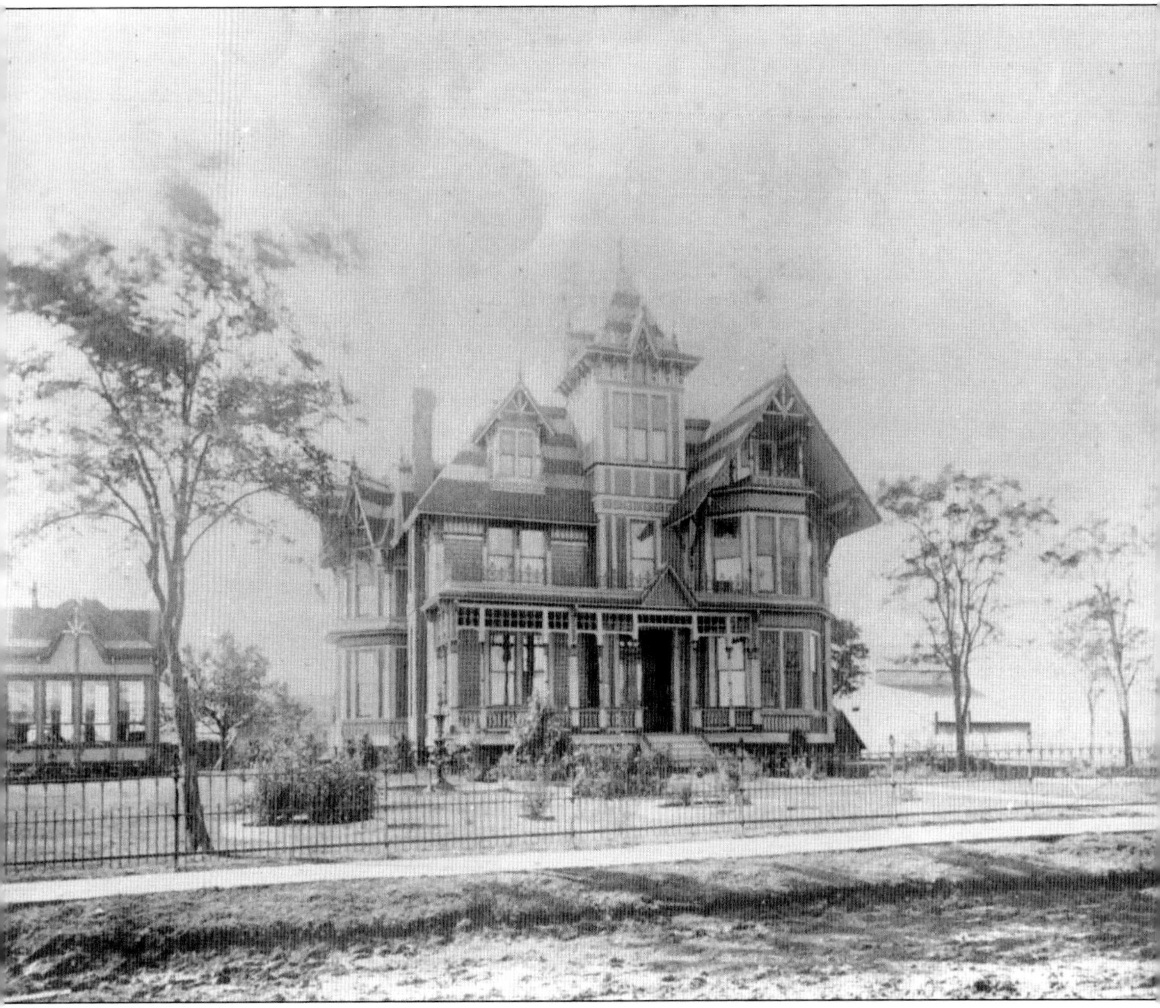

In 1884, Tom H. King (1848–1897) bought the old home built by McQuinney Howell Wright, donor of the original Greenville town site. King then built this elaborate showplace for his wife, the former Virginia Ann Oldham. The King's home became known for its lavish furnishings and the deer park, located on the east side of the house. Through smart investments in banking, cotton production, and in the cattle industry, Tom King became the first millionaire in Greenville. At an early age, King realized the value of the tall native grasses on the black land prairie. At first, he raised sheep before turning to cattle. He also invested in property in the town of Greenville, often paying in gold during the long recession of 1876–1879. When the First National Bank was chartered in 1883, Tom King was president. He formed the King Opera House in 1891. King's name was attached to such progressive projects as the water works. (Courtesy of Hunt County Historical Commission.)

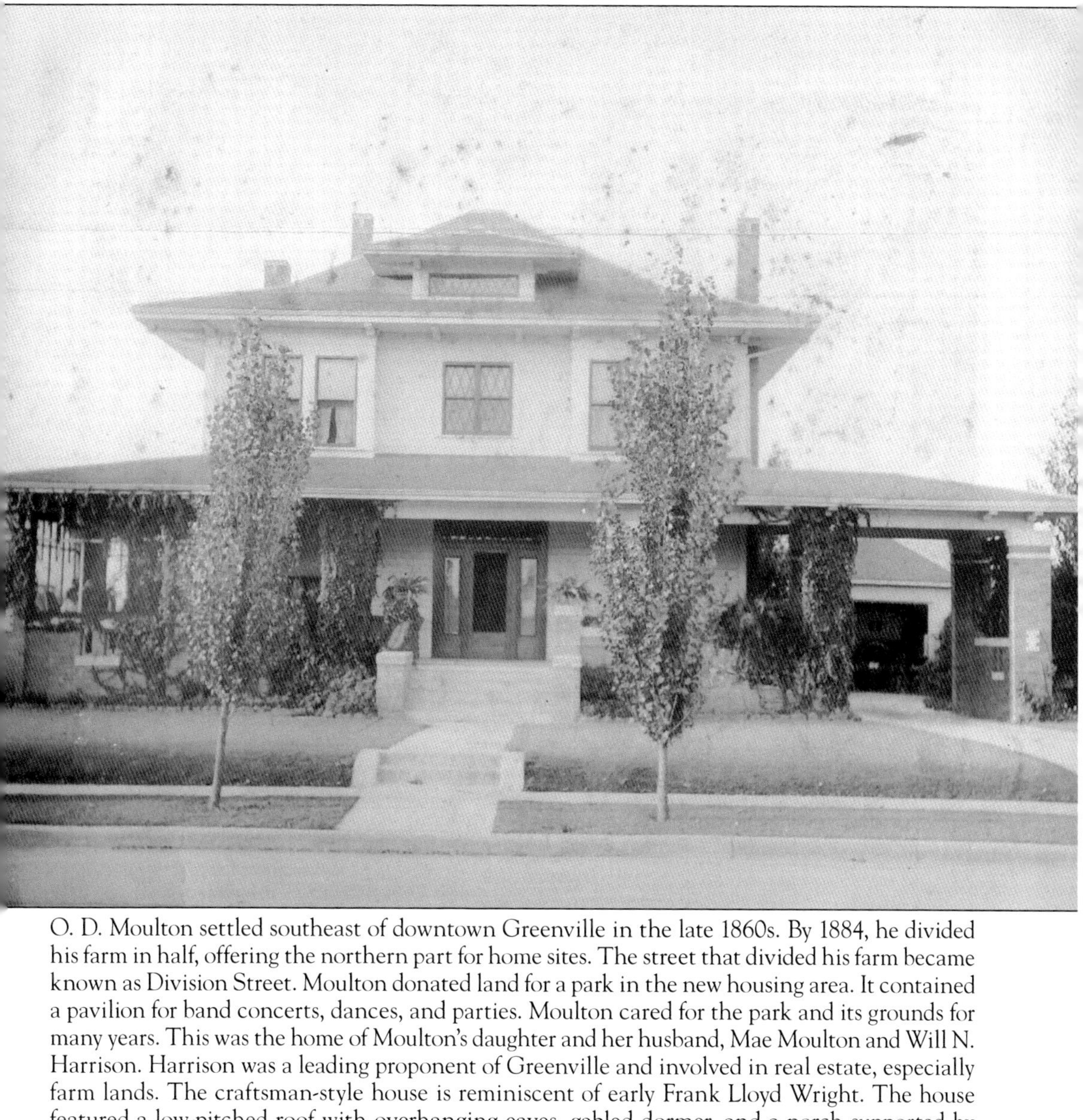

O. D. Moulton settled southeast of downtown Greenville in the late 1860s. By 1884, he divided his farm in half, offering the northern part for home sites. The street that divided his farm became known as Division Street. Moulton donated land for a park in the new housing area. It contained a pavilion for band concerts, dances, and parties. Moulton cared for the park and its grounds for many years. This was the home of Moulton's daughter and her husband, Mae Moulton and Will N. Harrison. Harrison was a leading proponent of Greenville and involved in real estate, especially farm lands. The craftsman-style house is reminiscent of early Frank Lloyd Wright. The house featured a low-pitched roof with overhanging eaves, gabled dormer, and a porch supported by thick square columns. The Harrisons entertained lavishly in their home. Overnight guests were treated to a private bath adjacent to the guest room complete with a porcelain tub, long before such amenities were standard. (Courtesy of W. Walworth Harrison Public Library.)

Consistent with our mission to preserve history on a local level, this book was printed in South Carolina on American-made paper and manufactured entirely in the United States. Products carrying the accredited Forest Stewardship Council (FSC) label are printed on 100 percent FSC-certified paper.

MADE IN THE USA